THE
SIMON AND SCHUSTER
BOOK OF

GIOVANNI CURATOLA

Foreword by John C. Hicks

SIMON AND SCHUSTER

NEW YORK

This book is dedicated to Giuditta.

Published by Simon and Schuster
A Division of Gulf & Western Corporation
Simon & Schuster Building
Rockefeller Center
1230 Avenue of the Americas
New York, NY 10020

SIMON AND SCHUSTER and colophon are trademarks
of Simon & Schuster

Translated from the Italian by Simon Pleasance

Printed and bound in Italy
by Officine Grafiche di Arnoldo Mondadori Editore, Verona

10 9 8 7 6 5 4 3 2 1

Library of Congress Cataloging in Publication Data
Curatola, Giovanni.
  The Simon and Schuster book of oriental carpets.

  Bibliography: p.
  Includes index.
  1. Rugs, oriental.   I. Title.   II. Title: Book of oriental carpets.
NK2808.C8713   1982   746.7-5   82-10268
ISBN: 0-671-45696-2

Contents

Acknowledgments

The publishers express their warm thanks for their co-operation to Federico Aborio Mella, Gabriele Mandel and all those collectors, organizations and museums who, by supplying picture material, have contributed greatly to the making of this book.

The U.S. publishers gratefully acknowledge the assistance of Bojtech Blau and Kirk Alan Igler in preparing the U.S. edition of this book.

The author wishes to thank the many friends and colleagues without whose help this book could never have been written. Without the constant encouragement and thorough research into sources and documentary material carried out by Sr. M. V. Fontana of the Oriental Institute, Naples, in particular, this book would most certainly have been incomplete. Special thanks are also due to Professors G. Bellingeri and R. Zipoli of the Institute for Iranian Studies at the University of Venice, and to the Professor of this Institution, Professor Giansoberto Scarcia who, among other things, read the typescript of the Introduction.

Blue Silk. Nain Carpet
Very fine Genuine Silk.

Foreword

Of making many books, we are told, there is no end. This maxim is certainly true of books about Oriental carpets, which in recent years have proliferated to an almost bewildering extent. This profusion is, however, rather to be applauded than condemned, reflecting as it does the great upsurge of interest in (and ownership of) Oriental carpets, rugs, and flat-weaves in the West during the last thirty-five years. For until this period, apart from one or two notable works that have become classics of Oriental-carpet literature, the whole fascinating and immense subject lacked anything approaching adequate coverage in print.

It is not really surprising that this should be so: until the present century Oriental carpets found their way to Western markets in only relatively small quantities, and they appear to have been regarded, as denizens of "the mysterious East," as being incapable of matter-of-fact description or down-to-earth analysis. Indeed, the aura of mystery that surrounded them could hardly have been swept away in days when communication was difficult and travel was expensive and protracted. Aren't the very names associated with the countries from which they came evocative of romance and legend: the far-distant Oxus, Bokhara and Samarkand, the Silk Road, Tamburlane and Genghis Khan?

The appearance and texture of the carpets themselves could only have enhanced this sense of strangeness. The exotic designs with unfamiliar though obviously significant motifs, the marvelously conceived dispositions of color, and the sumptuous "handle" of these fabrics must all have added to the feeling that they were alien—in this lay part of their attraction.

Then, too, the complexity of the subject, stemming from the enormous diversity of weaves, sizes, origins, and designs, must have baffled many a student of Oriental carpets and deterred many an aspirant from becoming their chronicler. Modern scholarship, systematic research, ease and speed of travel, scientific techniques—all these are only in our generation beginning to help us to classify, catalog, and analyze the vast quantities of information and knowledge that are there for our eyes to behold. Not that there can be any question of "explaining-away"; the object of our

studies is more than able to retain its elusive individuality, be our microscope ever so powerful.

A further obstacle on this road of exploration, daunting would-be scholars, may have been the obscurity of the origins of the hand-knotted carpet. There are conflicting opinions about the original place and earliest time to which its birth can be attributed. But whether the site was in fact Nineveh or Babylon, Persia or central Asia, and the date before or after 500 B.C., there is such an absence of documentary or pictorial evidence that the arguments will no doubt continue to rage for many years to come.

This brings us to a notable characteristic of many Oriental-carpet books—the great amount of heat (and small amount of light) generated by the scholars', students', and self-appointed experts' opinions on the subject, expressed often enough with an airy confidence totally unjustified by the weak support put forward for their hypotheses. It is almost as though the writers were writing only for each other rather than for the general reader or even for the specialist.

This volume avoids such pitfalls. It is designed and constructed to be of interest and profit both to the neophyte and to the amateur. That does not mean that it is not a scholarly work. On the contrary, the author is of an academic standing such as to guarantee the soundness of the book's text and the reliability of the information which it imparts. The research undertaken has been thorough and original. The general reader and the collector of Oriental carpets will both find here interesting and useful material of practical value, whether a first or subsequent purchase is being contemplated, or whether there is simply a wish to be better informed about a fascinating sub-division of the world of art where it meets and blends with that of handicraft.

There is a novel departure in the presentation of information on each of the illustrations in the Appendix: the use of codified symbols to convey the standard basic characteristics of each piece shown. This should enable readers to make comparisons more easily and help them to establish the various categories more clearly in their own minds—a prime requirement in any book of this kind.

John C. Hicks

How an Oriental Carpet Is Made

Take a warp or web of threads, or chains arranged lengthwise, and weave or interlace a weft of threads, crosswise. By tying knots between one or more threads of the weft you have a "knotted" carpet. This simple definition is not intended to disguise the complex and numerous factors involved in carpet making. Basically speaking the technique of knotting a carpet is one of the simplest skills of the artisan. It has undergone very few developments or changes down the centuries, and is still carried on very much as it used to be in olden times. Carpets are now part and parcel of our common cultural heritage. They have often reached the level of full-fledged works of art, revealing that perfection of proportion and balance, both technical and formal, which is the vital element of any art. In order to get some idea of the problems faced by the anonymous craftsmen (only the exceptional few are known by name) in pursuing their skills, and in order to go beyond the pure emotional reactions produced by works that are the fruit of man's genius and remarkable determination, it will perhaps be helpful to analyze the various elements that go into making a carpet; and we shall limit ourselves to those basic technical concepts that can be easily observed by watching an artisan at work.

Looms

The carpet is knotted upon a loom. Although there are various shapes and sizes of looms, the most common types are still the horizontal and the vertical. As a rule the horizontal, which is easier to operate, was and still is used by nomadic tribes, while the vertical was adopted by sedentary peoples. The technical and mechanical parts of both types are virtually the same, but the results obtained can be quite different. The horizontal loom consists of two usually not very long beams, fixed to the ground with pegs, to which the threads of the warp are attached. A tripod made of rods supports an upright post which in turn supports two axles. One of these acts as the heald or heddle and is attached to the warp threads. In this way a

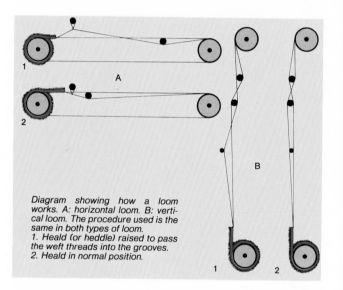

Diagram showing how a loom works. A: horizontal loom. B: vertical loom. The procedure used is the same in both types of loom.
1. Heald (or heddle) raised to pass the weft threads into the grooves.
2. Heald in normal position.

double arrangement of chains is formed, one upper and one lower. With this the loom operator can at will raise or lower the even (lower) threads or the odd (upper) threads, making alternate "channels" (partings) in which to pass the weft (or woof) thread. The operation begins with a fairly narrow woven border (with or without fringing), using the *kilim (ghilim)* technique (see page 10). Having thus secured the selvage (or selvedge), which serves to keep all the subsequent weave in place, the craftsman then starts knotting short, thin threads—which he chooses on the basis of color from large balls—to the warp chains. His technique will vary depending on the locale. Once he has completed a lengthwise line of knots, he will pass one or more weft threads, thus tightening the knots at the lower border of the carpet. The weft threads are knotted at the lateral borders in a variety of ways which differ from tribe to tribe. And so the work continues, with row after row of knots, until the

plane of the warp chains. To make a carpet that is larger than the length of the loom, the same method as for the horizontal loom is used: the completed part is rolled around the lower beam and the warp is then laid out again. Here too the principal defect is caused by the irregular linear arrangement of the carpet which can be produced by the uneven tension of the warp chains. In addition to vertical looms with fixed frames there are models of a different type which make it possible to weave carpets that are larger than the loom without any of the drawbacks already mentioned. In the so-called Tabriz loom the lower beam can be rotated: the warp is arranged on two parallel planes divided by beams, one in front and one behind; as the work gradually proceeds the completed part is pushed downward and then moves up the rear section of the loom, while the warp threads, which are initially on the second plane, gradually work their way in front of the craftsman. Carpets made in this way cannot be more than twice as long as the loom, but they keep the tension and the straightness of the warp even.

The third type of loom, on which regular carpets of any length can be made, has two rotating axles. As the completed section of the carpet is gradually wound around the lower beam, the warp chains are unrolled from the upper beam.

The advantage of the horizontal loom lies in its utter simplicity, its lightness, and the ease with which it can be operated—all qualities that are greatly appreciated by the nomadic and semi-nomadic peoples who still use it to this day. It cannot be used for making very wide carpets, but there are virtually no limits where length is concerned. The only drawback that recurs in carpets made in this way—as already mentioned—is the imperfect linearity.

Knots

The difference between a carpet and other textile handicrafts (tapestries, *kilim,* fabrics, etc.) lies in the fact that short lengths of thread or yarn are tied to the warp chains to form the pile of the carpet. These are ordinarily called "knots," an incorrect term, but one that is now commonly used and universally accepted, inasmuch as it is not an actual knot but rather a loop. There are three specific ways of tying this loop or knot on the warp chains: the Turkish system (*Ghiordes* knot), the Persian system (*Sehna* knot) and the Arab-Spanish system.

The Turkish system (*Turk baff*), known as the

carpet is finished. When part of the carpet is complete, the pegs are removed and the completed section is rolled around the beam. At the same time the tripod and the axles are moved forward. To keep the right degree of tension at the sides of the carpet, hooks are used, and these are attached to another set of pegs driven into the ground.

The vertical loom is similar in construction. There are two vertical poles (but not in every case because sometimes the walls of a room will be used as a support), which hold two transverse beams, one at the top and one at the bottom, to which the warp threads are attached. Opposite the craftsman is the pole which acts as the heald and enables him to shift the

Diagram showing the Turkish or Ghiordes knot. 1, 2, 3. The knot in cross-section and perspective, knotted to the warp chains at the three possible angles. 4. Two adjacent knots in perspective and with the threading of the weft. 5. Double knot or jufti, tied using the Turkish system; four warp chains are attached.

Diagram showing the Arab-Spanish knot, knotted to a single warp chain, drawn with the threading of the weft.

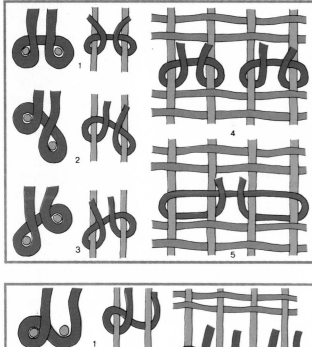

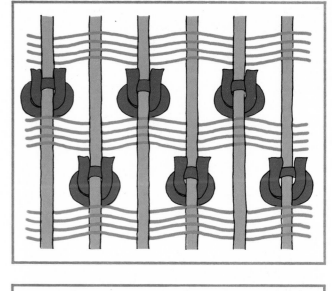

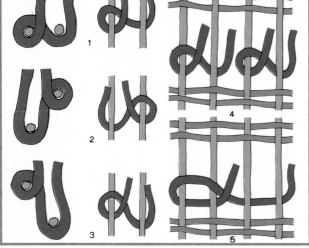

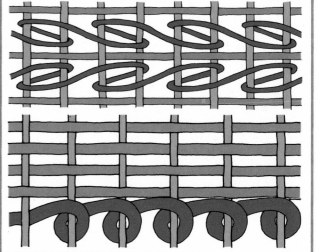

Diagram of the Persian or Sehna knot. 1, 2, 3. The knot in cross-section and perspective, knotted to the warp chains at the three possible angles. 4. Two adjacent knots in perspective and with the threading of the weft. 5. Double knot or jufti, *tied using the Persian system; four warp chains are attached.*

Above: Diagram showing the technique used in flat carpets known as sumak. *Below: Diagram showing the technique of flat carpets known as* kilim.

Ghiordes (or Gordian) knot after the name of the Anatolian city where, legend has it, Alexander the Great had to unravel that famous and most intricate knot, consists in making the loop in such a way that the two ends of the thread end up together in the space between two adjacent warp chains, around which they are passed.

The Persian system (*Farsi baff*), known as the Sehna (or Sinneh) knot (Sehna is present-day Sanandaj, a place in Iranian Kurdistan where, as it happens,

the knot was never used, and still is not!), consists in one end of the thread being looped around a warp chain to emerge between the second warp chain and the chain that will carry the loop in the following knot. The position of this second end of the thread, which may be to the right or left of the chain with the loop, determines whether the knot will be a right-hand or left-hand knot.

The Arab-Spanish system, which is the simplest of the three, consists in looping the thread to just one warp chain: the two ends cross at the back of the chain and are passed through again to the front. This last type of knot is the least used, and is limited to Spain (see page 10).

The Turkish knot is used in Turkey, in the Caucasian region, and generally in areas where Turkish is spoken. The Persian knot is used by peoples who speak Iranian, in India, and in China. The fact that both the Turkish knot and the Persian knot are irregularly spread throughout the carpet-making regions makes it difficult to establish whether one knot was more used than the other, except within a particular zone, and this has caused some experts to abandon the two traditional definitions in favor of a more scientific terminology: the symmetrical (Turkish) knot and the asymmetrical (Persian) knot. Because of the general approach of this book, however, we have preferred to stick to the more traditional and current names: the Ghiordes and Sehna knots, even though these are less correct in a technical sense.

The Turkish knot is the better one in terms of stability and solidity, but the Persian knot makes it possible to achieve sharper outlines and details in the design of the weave. If one examines the pile of a carpet made with the Persian knot it is possible to separate the two ends of the thread—if the knot is well made —which is not possible with carpets made with the Turkish knot.

The term "shared warp" is used when a knot is attached to a free warp chain and a second chain on which there is already a knot. This practice is common in certain Turkmen tribes, such as the Yomud.

Not only is it impossible to make rigid regional distinctions (designs, techniques, and craftsmen have always tended to move from place to place), it is also no less true that both types of knot can be found in one and the same carpet. This is because, in order to make the carpet more wear-resistant, Ghiordes knots are sometimes used on the warp chains nearest to the edges of the carpet, and these edges, incidentally, are knotted using the Persian method.

We should also mention the *jufti* knot, which is also known as the double knot or false knot. It can be used in both the most widely used methods, and it is quite straightforward: instead of making the knot on two warp chains, it is made on three or even four. The reason is fairly obvious; this method saves time and thread. But it is also obvious that this method affects the beauty and life of the finished product. Sometimes the carpet maker will include a *jufti* knot every so

often, and this does not have an adverse effect on the end result, whereas a carpet made entirely with this knot will be of poorer quality. We are obviously referring to modern knotted carpets. In earlier times the *jufti* knot was used in certain highly artistic Persian carpets, clearly not to reduce the density of the pile but because it is a very adaptable knot, particularly in the Persian system, permitting an extreme degree of precision in the detail; it also helped the weaver in his tiny circular designs.

There is a staggering number of variations that can be used (and is widely used) with such an apparently simple basic technique. Our observations are somewhat general in nature, so as to give some idea of this basic feature of the carpet: detailed technical publications are the best sources of information, although real knowledge can only be picked up by looking directly at the carpet in question, and practice makes perfect when it comes to classifying carpets.

When dealing with carpets the following type of equation is often made: the greatest number of knots per square inch equals the highest quality product. But there has been too much stress on this formula, which is simplistic and short-sighted. There are excellent carpets with a low number of knots per square inch—and we should not forget that over and above being things to buy, carpets are often works of art or show great craftsmanship deserving of serious study, regardless of their market price—whereas other carpets with a higher number of knots are of no interest whatsoever. Nevertheless a good carpet maker manages to tie, on average, about 14,000 knots a day. With this fact in mind and using reliable parameters, which we need not go into here, the time taken to make some of the most famous carpets in the world has been worked out with considerable accuracy. The Ardabil carpet (1128 x 534 cm/37' x 17'6"), for example, was made by eight or ten master craftsmen and took not less than 3½ years to complete. The carpet showing hunting scenes in the Austrian National Museum (680 x 320 cm/22'4" x 10'6") provided eight craftsmen with 3 years' work; the carpet showing hunting scenes in the Poldi Pezzoli Museum in Milan (692 x 360 cm/22'9" x 11'10") took seven or eight craftsmen between 16 and 18 months to finish. The number of knots per decimeter can be very high indeed: part of an Indian carpet made of silk in the first half of the 17th century has about 2,450 knots per square inch.

Motifs with a mainly floral decoration used on the various stripes of the border. 1. Wavy (vine) shoots with flowers, a Persian pattern. 2. Alternating stylized flowers, Persian. 3. The Persian boteh motif. 4. Alternating naturalistic rosettes and buds, Persian. 5. Wavy shoots with naturalistic flowers, Persian. 6. Elongated half-lozenges with the boteh motif, Persian. 7. Geometric shoot with flowers, a Persian motif used on the border. 8. Shoot with flowers and leaves, a Persian motif used on the border. 9. Stylized star-shaped flowers, Caucasian. 10. Stylized rosettes inside lozenges, Caucasian.

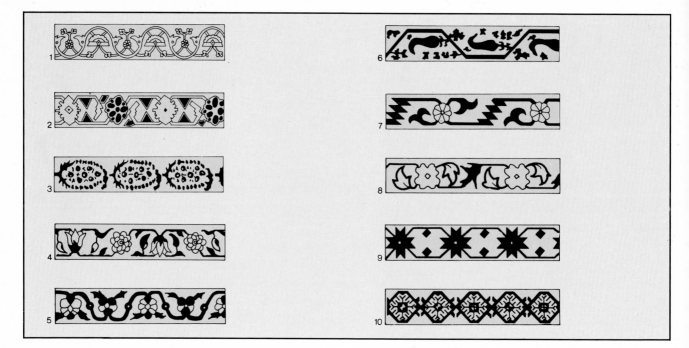

Techniques for Borders, Edges and Wefts

The border is a very important part of the carpet. In fact, it determines the strength of the carpet. The rows of knots are pushed against the border, with the result that its solidity is fundamental for the life of the product. The most commonly used technique for this part of the carpet is the *kilim* technique (*kilim* or *ghilim* is a Turkish term which is used throughout much of the Near East). It is used to make fabrics that have various uses (tents, blankets, mats, and rugs). Weft threads of various colors are woven onto the warp and passed (by means of a shuttle) alternately above and below the various chains. As the work gradually proceeds, the weft threads are squeezed tightly together. Unlike carpets, both sides of the fabric are identical. The strip used for the border of carpets, which may be fringed or otherwise, is usually very narrow and not decorated, but in some types, for example the Tekke carpets, it is decorated and can be up to 70 cm/27" wide, thus very much part and parcel of the carpet as a whole. A particular feature of some *kilim* is the vertical cracks or apertures in the fabric. This occurs when the pattern follows vertical lines parallel with the warp chains. The two differently colored wefts are in fact hooked to two adjacent chains which nevertheless remain apart from one another and cause these so-called cuts. This does not

happen if differently colored wefts are hooked alternately to one and the same warp chain, but this makes it difficult to form perfectly vertical lines in the pattern. Then there is another textile or weaving technique which must also be mentioned. It is known as *sumak*, and apparently is named after the city of Shemakhi in Azerbaijan (Transcaucasus). It is used by craftsmen in this region. The thread is passed at the front over four warp chains and from below ties two (or else it is passed over two and ties just one); the "stitches" made in this way end up on top of each other and give the impression of fish spines when the direction of the same stitches is alternated from row to row. To give the fabric the right texture and consistency, a weft thread is passed through every row or every other row of stitches.

The sides of a carpet—as opposed to the borders, which are at each end—can also be finished using various techniques. As a rule the first and last two- or three-warp chains are left free, that is, without knots. The weft is wound around these in the form of a figure 8, and produces a flat edge. In some cases quite large cords (one or two on each side) are laid beside the warp chains, equivalent in thickness to the chains with knots, and these are covered by the weft threads which are also tied with knots to the first two warp chains.

Geometric motifs. 11. With elongated lozenges, Persian. 12. Star-shaped designs alternating with stylized lilies, Persian. 13. Stylized rosettes and leaves, a Persian and Turkish pattern used for the border. 14. Geometric forms with fringes, Persian. 15. Design with square brackets or stylized Arabic lettering, Turkish. 16. Double intersected lozenges with alternating colors, Caucasian. 17. Shoots with flowers and leaves, highly geometric, Persian border pattern. 18. Zigzag line with alternate upturned Ts, Caucasian. 19. Continuous octagons with six-branched patterns, Caucasian. 20. Octagons with stars, Caucasian.

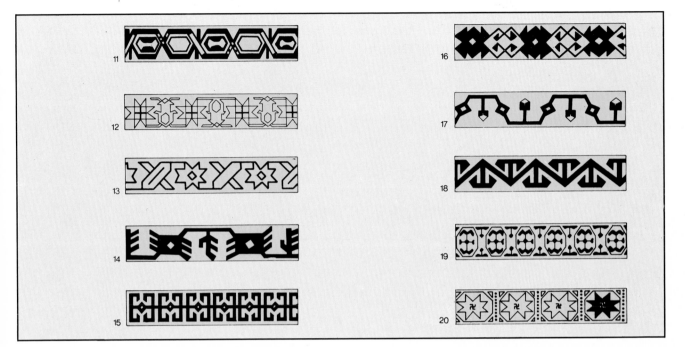

There are also numerous ways of inserting the weft. These can vary considerably in both thickness and number, and also in the way in which they cross the warp chains. For example, one might have a thicker weft passing across the taut warp threads, and a thinner weft passing across the slacker warp. In many cases the weft is hidden and is only strengthened by other threads at intervals of two or three knotted rows. In the Bijar carpets there may be up to five wefts (one large taut central one, with two thin slack wefts on either side). It is obvious that this system, as practiced in this part of the world, produces carpets that are extremely tough. As far as wefts are concerned, we should mention the practice known as "lazy lines." This was typically used in old Turkish carpets. These lines can occur when two weavers work at the same time on the same carpet. Their rhythms may obviously be different, and so instead of waiting until both weavers have finished their own line of knots before inserting the weft, they proceed separately, inserting the weft from the edge toward the center, but only in that particular part of the carpet for which each weaver is responsible. This can give rise to small void areas, and as the knotting proceeds a visible diagonal line is formed, although it is visible only on the back of the carpet. These lazy lines may be visible on the front of the carpet if the pile is worn.

It does, however, seem clear that there is no precise rule when it comes to making the border, whether fringed or not, or the sides or the weft of a carpet. All these factors vary from region to region, and it is not always the case that a specific feature to do with the making of a carpet is necessarily exclusive to a given geographical area. Classifications made on the basis of these features are extremely uncertain, given that any classification must be based on the sum of the various features of a carpet, and even then will invariably be empirical.

Tools

As we shall see, the carpet was probably invented by nomadic peoples living from sheep rearing. And as we have tried to establish already, it is an essentially artisan product (although quite capable of becoming a work of art), made with a great deal of talent and few tools. Even today the carpet maker's tools are very few in number: a blade to make the initial cut once the thread has been knotted (this blade may have a kind of hook at the tip, used for tying the Turkish knot, but found only in the Tabriz region); a sort of comb, made of wood or metal, used to push knots and weft tightly together; and a pair of very sharp scissors to cut the carpet to a perfectly even form once it is finished.

The main tools used by carpet weavers.

Two examples of twisting fibers:
1. The S-plied clockwise.
2. The Z-plied counterclockwise.

The main tools used by carpet weavers.

Where design is concerned, the nomadic peoples usually repeat a single geometric motif several times, sometimes adding variations. For the most part the designs are very old and have been handed down from father to son. For more complicated designs there are patterns or "cartoons" drawn by master craftsmen on squared paper, with each square corresponding to a knot. The importance of the design is also shown by the existence of special, jealously guarded books, filled with mysterious symbols, in which a carpet is described from the first knot to the last, just as the master craftsman dictates the knots, row after row, keeping to himself the secret of how the actual design develops.

Materials

The most important material in carpet making, on which the carpet's success or failure depends, is the type of thread or yarn used. By far and away the most widely used material, in the geographical regions where carpets are made, is wool, both for the warp and weft, and where the pile of the carpet is concerned. It may be sheep's wool or goat's wool. Cotton is used quite extensively, especially for warp and weft, and sometimes other materials are also used, such as hemp, jute, or camel's hair. Silk carpets, which are highly prized, may have a woolen or cotton warp. One specific technique consists in inserting a thin metal—usually silver—wire in the yarn (which is almost invariably wool or silk). This gives the carpet a sumptuous look, but it tends to dull with time.

The choice of the right wool to use is one of the secrets of good carpet making. The Persians, who are past masters in this type of craftsmanship, have had domesticated sheep from the Neolithic period onward. The quality of their wool is not among the best (it is inferior, for example, to the Merino sheep from Australia), but because of a certain resistance, or even hardness, and because of the special sheen it gives off, it is ideal for the main purpose for which it is used: making carpets.

Special care is taken in the selection of the best types of wool, and here one name, now a household one, instantly springs to mind: mohair. This term derives from the Arab-Persian word *mohayyar* which means "choice" or "selection" and refers to the underhide of a goat. We also owe the word "cotton" to the Near and Middle East. This derives from the Arabic word *quṭn* (Babylonian *kitiunu*) and not from the Sanskrit *karpasa* (although the Persian term *karbās* has been retained to denote a cotton garment—Hebrew *kirpās*, Greek *carbasos*, Latin *carbasus*). The term *pambeh* (middle Persian *pambak*) is also Iranian, whence Greek *pambax*, Latin *bambacium*, modern Italian *bambagia*, meaning cotton wool. The wool used has to be shorn. The wool of dead animals (*tabachi*) is definitely of lower quality (because it is less wear-resistant), as is wool removed from animals without shearing. The best wool comes from the shoulders and back of the animal.

Cotton, which as already noted is used mainly for the warp and weft, rarely appears in the pile of a carpet. In olden times silk was used in extremely delicate

Two nomads from the Zohreh valley in central-southern Iran busily at work weaving a kilim. In the foreground we can see the typical tripod-type of horizontal loom. Note also the distinctively bright color range of the warp chains. Carpet weaving and knotting is still one of the main economic activities of the nomadic tribes of Iran.

and elegant carpets, but the cost has always been so astronomical that silk was practically used only for luxury products. Camel's hair is sometimes used for areas requiring that particular color, but only to a limited extent. The frequent appearance of the term *sho-* *tori* does not always refer to actual camel's hair, but means "camel-colored," and this shade of color is often found in certain sheep. Hemp and jute are rarely used, and then only for low-quality carpets.

Inside a thatched tent in southeastern Iran. The furnishings are particularly scant and typical of a level of material life hovering just above subsistence. In the foreground we can see a carpet of average quality; the women, alone inside the tent, are tending to the latest addition to the family.

The way the wool is washed is extremely important. Washing does not always take place, in fact, and some people credit the natural fat content in the wool fibers with providing the sheen of some carpets and the fondness shown for them by household pets like cats and dogs, which are often not averse to chewing them. But when the wool is washed, one of the most important rules in the operation is that there should be plenty of running water with no alkaline substances in it. When the water is "hard" it is necessary to add chemical elements (potash or potassium carbonate) to offset the lower detergent properties of the water. It is certainly no accident that one of the most important imperial Persian "factories" in the 17th and 18th centuries was situated in the city of Isfahan, which stands in the middle of a vast oasis with an abundance of water. The next stage in the washing process is to separate the fibers on the basis of color and quality, to remove any remaining extraneous particles, and to comb the wool itself. Carding and the older method of "teaseling" or "raising" the wool is done with the string

of a heavy bow that is made to vibrate just above the wool, the vibrations having the effect of separating it.

At this point the wool is ready to be spun. Spinning requires a wool- or skein-winder, but in the East one can often see shepherds spinning their wool in the oldest and simplest way known to us: a spindle is held in one hand, balanced by one or more whorls in the other. The wool is added little by little, forming a yarn or thread that is rarely even in thickness or length. This is far from being considered a defect. Today wool spun in this way is still the most sought after. In conventional terms one talks of "S" spinning and "Z" spinning to indicate whether the fiber has been spun clockwise or counterclockwise. The distinction of S- or Z-twisted yarn is a very important one for the scientific study of carpets. Unlike the pattern of geographical diffusion of the two types of knots, there is no strict differentiation, either regional or technical, in the method of twisting the fiber with the S or Z technique, although as a general rule Z twisting is associated with nomad products or rural products, and S twisting is associated with urban products. In most cases several fibers twisted together form the thread of both the pile and the warp and weft. The method used for twisting is often explained in specialized exhibits or slides in museums. Z2S is an example of the most commonly used abbreviation. This means that the yarn is made up of two threads, each one twisted or plied like a Z, and then both twisted together like an S. (Z2S)4Z means that four "threads," all individually plied in the manner just described, are in turn twisted in a Z-shaped spiral. This type of yarn is known as a "cable," and is used as a weft.

Dyeing

Another essential operation is dyeing the materials used. Up until about 1860 carpets were made with fibers dyed with colors extracted from the vegetable or animal world. Slightly more than a century ago artificial dyes, known as aniline dyes, were introduced by Westerners. These were much easier to make and more practical to use, but considerably inferior as far as the fiber's resistance and color were concerned, and with regard to the infinite variety of color shades which the craftsman himself could produce. These colors have a tendency to fade quickly, and after a few years the carpet takes on a flat grayish color. The red obtained using aniline dyes can almost be identified by a fairly characteristic metallic blue hue.

In Persia, the major carpet-making center in the world today, where some excellent craftsmanship is still evident, the use of artificial dyes has dropped sharply in the past few decades.

These are the main materials with which colors used to be made:

Red—There are numerous possible shades of red. The most highly prized and sought after is obtained from the cochineal or scale insect, or more precisely from the body of the female. *Coccus cati*—found in Mexico and already widely used in the 17th century. The famous and very warm Armenian red is extracted from the insect *Porphyrophora Hamelii.* The insect *Kermes vermilio,* often confused with the cochineal insect, lives on a special type of oak. The color obtained is named after the term the Persians use for the grub, *kerm,* from which our words "carmine" and "crimson" are derived (and whence Kermes Oak, *Quercus coccifera*). An ancient Persian term for this color is *sakirlat,* whence the Latin *scarlatum* and our scarlet. When the insects have been caught, they are

Crocus sativus *flowers. Saffron is extracted from the stamens of these flowers and used for dyeing the silk and wool of valuable carpets yellow.*

killed (using acetic acid fumes, or by being plunged in vinegar or boiling water), dried, and crushed or crumbled. Their essence is fixed with alum, the best fixative of all, or urine. The color is water- or alcohol-soluble. It takes up to 100,000 insects to make one kilogram (2.2 pounds) of dye. Another widely used red dye is the madder extracted from the roots of the madder plant, *Rubia tinctorum,* a bush that grows up to 1 meter (3 feet) in height. It is of no use as a dye for 2 years: the roots reach their maximum potency between 3 and 9 years, and are at their highest strength between 5 and 7 years. It is thought that alkaline soil is the best for dyes of good quality: in fact the madder imported into France in the 17th century never achieved the dyeing strength of Middle Eastern madder. The plant is cut in the autumn, the roots are dried, then scraped and pulverized. The most commonly used fixative is again alum. A particularly bright red highlight with fine pinkish hues is produced by adding dried yogurt to the madder. Cinnabar is a dye with orange-red hues obtained from a resin from Zanzibar that reaches us via India and is known as "dragon's blood": it is the exudate from the leaves of *Dracaena cinnabari.* A dark red, almost brown, dye is obtained with *hennè* (henna), a powder made from the henna plant (*Lawsonia inermis),* which is widely used in Eastern cosmetics.

Yellow—One of the most beautiful and sought-after yellows, which was known as far back as the Achaemenid period in the 6th–4th centuries B.C., is saffron,

an extract from the stamens of *Crocus sativus.* It takes 4,000 stamens to make 30 grams (1 ounce). This most valuable product was used mainly for dyeing silk. The high cost of saffron has given rise to the need for less costly substitutes. One of the most widely used is *Carthamus tinctorius* (Meadow Saffron or Autumn Crocus), which is common in India, together with the powder of the turmeric root *(Curcuma longa),* which is the main ingredient of the spice known as curry. Another spice used in Eastern cooking, called *sumāc,* gives a deep yellow color. In autumn the yellow leaves of vines are picked, dried, boiled for 4–6 hours, and fixed with alum. These give a less intense yellow dye. One dye, used specifically for silk, is extracted from the flowers of succulents (containing latex) belonging to the family *Euphorbiaceae (Delphinium zalil),* which is known in Iran as *isparag* or *zalil.* The skin of pomegranates constitutes a useful combination of fixative, dye, and "tanning agent," with a mild, pale yellow color. The skins are kept when pomegranate juice is being made—this being very useful in cooking—then dried and pulverized. The active substance is obtained by adding water.

Blue—Blue is produced almost uniquely from indigo, produced in Baluchistan, Bengal, etc., extracted from the leaves of *Indigofera tinctoria.* These are kept for a long period of time in water. As a result of fermentation and oxidization processes, fibers soaked in the liquid take on the desired color. Blue dyeing using indigo is one of the most complex procedures, and the quality of the yarn and the chemical makeup of the water are especially important if good results are to be obtained. The Persians call a very deep blue *surmei,* and a very light blue *abi.*

Green—The best greens are made from berries of the buckthorn family *(Rhamnaceae),* such as *Rhamnus chloroporus* and *Rhamnus utilis. Rhamnus infectorius* used to be cultivated in the ancient city of Caesarea in Cappadocia (present-day Kayseri, in Turkey). Large quantities of the fruit were exported to Smyrna (Izmir). They were known as Persian or yellow berries.

A beautiful Nile-green color is obtained from the already mentioned *isparag,* a plant producing latex, which grows wild in places with a dry-to-arid climate. It is fixed with copper sulphate. The commonest way of dyeing fibers green is still the double-dyeing method: first yellow, and then blue (indigo).

Brown and black—For these colors, as for the various shades of white, wool that already has the respective coloration is generally used. A dark brown dye is made with the hulls of walnuts. Fibers dyed in this way become more shiny with an additional immersion in dye made from madder. The color prepared in this way is known as "camel." Camel is a shade of color obtained using the outside of acorns and the skin of pomegranate, ground up and boiled for several hours, with no fixative. A double-dyeing process, first with *hennè* (henna) and then with indigo, gives a very deep black. It is also good for dyeing hair.

Fixatives—Fixatives are necessary if the color is to stay the same shade with no alterations taking place. The best known fixative is definitely alum, in the form of potassium, ammonium, and aluminum alum. Iron and tin sulphate are also used. The fixative is often used in conjunction with astringents with a high percentage of tannic acid, serving both as a fixative and as an agent that rounds off the body of the color. One of the most widely used astringents is extracted from the leaves and skins of the fruit of the pistachio tree, either wild or cultivated. When the fixatives make a color that is too dark because of the high iron content in the alum or water, dyers use rainwater and pure alum. In ancient times dyers in the Middle East would treat aluminum sulphate with urine; the liquid was boiled and then cooled, and crystalized as pure aluminum alum. Last of all, it may be of some interest to include three "recipes" for dyeing fibers (all three examples are for wool), as described by Hawley who quotes, as his source, an Indian dyer hailing from Tabriz. The complexities and intricacies of the various processes clearly demonstrate the advanced technological levels of expertise achieved by the dyers, and the importance accorded to this branch of the art of carpet making.

Birbul's Blue. Take cinnabar, indigo, and alum, grind and sift lighter than the light dust of the high hills; soak for ten hours; keep stirring it; put in the wool and soak for many hours. Boil for three hours; wash in kurd water, water in which kurds and whey have been well beaten up; leave for three hours, and then wash and beat again in water.

A Fine Indigo Blue. Take indigo, soak it in water for twelve hours, grind it into a fine paste in a mortar, add some *Terminalia citrina,* pomegranate peel, and alum; and mix thoroughly. Boil; put the water into the hot bath and keep stirring till cold. Now mix in some iron-filings water, and boil steadily for another two-and-a-half or three hours; wash with a beating and dry.

Persian Scarlet. Take lac color, and if you choose, a little cochineal for richness, and soak from four to six days; strain it in two cloths and add alum and a little turmeric; let it stand for two hours. Put wool in and steep for twenty-four hours, then boil for two hours. Take out the wool and add mineral acid; re-enter wool and boil an hour more. Wash fifteen minutes when cold, and dry in the shade.

In any discussion of colors and the various features of them, we should not forget to mention that particular phenomenon known in the East as *abrash,* when there is a change of shade within an area of the same color. This happens, and becomes evident after the carpet has been washed or subjected to prolonged use, because of an uneven absorption of the dye and color by the fibers. *Abrash* is far from being considered a defect. If anything, the opposite is the case, with *abrash* being regarded by many people as proof of the genuine quality of the carpet in question.

Lastly, where colors are concerned, it should not be forgotten that we all see them in a different way. For example, it is a well-known fact that people in bygone times perceived colors in their own particular way, as is shown by the much abused example of the Parthenon, which had a red and blue decor. But going beyond this—in other words beyond the question of taste—it has been both historically and scientifically established that there are different values and "frequencies" between people living in large modern conurbations, and pastoral nomads roaming around Central Asia. These conflicting views are partly responsible for that flat or excessively gaudy appearance which we attribute to certain carpets—an effect that is totally alien to the effect intended by the weaver who made the carpet. An anthropological study designed to examine how much Western tastes and requirements have altered the sensitivity of the carpet maker would certainly be of great interest. A similar thing, if not exactly identical, happens, for example, when a Westerner listens to Asian music: on the whole his reaction is that "all Asian music sounds the same," whereas, in reality, the various forms of Asian music are the result of a different cultural upbringing, and this upbringing is not better or worse than Western upbringing, merely different.

The Stages of Carpet Making

It is necessary at this point to summarize the stages and basic elements in the process of making a carpet. Below we list the fundamental operations:

1. Setting up the loom as solidly as possible so as to avoid any distortions that will inevitably be reflected in the carpet itself.

2. Setting up the warp, having selected the most suitable fibers for the stress created by the knot.

3. Fiber selection, above all for wool, and dyeing.

4. Making the border, knotting the threads, passing the weft, and finishing the edges.

5. Following the design (using a pattern or from memory).

6. Compressing the knots and the wefts to make the fabric solid.

7. Final clipping of the pile of the carpet (usually left up to a very experienced master craftsman).

The art of carpet making calls to mind another decorative technique: mosaics. Just as every tessera is placed next to an adjoining tessera to complete a design in which every single piece is essential but where no single piece dominates, so carpets are made knot by knot. The major difficulty in making a carpet is the absence of a supporting base (mosaics have such a base), and the consequent likelihood of making mistakes. In larger carpets this problem is overcome by having a cartoon with the design on top which indicates every knot to be tied; and of course on rural looms the experience and skill of the carpet weaver counts for a lot.

In conclusion it seems obvious from these words about the technique of carpet knotting that this craft is essentially a job that requires various skilled hands. When one sees those marvelous knotted carpets, which are no less than masterpieces, one cannot avoid comparing them with the works of the great painters of the Renaissance, where everything was organized down to the tiniest detail with a great deal of care and attention, and where many hands had a part in the *oeuvre*. The major difference lies in the fact that the art of the carpet is what we would now call a collective art, in which individual genius, cultural heritage, and the meticulous patience of many an anonymous craftsman create one of the loftiest forms of artistic human expression, possibly because of the very simplicity of the end result: the carpet.

The History of the Oriental Carpet

We know only some of the long history of the knotted carpet, and in the evidence available to us, gaps often outnumber dates that are known with certainty. In the case of certain typological categories of products made by man we can be reasonably accurate about the origins and the decorative motifs by basing our findings on, in this instance, well-preserved, dated carpets; but for whole historical periods scholars and students in this field have to base their reconstructions on fragments, reproductions (in paintings or miniatures), or on simple, though ingenious, inference. Despite the generally robust appearance of carpets, they can be extremely fragile and delicate. There can be considerable problems caused by wear, damage by moths, and color changes. So it is not surprising that, with very few (extremely fortuitous) exceptions, very little remains from periods not that far removed from today, in which we know that carpet knotting was being done on a large scale. Furthermore, it seems more and more evident, given the relative uniformity of the geographical area where most carpets are made and where they are most widespread (Anatolia, Persia or Iran, and Central Asia), that any correct and valid interpretation of the carpet as artistic object must involve including it in the cultural, socio-economic, and political context of the places and peoples where this art has been developed down the ages. It is no coincidence that leading Orientalists and art historians have recently been making contributions of major importance to this area of study. Suffice it to mention Kurt Erdmann, who has based his own investigations on two principal factors: an extraordinary knowledge of carpets, acquired as a

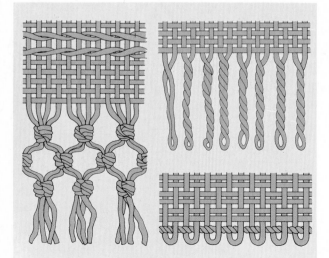

Diagram showing three ways of finishing off a carpet.

Inside the Nasir al-Molk mosque in Shiraz, which was built in the last two decades of the 19th century. This mosque echoes the decorative architectural style associated with the name of Karim Khan Zand, which flourished in the Shiraz region and represents one of the most interesting periods in Iranian architecture (influenced by European and Indian art), spanning the 18th and 19th centuries.

result of years and years of research and observation, and the equally extraordinary familiarity he shows for the various arts, major and minor, practiced in the East. This line of research has already borne much fruit, and will continue to do so, providing that the study of the complex artistic area of the history of the carpet, which implies a whole world, is no longer considered as a world completely separate from other worlds.

The major problem, which is still at the top of the list today for anyone whose subject is carpets, is classifying and cataloguing the material used. This is something that does not really concern the carpet trader, for whom one name (which is usually chosen at random or by convention) is much the same as the next, and the more high-sounding the name, the better it is for business. And in many cases the owner of a carpet will be more interested in its price than in its place of origin. But for anyone who takes a serious interest in carpets, the place of origin or rather the attribution of a carpet to a given group or typology is an essential step to take. Unfortunately, the shortage of certain data available to us is a cause of constant frustration for the specialist. In fact, there is still no standard method of classification and despite the dozens of books—some of which are clearly better than others—published in an apparently endless stream, our overall knowledge is still patchy. The publication of books is undoubtedly a positive feature and meets the public's general requirements. This revival of interest in carpets is being encouraged, but even more important are the still sporadic attempts to sort out and classify whole groups of carpets, which are of little concern to the lover of beautiful objects but nevertheless advance the actual study of carpets on scientific bases. These considerations are preliminary and basic to all our observations.

In fact, it should not be forgotten that the study of knotted carpets is still to a large extent an empirical one, based more on intuition and feelings than on hard facts. Our classification by type of material, type of knot, and type of decoration is one of many ways of grouping carpets, and it seems to us to be the most rational and easily interpreted method for a research subject, which is still unknown to very large numbers of people, and should possibly be taken out of that mystique-shrouded circle of "the initiated." The generic classification methods, however, are always subject to changes, and ours are no exception to this rule. In our analysis of the various carpets, we have tried to maintain a balance between an empirical methodology, based on associations between designs and materials, and a more scientific methodology that gives its most fertile results in the detailed analysis of the basic structures (warp, weft, and pile) and the manner in which these are organized. An American scholar has suggested the setting-up of a data bank to incorporate all possible information (and there is plenty of it) about a given carpet. There is no doubt that if scholars and students collaborated en masse in a project of this type, within a few years our knowledge about carpets would be a great deal fuller and broader, and the whole topic would probably be revolutionized.

But bear in mind that the movement of decorative motifs has always been associated with a migration of craftsmen—one of the more notable being the Armenians deported by Shah Abbas from Azerbaijan to Central Iran. We also know of movements and contacts between Turkmen (Turkoman) peoples and the inhabitants of the Caucasus and Azerbaijan between the 17th and 19th centuries. At the beginning of the 18th century, in the Caucasus again, we find the migration of members of the Turkmen Tekke clan. But in this respect a special mention, with greater detail, must be made of an outstanding historical figure, Nadir Shah Ashraf, the Persian sovereign with solid Turkmen ancestry, who dominated a whole historical period—the first half of the 18th century—to which we can trace large numbers of old carpets that still exist today. Nadir was born in the mountains in a tent not far from Mashhad, in 1688, and was crowned Shah in 1736. He reigned until 1747 when he was assassinated. In these ten years he found the time to undertake countless military campaigns which took him everywhere. In Persia these journeys took him, for example, to Isfahan, Qazvin, Mashhad, the Tabriz region, Kirman and Baluchistan, Shiraz, and the Gulf. More than once he passed through Herat, and he went to Qandahar and Kabul. He overran northern India, and stayed for a while in Delhi (and we know for sure that he took Indian craftsmen with him); he made raids into Transoxiana (Bukhara, Khiva, and Balkh fell to him, but he did not reach Samarkand); to the west he led campaigns to Daghestan (after his Indian and Central Asian exploits), and set foot in all the major Caucasian cities. He marched into Mesopotamia and laid siege to Baghdad. It goes without saying that the conquering Shah did not travel alone. He took armies with him, and the word "armies" embraced all manner

of backup units and an unknown and fluctuating number of "flankers." These armies usually numbered tens of thousands of men. And in their tents the carpet was, as always, the major article of furnishing. This observation nevertheless means that we must be extremely careful in our attributions, because this period (as were many periods both before and after it) was one of great geographical and social mobility. And the discovery of knotting techniques or decorative motifs typical of a region in some other area should not come as a surprise but rather strengthen our determination to concentrate on more and more detailed and in-depth research.

In other respects we can look forward to an increase in the number of scientific publications based on the various great private collections of carpets, we can hope for a series of exhibitions based on specific themes, and we can also hope that archaeological research will make available to us a great deal of useful material which will help fill in the blank areas in our knowledge of carpets.

Etymology

The etymology of the term "carpet" dates back to Greek *tapesetos* (which certain etymological dictionaries consider to be of Oriental origin; Berthold Laufer, for example, puts forward the case for considering it to be of Iranian origin. The modern neo-Persian term, in the Arabic lexicon, is *farsh*), whence Latin *tappetum* (and also *tapete* and *tapes*), and the derivative forms such as Italian *tappeto* (there is confirmation of the Bolognese term *tapedo* in the year 1290, and we also have evidence of the Venetian term *tapéo* and the Istrian *tapio*), Anglo-Saxon *taeppet* (whence modern German *Teppich*). From the Byzantine *tapetion* we get the Spanish and Portuguese *tapete* (of doubtful origin), the French *tapiz* (present-day *tapis*) and Provençal *tapiz* (from which we have the Catalan *tapit*). Arabic *tinfisa* is derived from the Byzantine *tapetion* as well, possibly by way of Aramaic.

The English term *carpet* comes from Old French *carpite,* which is in turn derived from the low or post-classical Latin *carpita,* from the verb *carpere* meaning "to tear," possibly because of the striplike shape. The Anglo-Saxon word *rug* is of Scandinavian derivation, from the Swedish *rugg* and Icelandic *rögg,* the original meaning having to do with the concept of ruffled or intricate, like a tuft of grass or a lock of hair.

The Arabic term *zarbiya* refers to carpets with a striped decorative motif, like a zebra's hide, and has a modern Italian derivative in *zerbino,* meaning mat.

The Origins of Carpets

We can only conjecture about the pre-history of the carpet. It probably originated from the dual need to cover the bare ground inside tents with a material that would provide as much warmth as possible (nothing is better than wool) without sacrificing the source of plenty represented by the wool-giving animal in the live state. If this is an accurate supposition, the inventors of the carpet would have been semi-nomadic peoples living off sheep rearing, living in a mountainous region of Asia, which cannot be precisely pinpointed, with steppelike vegetation. This region would have had a not particularly mild climate, or otherwise there would have been no need for a heavy floor covering; at the same time it would have been an area without too many fur-clad wild animals: this "identikit" picture points to the Caucasian-Armenian region, or certain parts of Persia and Central Asia. The first chunks of wool incorporated in fabric, aimed at copying the coat or fleece of animals, like a sort of artificial fur, probably developed into a technique very akin to the present-day one. There is every reason to suppose that the first carpets were made with variously colored wools, joined together at random, and in a subsequent phase, the need was felt to conceive simple decorative motifs. The wool must undoubtedly have been left for some time on the animal to provide it with warmth (even today some Turkmen tribes in Persia do not shear wool); and the carpet maker would not have started to shear until the aesthetic criterion of the design had been finalized.

The Oldest Carpets

After these few words outlining a somewhat imaginary but nevertheless probable reconstruction of the origins of the carpet, our historical inquiry will now base itself on numerous quotations and references from Antiquity which document the existence of carpets (for example, in the Bible, Exodus 36, III, and Acts 18, III). This evidence is plentiful and useful, but in some ways it is also awkward inasmuch as we cannot be sure whether it refers to knotted carpets rather than to fabrics, brocades, tapestries, or other similar products also used as coverings. The first certain dates, which are of fundamental importance, emerged

A tent belonging to Baktiari nomads in the Zagros range in Iranian Kurdistan.

A carpet decorated with the motif of a Persian garden, from northwestern Persia or the Caucasus, 18th century.

Detail of the Pazyryk carpet (4th—3rd centuries B.C.), the oldest known knotted carpet. The colors have been partly altered. It was found in southern Siberia and is now in the Hermitage, Leningrad.

as approximately 4th—3rd centuries B.C. and was saved quite by chance from being destroyed: after the chieftain's funeral the tomb was violated and a considerable quantity of water found its way inside; this water solidified inside the burial chamber and never thawed, not even on the hottest days of the year. In this way everything inside was perfectly preserved. The carpet is decorated with geometric-floral and animal motifs (possibly elk or alces) and a procession of twenty-eight horses, some with riders, others accompanied by attendants walking beside them, which bring to mind some of the motifs on the great stone panels of Nineveh and Persepolis. It would, in fact, seem evident that this carpet, which is of exceptional artistic and cultural importance, is not one of the first examples in the history of carpets, but rather a link in a long chain: unfortunately, the preceding links are all missing, and not many of the later ones are well accounted for either. In terms of evidence, the saddle fragments showing the technique of the knotted carpet, found once again by Rudenko in the Basadaj excavations (180 km/112 mi west of Pazyryk) confirm the existence of a possibly marginal but by no means casual tradition in Scythian art (although it also seems quite likely, on the basis of the information available to us, that these were imported goods); but this is of no help when it comes to defining a style. Similar observations can be made about the few fragments from Noin-Ula (Mongolia), discovered by the 19th-century Kozlov expedition, and to some extent about the finds of the expedition, mounted by Sir Aurel Stein and Albert von Le Coq, which went to Turfan in Central Asia in the early part of the 20th century.

only a few decades ago as a result of Soviet archaeological research: the oldest knotted carpet (but probably knotted, in Erdmann's opinion, using a different technique from the one described earlier, although the outcome is similar) was discovered by Sergei Ivanovich Rudenko (1949) in Kurgan V (Kurgan is the term for the tumuli of Scythian chieftains) in the Pazyryk Valley in the Altaj mountain range in southern Siberia. This find—a woolen carpet measuring 200 x 183 cm (79 x 72 in)—is currently in safekeeping in the Hermitage Museum in Leningrad; it has been dated

Once again, historical sources—though still not very precise about the real nature of the product—are of help to us in the form of the description of the carpet which was in Ctesiphon in the audience chamber. (25 x 65 m/80 x 200 ft) of the Sassanid ruler Chosroes I (531–579 A.D.). It is of particular interest because it constitutes an almost unique piece of evidence of the ancient origin of certain motifs found in 17th- and 18th-century carpets, the prototypes of which have been missing. This immense carpet (given that it almost certainly covered the entire chamber) known as "The Spring of Chosroes" was of the "garden" type. The materials of which it was made were among the very richest available (silk, gold, silver, and precious stones). The decoration depicted a flower garden traversed by streams (so that the ruler could enjoy the spring at all times of the year). The main colors used were blue, red, yellow, and white. The gemstones resembled flowers in bud; pale crystals acted as the running water, and according to one source, the green of the meadows was represented by large emeralds. As already mentioned, we know nothing about the technique (even though the descriptions that we do have would suggest that it was a brocade), but there can be no doubt that a carpet of this size must have been made by joining several sections together. This technique would have been particularly well-suited to the design, which was squared, if this corresponded to the design of proper Persian gardens which are divided by water channels into large rectangles.

We do know that the Arab conquerors sacked the palace of Ctesiphon in 637 A.D. and dismantled the carpet to sell the gems in it—not a difficult task given the probable way in which it had been assembled.

We have tried to stress the fact that carpets—and even those of exceptional quality like "The Spring of Chosroes"—existed before the arrival of the Islamic era. This period provided the art of carpet making with considerable momentum for reasons which we shall discuss further on (sometimes to the point where Islam was identified with carpets and vice versa). But this question of identification is also due to the scant amount of previous reliable material evidence.

Carpets and Islamic Art

There are certain specific characteristics peculiar to that vast and complex phenomenon, Islamic art—which, geographically speaking, involves the area that lies more or less between the Atlantic and the Yellow Sea—and to the peoples who have played the leading roles in the history of the carpet, which help to clarify some of the essential aspects of the problem confronting us (how and why the art of carpet making developed in the way we know it), and form the vital foundations for any accurate cultural consideration of the carpet.

The Prophet Muhammad died in 632 A.D., and from the year 633 A.D. onward the Arab tribes started to make inroads into the neighboring territories and thus started to build the Islamic framework. Their expansion was extremely swift: barely a century after Muhammad's death we find ourselves at the Battle of Poitiers. These far-reaching conquests were in the hands of semi-nomadic peoples with a not very high level of cultural and, in particular, artistic awareness and accomplishment (especially when compared with the people of the two great empires that they defeated —the Byzantine and the Persian-Sassanid), who were accustomed to living with few "home comforts." The basis of their thinking was the Quran (Koran), but it is not only in this book—which lacks uniformity and is rather a mosaic of heterogeneous pieces—that we should look for the ideological bases of Islamic art. Does it really theorize, for example, over what Oleg Grabar calls "iconophobia"? The ban on the reproduction of images is certainly never explicitly stated, nor is it even theorized over, but in the Koran there are in fact few illustratable "scenes" (and this tradition still holds today). In other respects there is no shortage of passages that exalt beauty and the image. But for all this, no artistic doctrine is expressed: socio-economic, political, religious, and cultural factors have created a sort of attitude toward that type of art which

is also encouraged by ideological questions. God is the supreme Creator. Only He can give life, and thus create a perfect image. Painters and artists, or people who represent figures, which is in effect an imitation of what is a divine prerogative, are to be condemned. In very broad terms the nub of the concept can be taken as the following: non-prohibition of the image as such but rather, and more prudently, the absence of competition with God on the level of representing the *real* or *actual*. And this statement becomes fundamental when it comes to art being associated, in any way whatsoever, with religious sentiment. The result of this was and is a marked move toward the abstraction and exaltation, in God, of the Name and the Word as his most perfect manifestation. The Word (the Koran) has become an extraordinary propaganda vehicle, and an image of synthesis inasmuch as it is an essence-cum-symbol that anyone and everyone can immediately and easily comprehend. Hence the representation of it in many varied forms, and in many art subjects, to the point where it reaches the paradox of writing conceived as a fine ornamental motif rather

than as a means of expression, which is shown by the invention and development of an extremely refined technique of pseudo-lettering, be it an imitation of writing or the repetition of written forms which are without meaning. Writing, on a par with architecture, is nevertheless the most exalted and important art form in the Islamic world, precisely because it is drawn from the Koran. At the risk of exaggerating a little, one could say that wherever you have a Moslem you find Arabic writing. It is a strange coincidence that for the highly refined culture of China, writing (which is seen as separate from painting and versifying and thus music, but regarded as a higher form than all these) is the highest possible expression of man's art. Another feature of Islamic art is the merger, or perhaps more accurately the complementarity, of the various forms of artistic expression, which thus avoids that distinction between major art forms (architecture, sculpture, painting) and certain minor art forms, which is a typical characteristic of the cultural history of the West. There is no doubt that in this respect Islamic art has been "helped" by having allocated precise roles to painting—as something for private use—and to sculpture, of which there are very few examples in existence. Rather than drawing a distinction between religious and lay art—which is the case in Western cultures—it is perhaps more valid, where the Islamic world is concerned, to make a distinction between public and private art forms. In Islam everything is important, but there is a specific emphasis on the Mosque, the house of God, and the house of God's people at one and the same time—in other words, a place of prayer and political association. Writing, often presented as the monumental presence of the word of God, is invariably to be found in mosques, and the carpet, that basic trapping of the Moslem, is also very frequently to be seen in mosques.

Remember that the Arabic alphabet, which is also the alphabet used in the Persian and Turkish languages with their host of dialects, does not always graphically represent the vowels; in poetic forms this permits a very specific form of metaphor and assonance, which in turn allows a high degree of ambiguity. And this ambiguity is used to the full in art forms as well: ceramics of the Abbasid period (750–940) (the so-called Samarra type) and the Samanid period (874–1001) have a basic scriptlike decoration (on the whole the sayings are auspicious), but the letters themselves are so "distorted" and stylized that the substance (the meaning) is no more than a pretext for

the presentation of some extremely elegant and "decorative" form. Some stucco medallions on the walls of mausolea at Qum, a city mistakenly qualified as "holy" and the seat of an important theological school of the Shiite branch of Islam, clearly show this decorative, "ambiguous" use of calligraphy as a favorite device of decorative art. Similar examples recur throughout "religious" Islamic art, especially in Iran. It is rare to come across these abstract, ambiguous elements in modern Qum carpets, but the repetition, with few variations, of the specific design is perhaps the only traceable survivor, if survivor there be.

Let us deal with abstraction: the component elements are divided into various segments or parts and then joined together in such a way that they produce a concrete motif (an animal or a flower, for example) by the union of abstract parts. We only rarely, if ever, find a background against which a subject stands out. The approach is different. Everything is background or everything is subject: one motif does not dominate the other. There is complementarity. And the whole is delimited, but not rendered finite, by a border. There is a constant contrast between light and shade (in architecture) and between colors (in carpets). We find a major emphasis, if not a predominance, on geometry and geometric figures in Islamic art which we might call "modular art" (this is quite common in carpets, for example, the groups known as "Holbein" and "Lotto"). A module—a fairly complex geometric figure, often constructed in such a way that its relation with

the space adjacent to it is left undefined and incomplete—is set up and then reproposed several times, but without the design becoming complete. It is this, together with the *horror vacui* (the taste for filling and decorating every part of a surface), that is a particular feature of certain periods of Islamic art. The figures are often composed in a symmetrical way in relation to a variable number of axes which act as centers for the development of a motif that is often reproduced in a specular or mirrorlike way. In this way many vanishing points are created, and there is the possibility for the observer to choose his preferred angle of vision. By changing the focal center of the image (this central point can be chosen at will, although the artist has various ways and means of suggesting his particular choice), the angle of vision is also changed. In fact the effect obtained is similar to that of a kaleidoscope.

Mathematical and geometric rules are part and parcel of a large number of decorative Islamic designs. The idea of the infinite, as a result of simple, perfectly rational mathematical operations, is very much part of the spirit of Asia, as shown, for example, by the invention of the so-called magic squares. The term "magic," when applied to mathematics, or to metal objects (cups that are regarded as talismanic or cabalistic) and other forms of artistic expression would seem to be an incorrect label coined during the Middle Ages in Europe when our forbears, who were unable to grasp the scientific meaning of these objects (which sometimes are designed around the central motif of the Ka'ba—in Mecca or Makkah—the undisputed heart of the Islamic world), relegated the whole activity to the level of superstition. But do not forget that Eastern science was extremely important, discovering, among other things, a practical application in the making of magnificent astrolabes, which are of great interest to both the scientist and the art historian.

In addition to geometric patterns and motifs, which are so frequent in Islamic art, another ornamental design that is very well represented is the *arabesque* (a term coined during the Italian Renaissance which describes a clearly defined set of aesthetics and tastes). In a synthetic sense an *arabesque* is an abstract and open floral form, which may be reproduced an indefinite number of times.

In the Orient, the textile industry has always been a factor of great economic importance. One need merely make reference to the huge variety of Chinese silks which so intrigued neighboring empires (the Romans even had to draw up legislation to check the outflow of money brought about by the importation of this valuable merchandise), and the close commercial ties between the Far East and the Sassanid empire (with mutual advantages), and the relations between the Sassanid empire and the great Byzantine tradition (and here, too, the trade was never a one-way affair). The Middle Ages and the Renaissance also saw flourishing trade between East and West. The main Italian trading centers—Florence, Venice, Genoa, and Lucca—all copied the fabrics being imported and were in their turn directly responsible for certain designs produced in the East. In some cases, for example, it is very hard to make a distinction between a 16th-century Italian velvet and a 16th-century Turkish velvet. During, and even after, the period of Arab domination, Sicily, like Spain, was an important bridge for this industry, which was extremely important for the spread of iconographic motifs, both qualitatively and quantitatively. The various reciprocal exchanges between textile industries and products have, up to now, been very little studied, but there is no doubt that any future studies in this area will yield a wealth of information.

There are many reasons why Islam saw significant developments in the art of making knotted carpets. The Arab tribes, as well as the Turkish tribes of Central Asian origin, which settled in Anatolia from the 11th century A.D. onward, have a consistent semi-nomadic tradition. They have very few "things," and the objects they do possess are for everyday use. Among

A detail of the façade of the Mosque with the Three Doors (866) at Kairouan in Tunisia. The writing is a Kufic script typical of the Maghreb.

these the carpet plays a leading part. We should, at this point, mention the function of the mosque (traditionally designed after the model of the house of the Prophet Muhammad), particularly as a meeting place and a center of social and political life for the community, as well as a place of prayer. Islamic ritual prescribes prayer five times a day, with appropriate ablutions so that the faithful are pure (clean) for the actual act of prayer. It is not difficult to understand the role of the carpet as a protective covering laid on the ground. It is worth noting that in the countries with a prevalently Islamic culture, the manufacture of furniture has never been developed as an art or handicraft. In the peasant's or shepherd's house, as in the Sultan's or Khalif's house, the furnishings consist principally of the floor covering: in other words, fabrics or carpets. The dominant dimension is the horizontal one, on the floor, where the household members sit, eat, and sleep, rather than the vertical one, on the walls.

When dealing with such a complex and varied topic as the development of Islamic artistic culture—and in particular the development of the carpet—do not underestimate one factor: the huge impact created by nomadic and semi-nomadic peoples and tribes on sedentary groups—in cities—and the importance enjoyed by this vital force in the development and formation of this culture. In fact, Islam exalts the urban

area (one simply has to think of the circular plan of the city of Baghdad, which is seen as the political hub of the world, although this concept of the circular plan is a very old Asian tradition), but at the same time does not deny the nomadic, Bedouin, or Central Asian cultures as such. The Mongol and Timurid rulers often lived in tents. They were extremely elaborate tents with plenty of trappings, but they were tents all the same. The physical mobility of the peoples of Asia, with their impressive migratory patterns (these are now mainly seasonal in nature) and the tight solidarity governing the various groups formed a background which has to be reckoned with if one wants to grasp the contradictory nature that seems to characterize some of the products of Islamic art—and carpets in particular.

Let us return for a moment to the question of ornamentation to discuss the commercial aspect as compared with the motif represented. A rough division indicates that carpets made to be given to a mosque or used in a mosque are never figurative, and are almost exclusively of geometric design (including the design group that includes highly stylized animals) or floral design. Conversely, carpets made at the bidding of princes, or more generally for private use, may depict naturalistic figurative scenes with a dominant typology embracing subjects such as hunting, and thus following a tradition that can be traced back as far as the Sassanid stone reliefs of Taq-i Bustan (4th century A.D.). From a chronological viewpoint, however, these latter, with hunting scenes, are later than the preceding ones, especially the geometric examples, and cannot be dated prior to the 16th century. Likewise, the carpets commonly known as prayer rugs or mats are more recent, although there is evidence of an artistic and ornamental tendency of this type in the 15th century. Additionally, the niche motif that typifies it— this is a stylization of the *mihrab* or niche which indicates the direction of the *qibla* (the Kaaba shrine in Mecca) and orientates the faithful at prayer, can obviously not predate the Islamic period. Furthermore, it is quite likely that a certain time must have passed before the sense of the *mihrab* was misrepresented (for it is neither necessary nor vital to the architecture of the mosque, but merely acts as a sign), to the point of identifying it with prayer in itself and therefore reproducing it in carpets.

There are very few cases where a single carpet will cover the entire surface, as in "The Spring of Chosroes," to which we can add the carpet in the sanctuary of Ardabil (16th century) in Persia; as a rule, in dwellings and in mosques, various carpets are laid side by side, with one often overlapping the other. In this way the carpet does not once more represent a finished space or design, given that it may run into the adjacent carpet. It is from here that we find, to some extent, the marked stylization or abstraction of the edges and outer squares of many carpets, which do not always serve as a mere frame. In other words, they may be part of a larger design. They are not always defined and isolated. In effect they become part of a space that may be much, much larger. Here again the garden carpets provide us with an example of immediate perception. Precisely because of their squared structure they are in themselves complete, but at the same time open to multiple "integration" without losing any of their originality. On the contrary they tend to acquire that modular value and quality (when the module is a carpet its artistic typology is of virtually no importance) which we have described and defined as a feature of Islamic art. This helps us to understand how completely different carpets can exist side by side in the world's great mosques without clashing—be they floral or geometric, ancient or modern. In some cases it is possible to link the medallion in the middle of the carpet with the cupola or dome of the room in which the carpet is laid, or for which it had been designed and in which it is intended to represent a symbolic pendant or reference. Because of its shape the cupola is associated with the representation of the celestial vault, but it is also sig-

Without warning, the arid Iranian landscape turns into a garden filled with flowers. This is one of the classical themes of Iranian literature and illumination. The association between landscape, literature, and painting has never been studied seriously in depth, although it represents a thematic key to an understanding of the artistic world of ancient Persia.

nificant that the same spherical shape is also typical of the tents of nomadic groups. A similar interpretation has been put forward for the medallion in the famous Ardabil carpet, although the symbology of this carpet is apparently much more complex.

The first evidence of a carpet with a *mihrab* is the one depicted in a miniature that is part of a manuscript (a *Khalila wa Dimnah* which is kept in the Egyptian National Library in Cairo) dated 743 H, or, in other words 1343—44 A.D. Similar considerations also apply to the group of carpets which show the "mosque-lamp" motif.

A separate problem is posed by the group of Caucasian carpets typified by the dragon motif. This is clearly identifiable in some examples, and stylized to the point of virtual distortion in others. It has a complex and rather blurred history behind it. The presence

of this imaginary creature, which has the clearly defined function of an amulet, a protection against evil (and particularly against earthquakes) in a mosque (although only in mosques in the Caucasus, Azerbaijan, and Anatolia) should not come as too much of a surprise, for two sets of reasons: the symbol of the serpent-dragon has always been a familiar one in this region, and became more widespread with the arrival of Turkish peoples from Central Asia who brought with them various elements of shamanistic culture and superstition (the shaman was a sort of magician who used dances and other ecstatic practices to enter into contact with the souls of the deceased and with deities). What is more, depictions of this theme appear on numerous gateways and arches (or walls) in religious or civil buildings in the area lying between eastern Anatolia and northern Mesopotamia. Nor should

Diagram showing niches (mihrab) on Anatolian carpets: 1–4. Ghiordes. 5–7. Kula. 8. Ladik. 9–10. Bergama. 11–12. Milas. 13. Mujur. 14–15. Konya. 16. Anatolia (non-representative). Diagram showing niches on Persian carpets, Caucasian carpets, and Central Asian carpets. 17. Ancient Persian. 18. Kermanshah. 19–20. Northeastern Persia. 21. Ancient Persian (16th century). 22. Kashan. 23–24. Shiraz. 25. Caucasian (very common). 26. Kazakistan. 27. Shirvan. 28. Karabagh. 29. Baluchistan. 30. Tekke Turkmen. 31. Khiva Turkmen. 32. Beshir Turkmen.

we overlook the fact that the stylization and hence the abstraction of this motif—and we shall find this point recurring frequently in the symbology and ornamental vocabulary of the carpet—make the image more acceptable in the eyes of the Moslem believer. If we can confidently assert that carpets with hunting scenes were not made for use in mosques, we cannot, on the contrary, exclude the possibility—in fact, the opposite is very probable—that carpets with floral and geometric designs were made to order for private use.

Where carpets are concerned, one of the most common distinctions drawn is between geometric carpets (from the Turkish-Caucasian area) and floral carpets (for Persia). It is commonly accepted that although this distinction is historically inaccurate—because old Persian carpets, as we see them in paintings, are essentially geometric—it has a certain validity as well. Obviously, there are plenty of exceptions, and we can point to carpets woven by semi-nomadic peoples of Iran and Turkish groups of the Ottoman period, which operated under imperial patronage. It is this system of patronage, in turn linked with the social organization of the day, which is one of the central points of the problem. As Kurt Erdmann has rightly maintained, there are various levels in the process of carpet making. The types of carpet most easily and immediately defined are village or rural carpets, woven for the private use of the weaver, and those woven on commission (imperial or less lofty) to a predetermined design. The former are usually made in small villages, on rudimentary looms that are on the whole horizontal. Carpets made to order, on the other hand, are made in larger urban centers on vertical looms. Another distinction, which is quite crucial in our view, has to do with design: the carpet made in a village has a predominantly geometric design which, to some extent at least, has to do with the natural tendency toward stylization that is peculiar to man's instinct. But today one can sometimes find carpets woven in small towns with floral or naturalistic designs. When this is so, the weaver has almost certainly bought a cartoon in the "bazaar" with the different knots indicated, and although the weaver works as an independent, he is making a carpet to order because he is keen to make a higher profit with that particular type of design which he would otherwise not have used. Between the village and the city there are also technical differences which we have already discussed. But city carpets are more elaborate and are the product of an entrepreneurial type of

PERSIA (Eastern Persia, Mashhad)

The Cleveland Museum of Art

Design Prayer rug
Date 19th century
Size 70 x 116 cm (2′ 4″ x 3′ 10″)
Warp Cotton
Weft Wool
Pile Wool
Knot Sehna
Density 10–11 knots per sq cm (65–66 per sq in)
Principal colors Brick red, yellow, blue, azure, cream
Description The field has the simple form of a rectangular *mihrab,* and in one section the border itself follows the shape of the niche. At the center of the field, and thus of the niche, there is a very stylized tree. The border is quite wide, consisting of a double inner guard stripe, a wider central stripe and an outer guard stripe. The first guard has a design of stylized lilies in alternating colors. The second guard stripe is identical to the first, and has a continuous zigzag line. The central stripe has highly stylized S-shaped diagonal bands in different colors.

PERSIA (Kashan)

Carpet Museum, Teheran

Design Prayer rug with floral and naturalistic decoration
Date 19th century
Size 285 x 395 cm (9' 8" x 12' 11")
Warp Cotton
Weft Cotton
Pile Wool
Knot Sehna
Density 57–58 knots per sq cm (355–360 per sq in)
Principal colors Various shades of red, yellow, and cream; black, white, brown, pink, and gray
Description The field has a lobed nichelike form which suggests the idea of a prayer rug. The form is achieved by the different background color of the corner areas, while the decoration is more or less the same all over the carpet. It is a very close knit and structured design with trees in blossom with leaves, buds, and other flowers; in the tree there are numerous animals, mainly birds, but also ducks and gazelles. The border consists of two guard stripes and a central stripe. The guard stripes have identical decoration consisting of rosettes and carnations, alternating with each other and joined by shoots with leaves and flowers. The stripe itself has a similar decoration to that of the field.

ANATOLIA (Ghiordes)

The Cleveland Museum of Art

Design Prayer rug
Date Late 19th century
Size 119 x 188 cm (3' 11" x 6' 2")
Warp Cotton
Weft Cotton
Pile Wool
Knot Ghiordes
Density 10 knots per sq cm (62–63 per sq in)
Principal colors Pale yellow, red, various shades of green, brown
Description In the middle we see the arch which represents the *mihrab* niche, consisting of two parallel zigzag sections supported by two basements which are in turn supported by flowering shrubs. In the center of the niche there is an area with stylized leaves, placed above a stylized mosque lamp. Another lamp hangs from the top of the arch. At the bottom of the niche, between the two shrubs, there is a complex motif of floral forms and geometric patterns. Two steles, each ending in a large leaf, branch off from the two halves of the arch. The border does not have a subsidiary strip. It is formed by the motif of a zigzagging shoot with leaflike forms which are very stylized. The edge of the rug has small *boteh* alternating with tulip buds joined together by short slender shoots.

Opposite: Ceramic tile panel decoration, 18th-century Turkish art, Iznik style. In the center, the famous mosque in Mecca with the Ka'ba, a rather common motif in Ottoman decoration.

Below: The mihrab *of the Mausoleum of Sajgda Rukaja. Islamic Museum, Cairo.*

ANATOLIA (Ushak)

Museum für Islamische Kunst, West Berlin

Design Prayer rug
Date 17th century
Size 118 x 185 cm (3′ 10″ x 6′ 1″)
Warp Wool
Weft Wool
Pile Wool
Knot Ghiordes
Density 14–15 knots per sq cm (90–91 per sq in)
Principal colors Varying shades of red and blue; brown, yellow, green, and white
Description The center of the rug is filled by a medallion in the form of a four-leaf clover. Each lobe contains a stylized floral shape. A thin line joins the central medallion with the upper part of the niche where a small lily-shaped medallion represents the direction of prayer. The arched areas above the niches have an arabesque decoration on a background of two colors. The border consists of a narrow inner border with an S decoration followed by a second red border without any decorative motifs. The central strip is quite wide and has stylized flowering buds alternating with other floral forms. The border is rounded off by an outer border decorated with a continuous wavy shoot motif with small alternating curls.

production organization: there are those who make the design, those who dye the fabric, and those who do the actual weaving. In villages all these processes are in the hands either of one person or the community, or there may be family groups who assume the different tasks. The man prepares the wool, the woman prepares the thread (although it is often the man who produces the twisted thread); the man does the dyeing, and the woman does the weaving. This does not imply that the rural product is more genuine than the urban product. Nowadays a geometric design can be flat and monotonous, just as a floral design can be lively and attractive. Both these major groups of carpets have important symbolical features. The rural carpet contains a whole old-world range of meanings, often spontaneous and traditional, although all memory and sense of those meanings

37

Detail of a Caucasian carpet showing a dragon. Note the conspicuous stylization of the animal.

the Shiite Persians had more freedom of action with the use of figurative motifs, whereas the strictly Sunnite Turks adhered closely to their strict observance of the rule not to depict anything animate. It goes without saying that even if this explanation is only vaguely plausible, the more specific reason for this

has long since vanished. The carpet designed by a draftsman or miniaturist (we are obviously referring to old carpets) embodies a series of more cultured symbolical indications, and cunningly hidden to make the object appear purely decorative, to our eyes at least. Many authors have written that the distinction between Turkish geometric carpets and Persian naturalistic, floral carpets is based on matters of religion:

CAUCASUS (Caucasian)

Museum für Islamische Kunst, West Berlin

Design Carpet with stylized dragon
Date Late 18th century
Size 160 x 294 cm (5′ 3″ x 9′ 8″)
Warp Wool
Weft Cotton
Pile Wool
Knot Ghiordes
Density 11–12 knots per sq cm (72 per sq in)
Principal colors Red, blue, brown, yellow, in various shades; violet, white, and black
Description A carpet with geometric decoration belonging to the group or type with a dragon design; it is a late example of this group. The design is almost perfectly symmetrical and specular, from the center outward. The central section has an oval indented medallion, elongated on the vertical axis which has a four-pointed star-shaped design in the middle. At the sides of the central medallion, in a space delimited by an elongated lozenge, there are two extremely stylized dragons. These are symmetrical except for the two feet, with two heads; each has two horns. They are based on the stylized designs commonly known as "flame" patterns. The remaining parts of the central area of the carpet have small stylized designs and mainly depict numerous animal species.

ANATOLIA (Ushak)

Islamisches Museum, East Berlin

Design Prayer rug, geometric
Date 17th century
Size 120 x 180 cm (3′ 11″ x 5′ 11″)
Warp Wool
Weft Wool
Pile Wool
Knot Ghiordes
Density 15 knots per sq cm (93–95 per sq in)
Principal colors Black, light green, cream, various shades of red
Description The central area has a three-lobed, unusually shaped niche. In the center of the niche, in the lower part of the central area of the rug, there is a ribbon motif; it is extremely arched and suggests a Persian influence. The ribbon has designs of rather wavy shoots which are very elegant. The rest of the background, inside the niche, has geometric motifs and a highly stylized mosque lamp design. The corner sections also have florally inspired geometric designs. The border is fairly small: it consists of two borders of equal size decorated with stylized floral motifs.

distinction, which is a fairly rough one, is, in our view, purely sociological in nature. In this respect it is, in fact, interesting to note how commonly used objects (various types of bags for example) and *kilim,* which are used every day, and which have only recently earned the attention of collectors, are in practice almost exclusively geometric in design.

Anatolian Fragments and Carpets

Having placed the carpet, even if very summarily, within a much wider context and in particular in a special relation with that Islamic art in which it plays a leading role, we can now turn our attention to its historical and artistic development. If we bear in mind that after the Pazyryk carpet, of the 4th–3rd centuries B.C., the first important carpet finds that are chronologically closest to it are the large and significant fragments unearthed in the mosque of Alaeddin in Konya (Central Anatolia), which date back roughly to the second half of the 13th century—to the height of the power being wielded by the Seljuk Turks who had come from Central Asia—we can see what a huge gap there is in our documentation, and how meager our present-day knowledge of carpets still is. Nothing remains of contemporary Iranian carpets. Marco Polo, who was in Anatolia in 1271 on his way back from Persia, refers to Turkish and Caucasian carpets as the best and most beautiful carpets in the world. The fact that this was not an exaggeration or a mere personal opinion uttered by the Venetian—who was, incidentally, a thorough and alert observer—is confirmed by other sources, and particularly by Islamic sources (the travelers Ibn Said and Ibn Battuta), who maintain that Anatolian carpets of the 13th and 14th centuries were so sought-after that they were exported to Egypt, Syria, Iraq, Persia, and even as far as India and China. Furthermore, indisputable archaeological proof is provided by fragments unearthed at Fustat (Old Cairo) dating back to the Seljuk period.

The Seljuk fragments from Central Anatolia are all of wool, and decorated with geometric patterns (the repertoire is very varied); they are not that large, either, when compared with the dimensions of the whole carpets, which were quite impressive. The motifs are arranged in lines, in a staggered way, giving the impression of a reticulated arrangement. Hexagons abound, either divided into four (thus suggesting flower petals) or within hooked squares. Another frequent motif consists of stars in squares separated by

ANATOLIA (Ushak)

Carpet Museum, Teheran

Design Floral rug
Date 17th—18th centuries
Size 140 x 142 cm (4′ 7″ x 4′ 8″)
Warp Wool
Weft Wool
Pile Wool
Knot Ghiordes
Density 25 knots per sq cm (156 per sq in)
Principal colors Red, blue, various shades of yellow; white, green, black, brown, and violet
Description The central area has a central stylized multicolored flower, inspired from the palmette design. Above and below this flower, enclosed by a pair of serrated leaves in a similar style, there are two large flower-buds, again rendered in a stylized manner. At the sides of the central palmette there are two more serrated leaves. The rest of the central area has floral designs of various sizes, all of them geometric. The border is quite small: it consists of a border and a wider strip lined with small bands. The border has a continuous design of stylized floral and plant motifs. The strip has broad oblique segments of different colors with a star-shaped rosette at the center.

Left: A beautiful detail of the famous Caucasian carpet from Marby, showing stylized birds and compositions of Greek frets.

a "grid" decorated with hooks (of the Greek type) and small squares. The borders are quite extensive—their function must have been important in every sense—and are sometimes also decorated with geometric figures. But they often bear rather vigorous Kufic inscriptions (Kufic is a type of stylized Arabic script, geometric in appearance and rather bulky). The colors are sober and two shades of the same color are frequently used: dark blue and light blue, dark red and light red. The other main colors are green, brown, yellow, and white (even though, in time, the fibers have taken on a coloration that differs from the original). The knots are not particularly dense, varying from 500 to 1000 knots per square decimeter (30 to 60 per square inch). A carpet fragment similar to those of Konya has been discovered by Riefstahl in the Beyshehir mosque (some 80 km/50 mi southwest of Konya). It was made in 1298. The use of already aged carpets does not come readily to mind, so a date in the second half of the 13th century would seem quite probable for the whole group. Fragments found in official and unofficial excavations on the outskirts of old Cairo are of the same period and essentially similar, that is, of Anatolian manufacture. They are now scattered in various museums around the world and also include older fragments (9th and 10th centuries). In this latter instance they may be of Egyptian origin, even though we do not have any definite dates or any tradition proven by references in written sources.

There is undoubtedly a continuity between the knotted Anatolian carpets of the Seljuk period and the carpets of the following period, the Ottoman period (named after the founder of that dynasty, Othman, 1299—1326). There are two similar typologies in the 14th and 15th centuries: carpets with depictions of animals (mainly birds and quadrupeds) which are very stylized, and carpets with geometric motifs. Unfortunately, there are very few examples of carpets that can be attributed to these groups and that still survive today. But there is no shortage of documentation. This is plentifully represented in contemporary European paintings, especially those of the Italian and Spanish schools. In both paintings and frescoes, carpets appear beneath thrones, at the feet of Madonna figures, and later on, as table coverings. There is a sort of encounter between two different arts. If the carpet, in that period, was used by European painters as a decorative element, European paintings are indispensable today when it comes to writing about the development of the decorative motifs of carpets.

We know of carpets with animals which date back to 1320, and they became an extremely popular theme in Italian painting. Take, for example, the "Wedding of the Virgin" (Sposalizio della Vergine, 1348) by Nicolo di Buonaccorso; a fresco of the "Annunciation," painted in the early 15th century, in the church of the Santissima Annunziata in Florence, and the mid-14th century "Madonna" by Lippo Menni.

The depiction of Oriental carpets in European art from the 14th century onward is the most conspicuous phenomenon of an Oriental influence that actually went a great deal deeper. Here, let us merely mention —still with regard to paintings—the huge spread of Oriental fabrics (recognizable by their inscriptions) and Arabic writing that sometimes appears in the halos of Madonnas, undoubtedly initially with precise symbolical meanings which subsequently degenerated into a purely ornamental use. These are just one or two of the most conspicuous examples of an influence that has been far reaching both in the material culture (for example, the whole Mediterranean area owes a huge debt to ceramic products coming from the Orient) and in the intellectual sphere, in particular where philosophical thinking is concerned.

The accurate and reliable representation of the carpets here, showing a stylized decoration of animals, handed down to us by these Old Masters, is illustrated by the correspondence between the famous carpet with the dragon and phoenix in the Berlin museum and the paintings of Domenico di Bartolo (Siena, Santa Maria della Scala hospital, painted between 1400 and 1444) and Domenico Morone (attributed, first half of the 15th century, now in Vienna). The Berlin carpet, or rather carpet fragment, is of exceptional importance not only because it is unique, but also because it confirms the fact that the carpets represented are real carpets—not fabrics and cloths, although these are also plentiful. In the Berlin fragment (page 157), as in the other well-preserved fragment (some smallish pieces in a poor state of conservation, which can be associated with the same typology, have been discovered at Fustat, once more) from the church of Marby in Sweden and known as the Marby fragment (it is now in the National Museum in Stockholm (page 158) there is clear evidence of the considerable influences wielded in this sector of Islamic artistic expression by Byzantine art. In fact we have a rich store of Byzantine fabrics which we can examine on a comparative basis. Similar observations have also been made (although they cannot be proven be-

cause carpets with this typology do not exist, or at least have not been preserved) about the detail—presumably a carpet—of a 1259 fresco in the church of Boiana in Sofia. There can be no doubt that the art of Byzantium and Coptic art in Egypt have a great deal to do with the stylized depiction of animals in carpets. Whether the center of production can be whittled down to the Konya region, the Caucasus, or western Anatolia, what seems certain is that these products were imported to Europe by Italian merchants (Venetians or possibly Genoese). In fact the Berlin carpet comes from a church in Central Italy where it was acquired in the last century by Wilhelm von Bode. In Spain, too, artists included carpets with depictions of stylized birds in their paintings. The Catalan painter Jaime Huguet, for example, included a carpet beneath the feet of an extremely lovely "Madonna with Child." The carpet differs from the one now in Sweden, but there are still obvious and striking similarities.

In addition to stylized animal motifs, we also find in European, and particularly Italian, painting of the same period carpets with exquisitely geometric decorations. But we must take a brief step backward, once geometric carpets are depicted (and there are noticeably less of them,) because these appear in Chinese painting, too, and somewhat earlier, toward the end of the Sung dynasty (960—1279). Geometric carpets appear in a scroll attributed to Chen Chü-chung (early 13th century) now in Taiwan. That these were knotted carpets and not of the *kilim* or similar types, which incidentally also appear in the scroll, seems obvious from the clear depiction of typical long fringes. This scroll—a classic pictorial invention of the Chinese, portraying a series of scenes, as in the narratives of balladeers—depicts scenes from Mongolian and Chinese life, and the carpets only appear in the former. It would thus seem plausible enough to attribute the origin of carpets with geometric motifs to the Mongols. They were semi-nomadic peoples living in Central and Eastern Asia. In China proper, as we shall see, the art of carpet knotting developed much later, probably in the Ch'ien lung period (1736–95). These differ from the Seljuk carpets which are characterized by designs that are very small in relation to the dimensions of the object. Here we find an emphasis on large format rhombi, hexagons, and octagons, filled in with geometric designs based on triangles, broken lines, and zigzag motifs. The under-saddle of a horse painted by the already mentioned Chen Chü-chung shows a knotted rug with a geometric design. The most interesting feature is the depiction of a Chinese ideogram that seems to be recognizable in one of the decorations; if this is the case, it is one of the oldest representations of writings to be found as a decorative element in a carpet, and possibly predates the Anatolian examples.

The Italian paintings of the 14th and 15th centuries offer a vast repertoire of carpets with geometric designs. Suffice it to mention, among others, the paintings of the Giotto school at Santo Spirito in Prato, the Assissi paintings, and the "Annunciation" at Santa Maria Novella in Florence. We can also add the paintings of the Flemish artist Jan van Eyck (1422–41). As a rule, and as is the case with the animal typology, the carpets are laid out at the feet of the Virgin, the most popular subject. The most frequently occurring motifs are lozenges or rhombi which fill the entire field, or else rosettes and star-shaped designs. As with the previous group, these carpets probably come from the Ushak district in western Anatolia.

The Holbein Group and Similar Typologies

Little by little, as the 15th century progressed, the geometric motif completely replaced the animal design, possibly because of natural evolution (or misrepresentation) of the latter. A geometric design with octagons (often within squares or arranged in rows) or other alternate closed forms (often somehow stag-

Jan Vermeer (1632–75). "Girl Asleep." Throughout the 17th century Flemish painters frequently depicted Oriental carpets in their works. This vogue was certainly offset by the diffusion of carpets throughout the Orient.

gered or irregularly arranged) is commonly called the Holbein type by scholars and collectors, after the German painter Hans Holbein the Younger (1497/8–1543) who depicted this type of carpet in some of his works. Holbein is not the only painter to show a preference for this type of Turkish carpet: before him a "Madonna with Child" by Domenico Ghirlandaio in the Uffizi Gallery, Florence, depicts the same sort of carpet. So the Holbein label is somewhat arbitrary, although it has now become part of the vocabulary associated with the study and business of carpets.

For the two groups of carpets previously dis-

ANATOLIA (Ushak)

Bardini Museum, Florence

Design Geometric, Holbein type
Date 16th century
Size 110 x 180 cm (3′ 7″ x 5′ 11″)
Warp Wool
Weft Wool
Pile Wool
Knot Ghiordes
Density 17 knots per sq cm (106 per sq in)
Principal colors Red, pink, blue, white, olive green, green, black, yellow
Description A geometric rug of the Holbein type. Two rows of four octagons. The cross-shaped area, which contains the octagons, is surrounded by a stylized motif of floral steles. The octagonal shape is suggested by an attractive interlacing that forms small squares and lozenges. In the middle there are octagons with star-shaped decorations with colors arranged in various combinations. Between the two rows of octagons we see alternating geometric motifs in the form of steles and small geometric forms that are either octagonal or lozenge-shaped. The border consists of a broad-edged strip, both inside and out. The decoration of this strip is pseudo-Kufic script. The two narrow edges have a dotted line, inward toward the inner edge and outward toward the outer, and a geometric motif.

cussed, many of our observations are inevitably based almost exclusively on second-hand data: paintings. But given that there is little or nothing remaining of the carpet production itself, we have numerous examples of the Holbein group, which enable us to compare and make a systematic study of the subject. The motifs are geometric, mainly polygonal, with other forms inscribed. The arrangement of the space follows the same pattern as we find in the dragon-and-phoenix carpets in Berlin, and the carpets showing birds and the tree of life in Stockholm. The outer border edge is typical and often has a pseudo-Kufic inscription joined by ovoid-shaped rings. The format is not that large, and the colors are clear and well-defined, with a predominance of blue, yellow, and red. The material used is wool. The knot is of the Turkish type with an average density of approximately 1,000 knots per square decimeter (60 or so per square inch). The carpets depicted, with a great wealth of details, by Vittore Carpaccio in the S. Orsola (Saint Ursula) cycle (in the Accademia in Venice), and more precisely those appearing in the scene showing the departure of the Saint (dated 1495) have many features in common, although they are by no means identical, with those described above.

Another type of carpet with, typically, a motif of intersecting arabesques which form a lozenge design, is clearly related to the group of major Holbein carpets, and even represents a typological variant or offshoot. Here, each "compartment," which is fairly small in size, has an octagon with a star or similar motif in the middle. Among the various empty spaces in the field we find star-shaped octagons. The borders may be decorated with pseudo-Kufic writing, with S-shaped motifs, semi-palmettes or ovals alternating with rosettes. The main colors in the field, that is, the central part or background of the carpet, are blue, red, and sometimes green. The geometric form may be created by a change of color in the field. A fact of great interest is that a similar arrangement occurs in Persian carpets depicted in the Timurid miniatures of the 15th century. The colors of the designs are the same (blue, red, and green) with the additional use of white and yellow. This carpet typology is also plentifully illustrated in painting: let us mention the Ghirlandaio ("Madonna with Child") in Naples and the Ognissanti fresco in Florence, Lorenzo di Credi ("Madonna with Child") in Pistoia cathedral, and the Mantegna ("Madonna with Child") in San Zeno in Verona.

Several carpets of this type have been preserved. One of the best examples, from the 15th century, is in Istanbul in the Museum of Turkish and Islamic Art. There are also carpets that combine the characteristics of both groups. These have a central part with an octagon (placed in another octagon and/or square), and in addition, a copy of the smaller motifs above and below this decoration. There are also arabesques —or very similar forms—which, it should be stressed, were not present in the Seljuk repertoire and which create closed geometric forms. The knot used is again the Turkish or Ghiordes type and these carpets probably come from the same Ushak district. The hypothesis given by some scholars, based on features that seem to some extent to anticipate the so-called Mameluk carpets, that these carpets were of Egyptian origin does not hold much water in the light of the present level of our knowledge.

A transitional typology between these carpets (Holbein of the second type and mixed) and the Mameluk carpets of Egypt is represented by a group dating back to the 16th century (see the carpet in the Bardini Museum in Florence, page 43). It was decorated with geometric motifs arranged in lines (hexagons or octagons created by the change of color of the field, which in turn contain octagons or hexagons), the number of which varies a great deal (from three to nine to thirty-two). They are surrounded by cypress trees, flowering buds, or lilies, all very stylized.

The Ushak district was also the center (or very probably) for the numerous carpets characterized by an elegant arabesque motif. This is generally yellow and arranged in a broad line on a red background, without ever ending or rounding off the design, in the sense of defining it. The border may have a highly stylized Kufic inscription, which is virtually unrecognizable as such because its function had by now become purely decorative, or consists of floral motifs. The finest carpets, which have a quiet and meticulous elegance, date back to the 16th century. In one corner some of these carpets bear the noble coat of arms of one of the aristocratic families of Europe (for example the Genoese Doria and Centurione families) who commissioned them in the East.

The more correct name for these carpets is Ushak carpets with arabesque motif, but they are also known as "Lotto" carpets, after the surname of the Italian painter Lorenzo Lotto (1480—1556) who depicted them in his work. (Ushak was certainly one of the

Andrea Mantegna. A detail from the "Pala di San Zeno" (now in Verona). The border of the carpet shows a pseudo-Kufic inscription.

ANATOLIA (Western Anatolia, Bergama)

Bayerisches Nationalmuseum, Munich

Design Geometric, of the Lotto type

Date 16th century
Size 124 x 264 cm (4′ 1″ x 8′ 8″)
Warp Wool
Weft Wool
Pile Wool
Knot Ghiordes
Density 9–10 knots per sq cm (59–60 per sq in)
Principal colors Red, various shades of blue, yellow, cream, white
Description The central area has a repeated and unfinished design of very stylized arabesques which merge into an overall pattern of extremely elegant geometric figures. It is not hard to pick out the palmettes and leaves that are the basic elements of the design which consists of elongated lozenges, octagons, and rhombi. The border is well proportioned, consisting of a double border with a wide central strip. The bordered edges have the same decoration, but in different colors. The strip has a design with squares divided into parts with opposite colors in pairs, and with a central rosette. The various squares are joined up by inverted brackets. The decoration is somewhat less precise at the corners. It is immediately obvious that this decoration is clearly inspired by and associated with the so-called pseudo-Kufic border.

ANATOLIA (Ushak)

Museum für Islamische Kunst, West Berlin

Design Fragment of a Lotto-type arabesque rug
Date 17th century
Size 210 x 381 cm (6′ 11″ x 12′ 6″)
Warp Wool
Weft Wool
Pile Wool
Knot Ghiordes
Density 11–12 knots per sq cm (72 per sq in)
Principal colors Yellow, red, green, blue, black
Description The geometric motifs of the highly stylized arabesque stand out against the red background in yellow, green, and blue. The principal feature is the variation of the colors, which follows no specific pattern, thus creating a certain degree of movement in the design. This is repeated and forms octagons; the intersecting lozenge motifs (almost starlike) stand out clearly. The border is quite narrow; it consists of an edge simulating a Kufic inscription. A wider second border is formed by a continuous motif with stylized flowers and leaves. The rug is rounded off by a narrow edge with small segments alternating in color.

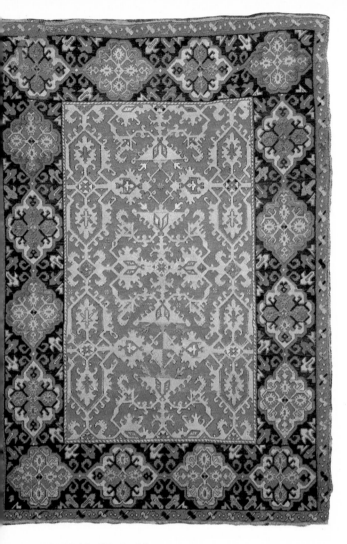

ANATOLIA (Ushak)

Metropolitan Museum of Art, New York

Design An arabesque rug of the Lotto type
Date 16th–17th centuries
Size 120 x 173 cm (3′ 11″ x 5′ 8″)
Warp Wool
Weft Wool
Pile Wool
Knot Ghiordes
Density 12–13 knots per sq cm (78 per sq in)
Principal colors Various shades of blue; red, yellow, orange, brown
Description The central design is made up of fairly well developed arabesques repeated several times over. As usual, the motif in this type of carpet is symmetrical and specular, but has no focal center, and is without beginning or end; it is quite simply a pattern that is reiterated. The arabesques are quite imposing, and decorated with hooks and other hooked motifs which are well delineated. The border is very wide. A small narrow edge separates the center of the rug from the broad strip which consists of elongated multifoiled medallions in alternating colors, containing stylized intersecting palmette leaves. The space remaining between medallions is decorated with hooked motifs and stylized lily flowers. The rug is rounded off by a border with a wavy shoot decoration with flowers and small leaves.

ANATOLIA (Ushak)

Bardini Museum, Florence

Design Arabesque, of the Lotto type
Date Late 16th–17th centuries
Size 124 x 200 cm (4′ 1″ x 6′ 7″)
Warp Wool
Weft Wool
Pile Wool
Knot Ghiordes
Density 12–13 knots per sq cm (76 per sq in)
Principal colors Red, yellow, blue, garnet, pink, white, black
Description Geometric motifs in two rows, separated by a design consisting of elongated and symmetrical lozenges. The design is not finite. The central area is fairly bright red, with yellow arabesques and additional blue elements. The border consists of two narrow borders surrounding a broad strip. The inner border has a geometric motif of steles, leaves and flowers. The outer border has a similarly stylized floral design. The strip has a motif of half-medallions, and leaf motifs of alternating colors. In the central part of the rug we can see that some areas have been recently restored.

major centers for the earlier production of carpets in Anatolia, but it is more than likely that some of the carpets now attributed—*tentatively*—to this region will in future be allocated to different sources of origin.) Within the Lotto category of carpets, Charles Grant Ellis has singled out at least three different ornamental styles, with numerous examples which we can call intermediate. This label was in all probability coined a few decades ago to emulate the Holbein type by a group of collectors and carpet admirers who gravitated around the Haji Baba Club in New York.

Great advances have been made in recent years in the study of carpets in painting. Special merit is due to John Mills who has published important articles both on the Holbein and the Lotto groups; these articles have greatly helped to clarify our ideas about these major carpet typologies. Attention is now focused not so much on the design of the central area of the carpet, but on the border motifs which, when compared with existing examples of carpets and rugs, enable us to try to establish a relative chronology. The sheer size is indicated by the following statistic: in Italian painting from the 14th to the 17th centuries there are more than 180 carpets depicted, including twenty-eight large Holbein carpets, twenty-nine small Holbein carpets and fifteen Lotto carpets. It goes without saying that there are probably many other paintings with carpets that have not been included.

Europe and the Carpet Trade

The large number of carpets depicted in the works of European, and in particular Italian, painters should not come as a surprise. Europe—where Italy played a role of considerable importance—had had a long tradition of carpet trading. In fact, carpets were one of the cornerstones of East–West trade, and this trade can be traced back to the early 14th century. In competition with the ports of southern Italy and then with Genoa, Venice gradually managed to win what was to become nothing less than a European monopoly. During this period the names of carpets also underwent changes because of trading practices. One type of well-known carpet was called "Rhodes," although there is little doubt that carpets were never knotted and produced on the island. As with ceramics, the name indicated the port of origin. More complexity surrounds the carpets of Damascus or Damascene carpets (which appear in the Venetian archives to-

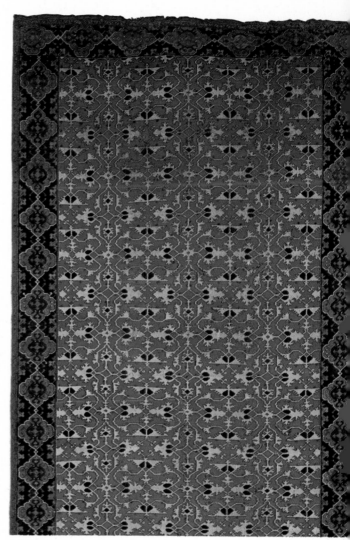

ANATOLIA (Ushak)
Bargello Museum, Florence

Design Arabesque, of the Lotto type
Date 16th century
Size 260 x 515 cm (8′ 6″ x 16′ 11″)
Warp Wool
Weft Wool
Pile Wool
Knot Ghiordes
Density 7–8 knots per sq cm (48–50 per sq in)
Principal colors Red, yellow, dark blue, light blue, pink, olive green, black, brown, and white
Description The repeated geometric motif forming rows of octagons stands out against the red background. The design is open-ended, to give the carpet a sense of continuity. From the top there are eight complete rows of octagons and only two horizontal ones, but an additional two are almost complete. The decoration is particularly dense, and the stylized motifs of palmettes and semi-palmettes are detailed and well proportioned. The border is narrow, with a series of small lozenge-shaped medallions. Those on the short side are slightly more elongated. Inside the medallions we see red and blue star-shaped motifs which stand out against the different and alternating background colors.

"Piazza S. Marco" by Antonio Canale, who was known to the foreigners who avidly collected his highly colored works as *"Canaletto."* Views such as this one of Piazza S. Marco were so popular abroad that few of them have remained in Venice.

gether with the already mentioned Rhodes carpets and the carpets described rather vaguely as *a la turchesca* or *à la turque*). Given that carpets were never made in Damascus, and given that it could not plausibly have been the port of origin or clearance, the name "Damascene" may define a particular type of processing carried out on fabrics, which lent a particular appearance to them. A Damascene carpet is characterized by color changes obtained by a fine juxtaposition of colors and small-scale motifs. The Venetian archives of the 16th century no longer use the term Damascene, which is replaced by the term (in Italian) *cagiarino,* which Erdmann interprets as synonymous with *cairota,* meaning "of Cairo." This would indicate that carpets imported to Venice were of the Mameluk type.

Two specific historical facts clearly show the basic role played by Venice in the carpet trade: firstly, the report submitted by Sebastiano Giustiniani, Venetian ambassador to London, dealing with the request made by Cardinal Wolsey in 1519 for 100 Damascene carpets. The transaction was helped along by several bottles of excellent wines from Rhodes, and the Cardinal was delivered sixty or so in the following year (it is clear from the large number of carpets and rugs entered in the inventories of King Henry VIII's wardrobe in Windsor Castle in 1547 that the monarch was certainly a keen admirer of Oriental carpets, even if he was not actually a collector as such); and secondly, the gift made to Venice—whose political sway was a force to be reckoned with—by the Persian emperor Shah Abbas (whom we shall be referring to later). This was a gift of finest silk carpets—some of them with brocaded parts—which still form part of the Treasure of San Marco (St. Mark) and are to be seen in the various city museums.

What Italy became between the 14th and 16th centuries was, quite simply, the world's largest importer of carpets, which is another reason why so many carpets occur in Italian painting. The bulk of the great collections in European museums was put together in the 19th century when for next to nothing it was possible to buy carpets in the churches of southern Italy which later turned out to be quite unique (an outstanding example being the dragon and phoenix carpet in Berlin, although it is not alone). Even nowadays, and apart from the public collections which have the very highest quality exhibits, the Italian standard in private collections is certainly among the highest, the only exception being those historical carpets that are now

scattered throughout almost all the world's major museums.

In Europe one is duty-bound to mention a geographical region that has played a leading role as far as the Oriental, and in particular the Anatolian, carpet is concerned: Transylvania. In this region, which now straddles Hungary and Rumania, there are a large number of churches that have well-preserved carpets in them. Because some of these are similar in type, and can thus be grouped together, they are known as Transylvanian carpets. There is still considerable debate over the origins of these carpets: some experts maintain that they were made in Transylvania itself, or in the European part of present-day Turkey; others propose Anatolian origins. This latter place of origin seems to be the most plausible, at least for the time being, and in particular because there is not the slightest documentary evidence to support the hypothesis that carpets were ever made in Transylvania. But one thing is beyond dispute: there is a very large number of carpets to be found in the churches of Transylvania today. Imports were probably gradual and started in the latter part of the 15th century, continuing to the 18th century. In the archives at Kronstadt (now called Brashov) more than 500 carpets were recorded for the years 1503–4; and today there are still many magnificent carpets on display in the Black Church in this city, and in the surrounding churches. The reason for the existence of this large number of carpets in this very definable geographical region is still not absolutely clear, even though considerable importance attaches to the fact that the Transylvanian area was—and to some extent still is—inhabited by Saxon peoples professing a Protestant faith with strict iconoclastic links. It is odd that to decorate a Christian church, people resorted to objects made by "infidels" (the origin of which was certainly not unknown to the decorators, who preferred to lower a veil of silence over it), which were hallmarked by their absence of figurative depiction.

The small number of carpets that have survived down to the present day (in relation to an art that is extremly ancient) is not in fact surprising. In the Orient carpets and rugs have always been considered as things to be used, in fact, the most useful and used of all household trappings. Up until recently carpets have not earned the same attention as other antique objects. The old carpets, which are now the pride of so many European and American museums, have survived because they were regarded as valuable ob-

The tiled portal of the Friday Mosque at Yazd, crowned by twin minarets, is the tallest in the country, and like many early mosques, it was constructed on the site of a Sassanid fire temple. Yazd's Friday Mosque was built over a forty-year period from 1324 to 1365, and is probably the best-preserved fourteenth-century mosque in Iran.

jects, worthy of being collected by the most noble and far-sighted families of Europe in bygone days. In Turkey old carpets have been preserved because once laid in a mosque (Turkish mosques differ architecturally from Persian mosques), sometimes as the result of a devotional gift, they then belong to the community, and it was—and still is—not considered right to destroy them. As a result they were simply covered over with other newer and more sightly carpets. In the Orient it is very rare to find a carpet that has been carefully preserved in a private home.

The First News about Persian Carpets

For the moment certain important categories of carpet have still to be included in our historical reconstruction, but thus far we have dealt with Turkish carpets and completely ignored what was happening in the very same period in the other great landmark in the history of carpets: Persia. The fact is that chronologically speaking Anatolia comes before Iran.

In fact we have little information about Persian carpets up until the 15th century. What we do know is derived from literary references or travelers' descriptions. There is no visible documentation, either direct or indirect. For the Seljuk period—during which carpets were almost certainly knotted, there being no reason to believe otherwise—the sources are extraordinarily low on information and there are not even any miniatures to help us out. The step forward came in the Ilkhanid period (1221—1353) with one or two more bits of information and, more important, the first illuminated representations. From the end of the Ilkhanid period to the late 15th century the Persian carpet is excellently documented by the precise depictions contained in the illuminations. But not even a fragment has survived. The designs are all geometric, with the various types of octagon most frequently used (sometimes there seems to be a certain similarity with certain Holbein carpets). The octagons are either separate or joined together by linking motifs. Octagonal motifs alternating with stars with several points or with crosses are also used very frequently. This decoration is common in paving tiles (often cobalt blue and gold). The idea is probably to create a continuous space between floor and walls. As a rule the designs are schematic, fairly simple, and stripped of any affectation. In the 15th century there occurred a profound change in design in Persia. It was almost like a radical turnabout of the whole decorative philos-

Carpets are dried naturally in the sun, following the ancient Persian custom.

ophy. There was a shift from the simple geometric forms (of which there is a fair-sized repertoire of varieties, taken from illuminations), which can be open or closed and are often arranged in alternate or staggered rows, to a dominant emphasis on floral motifs and/or motifs with a floral shoot, with an organization and distribution of the space that is completely different from previous arrangements and does not occur elsewhere. One can only make conjectures, based on historical observation, about the whys and wherefores of this change. The change in inspiration was probably a result of the clash with Eastern art, or Chinese art, which was responsible for an already extensive influence in the Mongolian (Ilkhanid) period. It is easy to detect in illuminations. Under Tamerlane (1335—1405), the mighty central Asian commander, the forms were then assimilated and we find an appropriation and re-elaboration of the artistic theme. It is beyond any doubt that the Timurid period (1370—1506) was a golden age in which there were major achievements in every artistic domain. There was, moreover, a happy synthesis between different attitudes, scholarship, and cultures, and the center where all these elements merged was Herat. Artists flocked to the court here, ready to help in the great royal project.

Motifs of Persian Carpets and Illuminators

The simultaneous presence in one place of highly skilled artists promoted the art of carpet making too.

Diagram showing various types of floral motifs: 1. Lotus palmette, from eastern Persia. 2. Lotus palmette from Kashan. 3. Goa. 4. Lotus flower in the Rockefeller-McCormick Vase carpet. 5. Jawshaqan Qali. 6. Palmette with leaves, eastern Persia, 16th century. 7. Palmette with leaf, eastern Persia, 16th century. 8, 9, 10, 11, 12. Lotus palmettes, from carpets made in northwestern and eastern Persia in the 16th–17th centuries. 13. Palmette with leaf from northwestern Persia. 14. Palmette with leaf from eastern Persia, 16th century.

53

Arches in ceramic (Kashi) mosaic in the Safawid caravanserai in the town of Kirman. The decoration, on a very elegant floral background, consists of winged figures in medallions, and of dragons and phoenixes confronting one another. A very similar decoration can be seen in certain carpets too: many experts maintain that the basic cartoon for these ceramics and carpets was prepared by the same artist.

Left: The iwan at the entrance to the Mosque of the Shah of Isfahan. The stalactitelike structure is typical of the Safawid period, as is the ornamentation based on medallions, arabesques, and floral motifs; the same features recur in carpet decorations.

To a large extent it was the illuminators who influenced design. In fact experts have pointed to the close tie that exists—particularly in the 16th century—between books and knotting. More specifically, carpets use designs that are peculiar to the bindings of manuscripts. With their long tradition, books therefore prevailed over carpets. In fact, rather than being inspired by the forms used in manuscripts, artisans simply borrowed them, without making any modifications. The space is dominated by a central medallion, either circular or ovoid in shape, and elongated at both ends, decorated in various ways with floral shoots being predominant. The corners often have a quarter medallion with a design that is part of the central medallion. The borders are clearly defined and often characterized by scrolls with floral forms or inscriptions inside them in some cases. Motifs with a geometric allover design, which sometimes decorate the covers of manuscripts, are also reproduced in carpets. Illuminators are also responsible for the appearance of naturalistic scenes in the carpet repertoire. We find many a hunting scene set against an imaginary landscape with a great many trees (usually cypress), spectacular blooms, peonies, and lotus flowers, obeying what can be called an exotic taste. Chinese motifs, such as cloud or ribbon designs (known as *chi-chi*), as well as Indian motifs, are by now part of the decorative grammar of Persian carpets. If the carpets that borrowed the motifs used in book bindings did not require any particular procedures or technical skills for the reproduction of the design, those with hunting scenes were first painted by capable artists on squared boards. This suggests not so much an association with the illumination but rather, in some cases, a dependence on it. The appearance of a large number of carpets with figurative scenes was certainly not an overnight phenomenon. It must be viewed in relation to an increased private interest in carpets, as opposed to public commissions or, in other words, carpets ordered for mosques by the faithful congregation.

The Great Safawid Period

At this juncture we should briefly outline the social conditions of what was to be the golden age of Persian carpet making. The Safawid period (1501–1732) was hallmarked by a certain degree of political and social stability, as well as by an overall increase in commerce and trade which brought wealth to certain classes of citizens. In this atmosphere of well-being we find the outstanding figure of Shah Abbas (1587–1628), who was more or less contemporary with other grandiose sovereigns, such as Elizabeth I of England, Philip II, Ivan the Terrible and Moghul Akbar, emperor of India. Shah Abbas was a great patron of all the arts, and the arts received encouragement and assistance of every kind during his reign. In this period sights were set at achieving a degree of equilibrium among the various artistic endeavors which would come as close as possible to formal perfection. The sovereign championed the employment of palace weavers, an appropriate and accurate label given that various travelers reported seeing excellent carpets being made at court. There was great opulence and a consequence of this was the great enrichment of the "palette" available to the craftsman. Dyeing techniques were also becoming increasingly specialized and of a higher quality. The various colors, and their various shades and hues, offered a range of possibilities hitherto unexplored by artists. The other major technical innovation was the introduction of silk, which was used not only for the fibers making up the warp and weft, but also for the pile. The use of silk permitted a very high knot density and the consequent possibility of depicting highly detailed naturalistic scenes—not least because of the superiority of the Persian knot in this respect. The combination of all these technical, artistic, and socio-historical factors brought about the golden age of the Persian carpet

during the 16th and 17th centuries, under the great Safawids.

The Major Production Centers: Tabriz

One of the major centers where carpets were produced was undoubtedly northwestern Persia, with its epicenter at Tabriz. Here, in the early years of the Safawid dynasty, the region underwent an extraordinary economic boom. Tabriz, the first Safawid capital, is not far from Ardabil, a city greatly esteemed as the birthplace of the royal family. The first sovereign of the dynasty, Shah Ismail (1502–24), was a descendant of the Shaih (meaning spiritual master and guide) Safi-ed-Din (hence the name Safawid), who is buried there in an impressive mausoleum. The carpets here followed the scheme of manuscript cover-designs, as mentioned before. The most typical forms are those with central medallions, characteristic of the area. The design of the field often consists of a closely interwoven series of variously colored floral shoots, overlaid in an "ad infinitum" design, in which it is not always easy to pinpoint the basic module. The background often contrasts deliberately with the center of the carpet which is dominated by the well-defined form of the medallion. Above the uniform background of shoots there may also be naturalistic scenes, especially of hunting. The limelight is also stolen by a carpet in

The central medallion of a modern carpet coming from Tabriz. The medallion is the only feature that we can associate with the glorious tradition of the past.

which we find depicted all the known and imaginable flora and fauna. This carpet is seen as a garden (a modern wildlife park), and as a part or depiction of paradise. This is confirmed indirectly by the texts on the scrolls at the borders which are inspired by images of paradise. There are a great many excellent carpets knotted and produced either in Tabriz or attributable with reasonable certainty to local production in the immediate vicinity. From the artistic viewpoint and as documentation, we should mention two very important ones: the so-called Ardabil carpet in the Victoria and Albert Museum, London, and the carpet with hunting scenes in the Poldi Pezzoli Museum in Milan.

Because of its quality, place of origin, and the history of its acquisition, the Ardabil carpet is an exceptional and unique example in the history of knotted carpets. It is huge, measuring 11.50 x 5.34 meters (37′9″ x 17′6″), and dated by an inscription in the year 946 H, in other words 1539–40. This inscription also includes the name of a certain Maqsyd Kashani, who was probably the superintendent in charge of organizing and supervising the various stages of production. This carpet, it has been calculated, probably took 3 years to complete. The carpet appears to have been ordered by the Safawid sovereign Shah Tahmasp (1524–76) for the central hall of the mausoleum of the Shaih Safi-ed-Din. As is often the case in Persia there were two carpets knotted with the same design.

It was only after much patient restitching and restoration work in the 19th century that one complete one was successfully put together of more or less perfect appearance. The remains of the other one form a smaller carpet (whose central part is nevertheless well-preserved) currently in the Los Angeles County Museum. Other relatively small fragments are scattered throughout various European museums. (For a description of and further information about the Ardabil carpet see page 176). A sensational press campaign was launched over this carpet which was labeled "holy," and when it was put on display in 1892 in the premises of the well-known London firm of V. Robinson and Co., it stirred up a great deal of excitement. The carpet was sold by the religious authorities of Ardabil to enable them to restore the dome of the sanctuary, and via a firm of import-export agents in Manchester it eventually ended up in the hands of the Robinson company. Here, four years were required to turn the "faded carpet remnants" observed by the overly pessimistic traveler Holmes in 1843 into a carpet in a perfect state of conservation. The sum of money in question was £2500, an unheard-of amount at that time, and an amount that no individual or museum budget could possibly afford. In the end it was only by public subscription, to which William Morris devoted much of his own time and energy, that the carpet finally ended up in 1893 in the Victoria and Albert Museum.

This is the story as it is traditionally told. But to a large extent the Ardabil carpets are still shrouded in mystery. In a detailed monograph on the famous pair (Rexford Stead, *The Ardabil Carpets*), we find all the doubts and uncertainties surrounding these carpets fully expressed. First and foremost, and using historical bases, a question mark is raised over the traditional and prevalent attribution of them to the looms of northwestern Iran (and reference is made to the Turkish occupation of Tabriz more or less at the time during which the carpets were being made). But the alternative attribution to Qazvin does not seem very plausible either, and the likelihood that the more important center of Kashan was the place of their manufacture seems more convincing. But it must be said that the addition of the family's place of birth or origin to the signature is a practice common among Persian artists (and not only Persian—Leonardo da Vinci is a good example, and he certainly did not actually execute his works at Vinci), and in some senses it backs up the hypothesis of an émigré proudly claiming his own origins from some renowned city for his own carpets. But all this is mere conjecture. And the suggestion that the carpets came from Ardabil is also questioned: in the sanctuary (associated with an important tradition to do with donations received—apart from the possible gift of the carpets, the most amazing gift, now in Teheran, was the collection of Chinese porcelain given by Shah Abbas I), in the 17th century, there was not a large enough space to contain the carpet and even less room for two carpets. Another proposal is that they came from the sanctuary of the Imam Reza in Mashhad, although this conflicts with the evidence presented by Holmes who, he says, saw a carpet that was knotted 300 years ago—with a date at one end—precisely at Ardabil. To sum up, the problems which these carpets pose for the art historian are many and major (not least of which is the fact that the carpet in Los Angeles is more closely knotted than the one in London). But what nobody can cast any doubt on is the extraordinary beauty of these objects which justly merit the qualification "masterpiece."

We have dwelt somewhat on the vagaries of the Ardabil carpet because it has had an extremely significant role where Western knowledge of the knotted carpet is concerned. The sale of this carpet galvanized the attention and interest of numerous new collectors of Eastern and Oriental carpets. The first important books about carpets were published (Von Bode's work, which was more than once updated and republished by Ernst Kühnel, dates back to 1901 and is still a definitive study), and there were the first attempts to mount major exhibitions, like the one in Vienna in 1891 with some 515 items in the catalog, followed by a series of other exhibitions.

The very important carpet showing hunting scenes, in the Poldi Pezzoli Museum in Milan (page 175), is almost certainly dated 1542–43. There has been a great deal of discussion about this carpet (one figure in the date is not totally legible and it might just as easily be 1522–23), as to whether, as is Maurice Dimand's view, it predates the group of silk carpets (from Kashan, the best-known example is the one in Vienna, page 185, or whether, as is Erdmann's view, it is contemporary or even later. The carpet has hunting scenes set against a floral background. In the center there is a many-lobed medallion with a heart-shaped motif with birds in flight against a floral background. On the basis of style, it is our view that the older appearance (or the appearance of a later copy) is created by the lesser degree of precision in the definition of the detail, caused by the material used—wool instead of silk—and by the less dense knotting. Both carpets owe something to the illuminator's art and are artistically very close.

There are two other important carpets with hunting scenes, in addition to those of Vienna and Milan. One is in the Royal Swedish collection; the other, originating from an old Florentine collection (Torrigiani), then passed into the hands of the Rothschild family and is now in the Museum of Fine Arts in Boston. The theme of these carpets is the hunt (cf. the chapter dealing with symbology). It seems very likely that they were made for ceremonial reasons and are representative objects. They were laid in the middle of the audience chamber, where the sovereign sat on his throne. The throne was placed over the central medallion—an age-old custom, illustrated in countless miniatures painted as early as the 15th century with sovereigns perched on thrones, and one which we can nevertheless date right back to the pre-Islamic tradition.

Tabriz, again as capital of the Azerbaijan region, is also associated with carpets that have very detailed floral shoot motifs, carpets with fairly varied divisions of space in relation to the plan of the central medallion with pendants on a background of foliage and the frequent inclusion of animals, and also carpets belonging to the group that has compartments. The decoration of these consists of a series of small many-lobed medallions surrounded by slightly more elongated ones which form the same number of compartments, arranged in such a way that they produce the design of a grid (which is better defined by color changes in the backgrounds of the medallions); inside these we find fighting animals, lions, arabesqued forms, etc. On the borders there are wide elongated scrolls with animals facing each other as decoration (the most frequent motif of Far Eastern inspiration is that of dragon and phoenix), or large floral shoots and volutes together with cloud or ribbon motifs (chi-chi).

The Orient was "rediscovered" in the 19th century. Even now it is hard to remain unamazed by all the journeys, the archaeological finds, and the profound knowledge of both the Near and the Far East which hallmarked the entire culture of the 19th century. But it is also true that contradictory attitudes existed. On the one hand we find an explosion of a taste for the exotic and a bewildering fascination with the mysterious, veiled Orient. This attitude is illustrated by the host of *genre* painters, a few of whom are worth mentioning on the basis of their own original approach to

Eugène Delacroix was one of the most authoritative "Orientalist" artists of the 19th century. In this painting, "Women of Algiers," we find a pleasing blend of Western features (the faces are typically European) and observations resulting from a journey made by Delacroix to North Africa in 1832. Although it does not achieve the descriptive precision of other great artists, this magnificent canvas is a fine example of the charm of the East which so fascinated the 19th-century artist.

PERSIA (Northwestern Persia)

Private collection

Design Floral and geometric
Date 20th century
Size 140 x 410 cm (4' 7" x 13' 6")
Warp Wool
Weft Wool and cotton
Pile Wool
Knot Ghiordes
Density 15–18 knots per sq cm (95–115 per sq in)
Principal colors Various shades of red and blue; mustard, yellow, white
Description The long, narrow central area is decorated with a single, repeated, florally inspired ornamental motif. It consists of rows of very stylized flowers, with alternating colors, which are staggered between rows. The motif itself consists of a stem, with two pairs of leaves and a bud at the top. The design is very schematic. The border is fairly small, consisting of a wider band and an outer border. The band is decorated with squares, with internal divisions as in a flowerbed, with the colors alternating, but following a precise pattern. The outer border has a decoration of wavy plant shoots with stylized flowers, alternating in color, at the center of the curved areas.

PERSIA (Tabriz)

Private collection

Design Floral
Date 19th century
Size 130 x 200 cm (4′ 3″ x 6′ 8″)
Warp Cotton
Weft Cotton
Pile Wool
Knot Ghiordes
Density 50 knots per sq cm (310—315 per sq in)
Principal colors Various shades of blue and green; yellow, brown, black, and red
Description In the middle of the central area there is an elongated oval form with two pendants at either end. This oval with its pale-colored background has a serrated outer edge and is decorated with a schematic interweave of plant shoots, floral forms, and leaves. The central oval medallion is set within a similar form of larger dimensions, with a dark-colored background: this latter has a thick network of plant shoots with numerous different floral motifs such as rosettes, palmettes, and flower buds. The border is small with two borders flanking a wider central band. The borders themselves are narrow and have a simple chevron motif. The central band has a continuous wavy motif with flowers and leaves, again very stylized.

PERSIA (Western Persia)

Private collection

Design Floral
Date 19th century
Size 320 x 550 cm (10′ 8″ x 18′ 4″, approx.)
Warp Wool
Weft Wool
Pile Wool
Knot Ghiordes
Density 56 knots per sq cm (350 per sq in)
Principal colors Various shades of blue, red, and yellow; brown, green, ivory
Description A carpet with floral decoration. It belongs to the group of so-called garden carpets. The center has large rectangular panels which represent the various parts of a classical Persian garden. At the center of the area illustrated opposite, there is a round medallion with floral decoration and the right-angled (vertical and horizontal) axes with a design creating the effect of rippling water. Each of the four rectangles thus created has three squares, each one edged with floral motifs. The two squares at the edge are decorated with flowering shrubs with very elegant foliage. The central square has an octagonal star decorated all over with schematic floral motifs.

PERSIA (Tabriz)

Private collection

Design Naturalistic
Date 19th century
Size 181 x 273 cm (5′ 11″ x 8′ 11″)
Warp Silk
Weft Cotton
Pile Wool
Knot Ghiordes
Density 42 knots per sq cm (260–265 per sq in)
Principal colors Various shades of red, cream, and brown; gray, yellow, pink, and blue
Description Rug with naturalistic decoration. The scene depicts the well-known biblical episode of Joseph being sold by his brothers. The style is one rich in detail; we see the well, a pair of camels, the brothers, and the merchants. The surrounding landscape is also highly detailed. This rug is strikingly and skillfully woven and seems, in its artistic style, to echo something of the craft of Western tapestry weaving, with an emphatic descriptive style that also keeps a keen eye on perspective. The border is quite wide and has the customary three-part structure.

the topic (they are towered over by Ingres and Delacroix, and then there was Van Gogh, for example, who collected Japanese prints). It was a phenomenon with mass appeal, no less, and it involved the French, in particular, in the Near East and the Middle East, whereas the English, as we well know, went mainly to India. It was roughly in the middle of the century that the important complete translations of the *Arabian Nights* were published, spreading all the myths far and wide, and markedly stimulating a romantic desire for knowledge of those extraordinary civilizations. On the other hand it was also the period of the first basic scientific efforts to study and understand the cultures of Asia. In some fields our knowledge has in fact advanced very little, and it is surprising how some of the intuitive observations made about carpets by experts such as Von Bode (1901) or Martin (1908) are still considered valid and up to date.

Kashan

Another place of great historical importance for the production of Persian carpets is a small town in central Iran called Kashan. The finest, most delicate, and elegant carpets made during the golden age of the Persian carpet (16th century) were produced here. And Kashan enjoyed the status of having imperial protection. Kashan was a hugely important center in terms of the development of Persian art. In this city there was a well-renowned ceramic tradition; ceramics were made with a highly artistic metallic luster. Furthermore, in the Safawid period in Kashan, a large number of fabrics—velvets in particular—were also worked, and these are among the most beautiful and technically most complex examples of this important art. It should not be forgotten that many artists in the various disciplines, whose names have lived on because they signed their works, were either born in Kashan or came from a family that originated from Kashan.

The principal technical feature of the carpets from Kashan is the use of silk in the warp, the weft, and the pile. Silk has always been very costly. Its best qualities are the sheen of the fiber (dyed with great precision and in a very wide variety of shades) and its combination of thinness and strength, which makes for a very high knot density. This in turn makes it possible to depict the details of a scene or design so precisely that the outcome is every bit a match for the illuminator's pen. In fact, these carpets are nothing

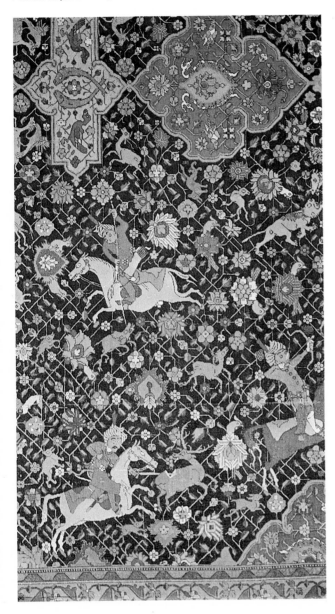

Hunting scene on a floral background. This is a detail from the famous Persian carpet of 1522, now in the Poldi Pezzoli Museum in Milan.

short of knotted illuminations. They are made, once more, using the Persian knot, and are rarely that large. But the carpets of Kashan are among the most beautiful ever made.

One of the recurrent themes in Islamic art, associated with the idea of royal legitimization, is the hunt. It is a very ancient thematic device, undoubtedly pre-Islamic, as is shown, for example, by the numerous scenes of this type which can be dated back to the Sassanid period. But it is also a universal theme, found in different regions and cultures. One has only to think of China, or Assyrian reliefs, or Greek art. In the hunt the virility and skill of man is exalted. For centuries hunting has been the favorite sport of kings, whose famous exploits have been handed down to later generations by various epic writings. The sport of polo, which is still so fashionable today among the English aristocracy, was invented in Central Asia. Polo was extremely popular with Persians (the magnificent royal square in Isfahan is the most amazing "stadium" ever built for this sport), and its origins lie in the struggle between two tribes over the pursuit of a prey (later transformed into a standard), the eventual taking of which was a symbol of supremacy. It is therefore not surprising to find the large numbers of prey depicted in these carpets, and the variety is not always the outcome of rhetorical exaggeration by the artist. Real hunts were organized by channeling large numbers of animals into narrow valleys, the ends of which were then sealed off with large nets and barricades so as to give those taking part in the hunt plenty of chance to make a kill. The hunt, together with going to war (for which hunting acted as a substitute in times of peace), was the most noble and in fact the only occupation worthy of a king. It was hymned in Persia in the *Shahnama* epic *(The Book of Kings),* composed by the famous poet Firdausi, and in the works of another great name in Iranian literature, Nezami. These themes have been widely used and illustrated in miniatures, the importance of which as an iconographic source for carpet decorations has already been discussed.

The absolute masterpiece in this group, with naturalistic hunting scenes, is the famous carpet, now in Vienna (page 185), which was probably commissioned by Shah Tahmasp (1524—76). An elegant octagonal medallion in the form of a floral corolla with slender pendants at the tips has an internal decoration of dragons and phoenixes. This motif is repeated in the quarter medallions in the corners as well. The field shows hunting scenes. The accuracy of the design of the saddle and the horses' harnesses shows up well under the camera. The background shows flora with low bushes and flowers. The border is divided into three sections: the larger central one is decorated with houri figures—angelic creatures in the Islamic paradise—against a background of flowers, ribbons, and birds. The type of design is fairly reminiscent of the 1542—43 Milanese carpet (in fact the period more or less tallies), but there is less symmetry about the depictions, being merely hinted at. The design is freely executed, with a mastery that calls to mind Sultan Muhammad—the "official" artist at the court of Tahmasp—as the possible author of the cartoon.

As already mentioned, two further important carpets with a hunting theme exist, besides those in Vienna and Milan. One is in the Swedish Royal Collection and the other, which comes from a very old Florentine collection (the Torrigiani) via the Rothschild family, is preserved in the Museum of Fine Arts, Boston. The theme of these carpets is hunting (see chapter on symbology). They were most likely woven for a ceremonial purpose, and depict specific scenes: they would be placed in the middle of the royal audience room, and the sovereign would sit on the throne placed on the medallion at the center of the carpet. This practice is an ancient one, as revealed by countless miniatures painted as far back as the 15th century, showing sovereigns sitting on their thrones, which we can, however, date back to the pre-Islamic tradition.

In addition to carpets with hunting scenes, Kashan also produced smaller silk carpets. The decoration here consisted of a central medallion, often with a fairly large four-leaved clover design, and floral designs in the field and at the borders. Others have animal motifs, often with the animals doing battle together. The designs are invariably pictorial in style, and executed with considerable refinement.

Isfahan and the So-called Polish Carpets

Isfahan is a city situated in the middle of a beautiful and lush oasis in the heart of Persia. Shah Abbas wanted to set up the capital of his kingdom there. Although looms certainly existed already in Isfahan, and had for some time, Isfahan is in some sense the heir of Kashan. During the reign of Shah Abbas (1588—1629) the city underwent extraordinary development, with the construction of mosques, baths, palaces, and pavilions swathed in lush green vegetation

The school of Sultan Muhammad: "Garden Scene." Miniature of the Shah Tahmasp period, 16th century.

PERSIA (Qum)

Private collection

Design Floral
Date 20th century
Size 115 x 195 cm (3′ 9″ x 6′ 5″)
Warp Cotton
Weft Cotton
Pile Wool
Knot Sehna
Density 45 knots per sq cm (280–285 per sq in)
Principal colors Various shades of red, blue, yellow, and green; white, cream, black, pink, and brown
Description The field has five stripes, with different background colors, decorated with the same floral motif with rosettes, buds, other floral forms, and small birds at regular intervals. The design of each stripe is divided into two halves by a central stem and repeated with the same motif. Between the stripes there is a dividing strip decorated with detailed floral motifs. The border is small, with two guard stripes and a central stripe. The edged guard stripes have a repeated and continuous design of stylized palmettes. The central stripe has a motif of geometric shoots with rosettes, buds, and other floral forms.

PERSIA (Kashan)

National Gallery, Washington, D.C.

Design Geometric and floral
Date 16th century
Size 165 x 241 cm (5′ 5″ x 7′ 1″)
Warp Silk
Weft Silk
Pile Silk
Knot Sehna
Density 40 knots per sq cm (250 per sq in)
Principal colors Various shades of red and blue; yellow, green, brown, cream, and white
Description The field is dominated by a lobed and eight-pointed medallion with a lozenge in the middle of it and a palmette joined together by half-palmettes and slender shoots with small flowers. At the four cardinal points of the medallion there are crownlike designs. Outside the central medallion there appears to be another medallion, interrupted by scrolls decorated with ribbons or fairly large chi-chi designs. The remainder of the central area is decorated with slender shoots which support palmette flowers, peonies, rosettes, and other flowers. In the corners there are compartments decorated with buds and stems, but not using the same design as in the main medallion.

and surrounded by playing waters. All the arts, which were protected and greatly encouraged, developed rapidly. This included the art of carpet making, spurred by the establishment of *karkhana* or state "factories," and carpet making was in no way regarded as a lesser art. Because of their lofty clientele, carpets with hunting scenes were undoubtedly regarded as the most important products made in the workshop and were also certainly worked on by the best-known artists of the day with costly and carefully selected materials. These imperial carpets have been seen by numerous Western travelers, such as Chardin in 1673 and Tavernier in 1687, who recalls them as follows: "The *Karkrone* is the House for the Royal Manufactures, where the Gold and Silver carpets are made, as also those of silks and worsted, together with Tissues, Velvet and Taffetas."

The looms of Kashan and Isfahan are also renowned for their production of smaller carpets or rugs, some of which were invariably made to imperial order. These carpets were less exacting on a technical and decorative level, but embodied a high degree of artistry. They are known as "Polish" or "Polonaise" carpets (see below), and were made in palace workshops and used as gifts for ambassadors. It is, however, likely that similarly manufactured carpets, though possibly less sumptuous in their use of gold and silver brocade, were also used in court surroundings. The decorations are varied but invariably floral and use several different styles. The carpet is usually part of a more complex and repeated geometric floral motif, of which only a part is actually used (though on a larger scale). Many of these floral designs are to be found in the decorative ceramic art—*Kashi*—of the great mosques, and in palace paintings, around the huge royal square in Isfahan.

Silk carpets—but other types too—are the boast of Isfahan. If Kashan represents perfection and, in all probability, the best that has ever been achieved in this area (in terms of an art developed technically to the highest pitch, and absolutely mature where pictorial expression is concerned), Isfahan cannot escape, almost by force of circumstance, being vaguely decadent and slightly redundant in its decorative themes. But it did maintain a level of quality that can only be called excellent. The decorative motifs are predominantly floral. In some cases a color change in the field produces a spatial division resembling the division created by medallions. Floral shoots, intermixed with cloud motifs and ribbon motifs (*chi-chi*)

PERSIA (Kashan)

Private collection

Design Rug with naturalistic design
Date 20th century
Size 116 x 218 cm (3′ 10″ x 7′ 2″)
Warp Silk
Weft Silk
Pile Silk
Knot Sehna
Density 50 knots per sq cm (310–315 per sq in)
Principal colors Red, mustard, brown, gray, yellow, black, white, and cream
Description The field is dominated by the depiction of an ancient Iranian legend: the hunt of King Bahrām Gūr and his favorite maiden. The scene, which has been described and narrated by all the classical authors of Persian literature, shows the marksmanship of the monarch who shoots a gazelle in one mighty blow in the leg and ear, before an awestruck group of onlookers. The depiction is detailed and follows the spirit and iconographic style of the *qajar* period. The inscriptions, including those in the center of the field, refer to the text of the legend.

A tile with a metallic luster made in Kashan in the 13th century. The ceramic industry in Kashan was one of the most advanced in the whole of Persia, and was particularly skilled in techniques to do with the luster, a typical invention of the Near East. Tiles such as this, with their epigraphic content, decorated the walls of mosques and sanctuaries throughout Persia.

PERSIA (Kashan or Isfahan)

Correr Museum, Venice

Design Floral
Date 17th century
Size 140 x 230 cm (4' 7" x 7' 7")
Warp Silk
Weft Silk
Pile Silk, with silver brocade
Knot Sehna
Density 23 knots per sq cm (140–145 per sq in)
Principal colors Three shades of green; olive, blue, pink, yellow, black, and white
Description This rug is hallmarked by the technique with which it has been woven, a brocade of silver threads on silk. At the center of the carpet a lozenge contains flower buds with plant forms; at the four corners of the lozenge, facing one another, we have two pairs of lily-shaped medallions with plant forms within them. The central area is delineated by conspicuous floral shoots with embryonic half-palmettes which suggest the form of a central medallion, but only in a vague sense. Inside we have rosettes and other floral motifs, in a sparsely decorated area.

This rug was probably part of the gifts presented by a legation of Shah Abbas (1587–1628) to the Venetian Republic in 1603 or 1622.

PERSIA (Isfahan or Kashan)

The Cleveland Museum of Art

Design Floral
Date 17th century
Size 169 x 398 cm (5′ 6″ x 13′ 3″)
Warp Silk
Weft Silk
Pile Silk, with silver brocade
Knot Sehna
Density 47—48 knots per sq cm (295 per sq in)
Principal colors Blue, mustard, green, salmon-pink; silver and gold
Description The field has a gridlike design which forms rows of staggered medallions. This design can obviously be repeated ad infinitum, and the pattern is an open-ended one. The brocaded medallions have two opposed palmettes at the farthest ends, and four flower buds at the center. The decoration of the medallions is rounded off by lanceolate leaves and plant shoots with flowers which act as a contour to the central flowers and join the palmettes together. The vertices of the medallions are joined together by a four-lobed floral shape. The border has the customary structure of two narrow guard stripes of floral design, with a wider stripe in between.

Ribbon motifs in 16th-century carpets. 1, 2, 3. From carpets of northwestern Persia. 4. From carpets made in eastern Persia.

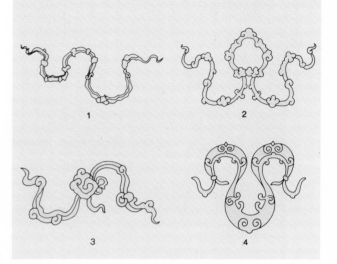

with individual flowering buds sometimes fill up the entire field of the carpet with a pleasing airy movement. The borders are almost exclusively floral in design. The flowers themselves, in these designs, are full and lush: lotus, peony, chrysanthemum, and other species, often tending toward abstraction in their form but designed with a naturalistic vigor. A typical feature of the Safawid period and of Isfahan, although it was also known and used in Kashan, is the brocaded carpet, usually in silver with some use of gold. This lends a sumptuous and visually most effective look to a carpet. The most fashionable colors in the time of Shah Abbas were warm pastel hues. Carpets of this type, produced in Kashan but mainly in Isfahan, were once considered to be of Polish origin, whence the name "Polonaise," which is still in conventional use. The name dates back to the Paris World's Fair in 1878, where there were carpets belonging to Prince Czartoryski on display with coats of arms of his own family of Poland, and of other great European families. The muddle was cleared up a long time ago and is not unlike the confusion over the term "transval" as applied to carpets found in large numbers in churches in Transylvania, which was under Turkish sway from 1526 to 1699. But these carpets were still produced by looms in Anatolia.

Central-Southern Persia: Kirman

The so-called Vase carpet is associated with the Kirman region in central-southern Persia. There is dis-

Cloud motifs in 16th-17th-century carpets. 1. From northwestern Persia. 2, 3. From the Viennese hunting carpet. 4. Possibly from the Kirman carpet.

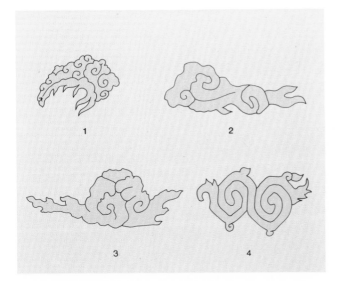

PERSIA (Isfahan)

The Detroit Institute of Art

Design Floral, so-called Polonaise (Polish)
Date 17th century
Size 329 x 337 cm (10' 11" x 11' 3")
Warp Silk
Weft Silk
Pile Silk
Knot Sehna
Density 50–60 per sq cm (312–375 per sq in, approx.)
Principal colors Various shades of red and green; yellow, blue, brown
Description The field, which is an almost perfect square, is decorated with a floral design. The whole composition is symmetrical and specular in relation to the central right-angled axes, and is formed by large shoots that form a lozenge at the center and support spiked leaves and palmette flowers, as well as buds and rosettes. The border consists of a fairly narrow pair of guard stripes and a central stripe decorated with alternating palmettes and rosettes joined together by flowering shoots.

agreement among experts about this. For example, Friedrich Spuhler thinks that there is not enough documentation to attribute these carpets to the looms of Kirman (or of southern Persia in general) rather than to those of another province. But the Persian origin of the group is not in dispute. The name of this group of carpets (the oldest examples of which do not pre-date the mid-16th century) derives from the fact that in some cases the design is in the form of a vase, although this is not by any means the dominant decorative feature.

The most appropriate definition of the technique used by the craftsmen, which hallmarks this group, is perhaps the one coined by May Beattie, who was responsible for the catalog for the exhibition mounted in England in 1976, and dedicated to this particular typology: ". . . a type of weave in which the tightly stretched first and third wefts separate the warp threads of Z4S or Z5S cotton into two planes. These are held together by the fine second weft, which passes back and forth from one plane to the other, and also by the knots. The first and third wefts are usually 2 strands of Z-spun wool, often loosely piled. . . . The second weft is usually two strands of fine silk or Z-spun cotton, or both in one rug. . . . The pile of the Vase-technique rugs is of Z2S wool and is attached by means of the asymmetrical *knot* open to the left."

The design has floral motifs with palmettes and fairly stylized semi-palmettes, rosettes, lilies, and other types of flowers. Fairly large stylized flower

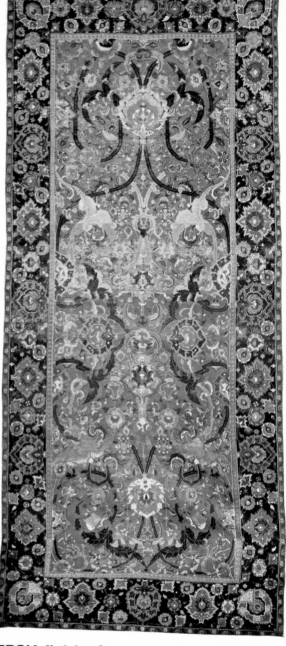

PERSIA (Isfahan)

The Cleveland Museum of Art

Design Floral, so-called Polonaise (Polish)
Date 17th century
Size 142 x 206 cm (4′ 9″ x 7′ 9″)
Warp Silk
Weft Silk
Pile Silk, with silver brocade
Knot Sehna
Density 34—35 knots per sq cm (210—215 per sq in)
Principal colors Shades of green, yellow, and blue; orange, brown, pink, black, silver, and gold
Description The field is divided into two almost equal parts, in relation to the decorative scheme. At the center of each of the two parts there is a floral lozenge from which issue four floral stems supporting two curved and featherlike leaves, each forming a sort of octagonal, lobed medallion. Within this structure there are two pairs of symmetrical palmettes joined together by slender shoots with small leaves and flowers. The remainder of the central area is decorated with half-palmettes with leaves or plumes, similar to those forming the medallions, and using a lively range of colors. The border consists of two guard stripes and a central stripe.

PERSIA (Isfahan)

Metropolitan Museum of Art, New York

Design Floral
Date Early 17th century
Size 210 x 480 cm (6′ 11″ x 16′)
Warp Cotton
Weft Cotton
Pile Wool
Knot Sehna
Density 30 knots per sq cm (188 per sq in)
Principal colors Various shades of red, blue, and green; white, pink, orange, yellow, and black
Description Attributed to the Isfahan region, although numerous features in the design can be readily associated with the eastern region of Herat. The field shows a striking and energetic movement of floral shoots intersected by ribbon motifs and *chi-chi* designs. The central axis divides the carpet into two similarly decorated parts. The design consists of shoots with large-ish serrated half-palmette leaves, rosettes, peonies, flower buds, and large palmettes. The border consists of two narrow guard stripes and a central stripe.

Young women dancing, using multicolored ribbons to accompany their movements. This is the wedding feast of a young couple. The photograph was taken in the Sistan region in June 1975.

buds, ovoidal in shape and of various forms, are set against backgrounds of different colors which creates an almost geometric spatial division. A typical feature is the fairly inaccurate definition of the border designs, and this suggests that they may well have been made for use in mosques. The colors are very rich and particularly intense. The knotting (again the Persian knot is used with wool, sometimes with a cotton warp and weft) is not particularly dense, but despite this these carpets are very robust. One body of opinion asserts a similarity with and possible derivation from the Caucasian carpets with the dragon motif, especially because of the resemblance of the respective spatial arrangements. This brings up the question of the Armenians who were deported by Shah Abbas from Julfa in Azerbaijan to Isfahan, near where they founded a "New Julfa." Some scholars have recently proposed bringing up this matter again and examining a contrary migration: in this view the carpets of Kirman would be the prototypes of the Caucasian

dragon carpets. This is an interesting hypothesis, but it requires further research in order to be proven and thus accepted.

The Herat Region

Herat, which is situated in present-day Afghanistan, was an important center for the production of carpets from the mid-16th century to the early 18th century. The carpets made at Herat are of the floral type. A common element in the borders of these carpets—lanceolate leaves symmetrically positioned with a lozenge formed by shoots and flowers—is often known as *herati* (of Herat), and also occurs in carpets made in other areas. The motif that dominates the field of the carpet consists of minute spiraled floral shoots with arabesques and cloud or ribbon motifs which interweave and are superimposed. In the early example one feels the undoubted influence of the decorative paintings of the late Timurid period and of Far Eastern

PERSIA (Isfahan)

Private collection

Design Floral
Date 19th century
Size 130 x 210 cm (4′ 3″ x 6′ 11″, approx.)
Warp Cotton
Weft Cotton
Pile Wool
Knot Sehna
Density 45 knots per sq cm (280–285 per sq in)
Principal colors Various shades of red, green, and blue; yellow, cream, and white
Description The field is divided into sections with a floral decoration. In alternate rows we see lobed medallions with fairly stylized floral motifs. Between the rows of medallions there is the rather imprecise motif of a floral bouquet, with rosettes, buds, and lanceolate leaves. The border consists of a double guard stripe, edged in both cases with a wider stripe between them. The guard stripes have similar decoration, of different proportions, consisting of rosettes in alternating colors joined up by slender spiked leaves. The central stripe has elongated scrolls decorated with a bird perched on branches in blossom.

PERSIA (Indo-Persian)

Bardini Museum, Florence

Design Carpet fragment with floral decoration
Date Late 17th century
Size 265 x 275 cm (8′ 8″ x 9′)
Warp Wool
Weft Wool
Pile Wool
Knot Sehna
Density 16–17 knots per sq cm (103–105 per sq in)
Principal colors Red, pink, blue, yellow, white, cream, brown, and green
Description This is a fragment—about one third of the original—of a carpet with floral decoration and a busy and spacious design. The field is decorated with buds, stems, and leaves, and dominated in the center by a sizable palmette that is fairly brightly colored and surrounded by two fleshy lanceolate leaves. The decoration, which is at once energetic and peaceful, gives the impression of a good-quality carpet which is striking in appearance rather than subtle and detailed. The border is complete on three sides. It has a very narrow inner guard stripe with highly stylized stems and leaves, and a central stripe with various types of palmettes that alternate with groups of five flowers, with the four smaller ones surrounding the single larger one.

Examples of leaf motifs: 1. From northwestern Persia, 16th century.
2, 3. From the Polonaise carpets. 4. From northwestern Persia.

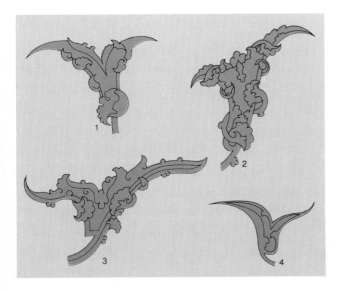

PERSIA (Herat)

The Cleveland Museum of Art

Design Floral
Date 17th century
Size 317 x 772 cm (10' 5" x 25' 9")
Warp Cotton
Weft Cotton
Pile Wool
Knot Sehna
Density 6—7 knots per sq cm (39 per sq in)
Principal colors Various shades of red, blue, and green; yellow, violet, cream, brown, black, and white
Description The field of the carpet has large palmette flowers and peonies arranged to a design that is symmetrical and specular. The border is well proportioned and worthy of a carpet of this quality. It consists of two guard stripes with a wider stripe in between. The inner guard stripe is edged by a narrow barber's pole band and another band decorated with S-shapes of varying color.

PERSIA (Herat)

Poldi Pezzoli Museum, Milan

Design Floral
Date Late 16th–17th centuries
Size 258 x 432 cm (8′ 4″ x 14′ 2″)
Warp Wool
Weft Wool
Pile Wool
Knot Sehna
Density 41 knots per sq cm (256 per sq in)
Principal colors Various shades of red, blue, green, and yellow; white, black, and orange
Description The field is completely dominated by a design of plant shoots and flowers, which could be repeated ad infinitum. Based on a scheme traditional to this type of carpet, the most commonly used decorative motifs are large palmette flowers and peonies. The field is densely decorated with an intricate and well-planned juxtaposition of colors. The border consists of two guard stripes with a central stripe between them. The wide stripe has a classical and elegant design of palmettes alternating with smaller flowers, arranged in alternate directions and with different colors. The stripe is rounded off by wavy plant and floral stems, and the decoration at the corners appears to be well executed with the use of diagonal flowers.

floral forms. From the beginning of the 17th century onward we find a change of layout. The flowers increase in size, the proportions of the lanceolate leaves also increase, as does the scale of the spirals which becomes fuller and more imposing. The result is a progressive "loading" of the design which falls prey to a repetitive formula, even though it has vast possibilities of expression.

The attribution of this group to the Herat region is a matter of debate. For some of these carpets (pages 73 and 192), the term "Indo-Persian" has been proposed. This is a very ambiguous term which suggests Indian manufacture to a Persian design. But as yet no precise place has been put forward to which the actual manufacture of these carpets can be traced back. It is nevertheless important to underline that even if they were made elsewhere than in eastern Persia, the carpets of this type are clearly based on the stylistic approach of this region.

Strangely enough the commercial name for this group is Isfahan. These carpets were highly successful in the West and were imported liberally by Europe, and in particular by Portugal, Spain, and Holland. They were reproduced on numerous occasions in works by major Masters, such as Vermeer, Rubens, Velasquez. The design has been one of the most copied by craftsmen (especially in Isfahan, Azerbaijan, Kurdistan, and the Caucasus), and not only in recent times. The imitations are recognizable from certain decorative details executed in a style or with a motif that is alien to the Herat repertoire.

The Other Major Centers of Persian Craftsmanship

These five centers (Tabriz, Kashan, Isfahan, Kirman, and Herat) whose production we have discussed with the help of some famous examples of carpets, in no way account for all of the huge production of Persian carpets in terms of type and quantity and age. Our brief introductory remarks obviously exclude other important and historical production centers. One such is Shiraz (and the region frequented by the Qashqai nomads). Others include Hamadan, Joshagan, Baluchistan and Kurdistan. Other names familiar to those who have dabbled in the world of carpets, such as Ardabil, Varamin, Sehna, Kermanshah, Kum, and Nain (to name just a few), derive from commercial definitions given to relatively recent carpets which do

"Jacob Receives His Coat from Joseph" (1630), by Diego Velasquez. Now in the Escorial in Madrid.

PERSIA (Bidjar)

Private collection, Milan

Design Floral
Date 19th century
Size 342 x 245 cm (11' 5" x 8' 1")
Warp Wool
Weft Wool and cotton
Pile Wool
Knot Ghiordes
Density 25 knots per sq cm (155–160 per sq in)
Principal colors Various shades of red, blue, and yellow; green, gray, black, pink, and white
Description The center is dominated by a series of lines of floral motifs. The regular arrangement of the flowers is achieved by their being set very close together; alternating colors are used and they are joined together by slender shoots. The border is well proportioned and in three sections, consisting of a double border with motifs of flower buds joined together by flowering shoots edged by a Greek fret and a small band with a linear zigzag motif. The third central section has a different background color and a rosette design within a lively pattern of buds and other plant and floral forms. The specific structure of this carpet, with five weft rows, makes it a particularly hard-wearing one.

PERSIA (Herat or Tabriz)

Osterreichisches Museum, Vienna

Design Floral
Date 16th century
Size 270 x 540 cm (8' 10" x 18')
Warp Cotton
Weft Cotton
Pile Wool
Knot Sehna
Density 28 knots per sq cm (175 per sq in)
Principal colors Various shades of red, blue, and green; yellow, white, cream, brown, pink, and black
Description The field has a network of shield-shaped or lily-shaped medallions of similar form, decorated in alternate rows by medallions with the same motif repeated in alternating directions, and other medallions with a background of a different color and varying decoration. The latter medallions have palmettes surrounded by arabesques, fairly elaborate *chi-chi* motifs of varying designs, birds facing one another on branches, and flowering plant shoots. The decoration of the medallions with red backgrounds consists of a tree in blossom and a pomegranate.

A fine example of boteh *in a Ferahan Persian carpet.*

not always have a precise typological appearance, and can be taken for "samples."

One specific object of interest where Oriental carpets are concerned is the *waghireh*. This is a carpet made up of differing designs placed adjacent but in no particular order. They are the "guides" that help carpet makers to reproduce a design by copying the knots as they appear on the back of the "model." These carpets are quite common in northwestern Persia.

PERSIA (Saruk)

Private collection

Design Rug with geometric and floral decoration
Date 19th century
Size 210 x 125 cm (6' 11" x 4' 1")
Warp Cotton
Weft Cotton
Pile Wool
Knot Sehna
Density 50 knots per sq cm (310–315 per sq in)
Principal colors Various shades of red, blue, and green; brown, black, pink, cream, and white
Description The central area is dominated by an elongated hexagonal lozenge. This is decorated by large and extremely stylized floral forms. The flowers are joined together by slender shoots, rosettes, buds, and other designs, all in a geometric style. Each of the four corner areas has a very similar decoration, but with smaller flowers. The border is well proportioned, consisting of a double border with a central band in between. The edged borders have the same decoration of very angular shoots which support stylized tulip buds. The central band has a complicated geometric decoration of floral inspiration formed by shoots with leaves which support flowers of alternating colors.

PERSIA (Northwest Persia)

Carpet Museum, Teheran

Design Floral
Date 19th century
Size 208 x 492 cm (6' 10" x 16' 5")
Warp Wool
Weft Wool
Pile Wool
Knot Ghiordes
Density 40—41 knots per sq cm (250—255 per sq in)
Principal colors Various shades of red and blue; green, brown, cream, orange, and pink
Description The central area has a series of horizontal bands decorated with floral motifs which are staggered in adjacent rows. The design is open-ended and could extend over a much larger area. Each band is decorated with stylized tree motifs, repeated over and over: there are cypress trees, willows, and possibly plane trees. The decorative scheme is quite simple and the design a very close-knit one. Taking into account the dominant warm brown tones, the effect is a very elegant one. The border is noticeably small, consisting of a double border with a central strip. The borders themselves have a continuous design of flowers supported on a plant shoot. The strip has a motif of double shoots with flowers.

PERSIA (Saruk)

Carpet Museum, Teheran

Design Floral rug
Date 20th century
Size 125 x 204 cm (4' 1" x 6' 9")
Warp Cotton
Weft Cotton
Pile Wool
Knot Ghiordes
Density 42—43 knots per sq cm (260—265 per sq in)
Principal colors Various shades of red and blue; mustard, pink, cream
Description The center is dominated by an elongated oval medallion with additional smaller medallions forming a slightly stylized corolla of a magnificent flower. The rest of the principal medallion, which has lily-shaped pendants at the ends, is decorated with geometrically described shoots. The center of the rug changes its background color, except in the sizable corner areas, and is decorated with floral motifs. The four corners are decorated with similar motifs and more extensive flowers. The border is very narrow. The band has oblique palmettes alternating with flowers of varying designs.

PERSIA (Persian or Anatolian Kurdistan)

The Cleveland Museum of Art

Design Geometric
Date 20th century
Size 97 x 130 cm (3′ 2″ x 4′ 3″)
Warp Wool
Weft Wool
Pile Wool
Knot Ghiordes
Density 9 knots per sq cm (56–57 per sq in)
Principal colors Blue, red, white, green, brown, black, yellow, ochre
Description The central area has an irregularly shaped medallion. The decoration is not regular inside the medallion: the most recurrent motif is that of a square surrounded by stylized petals. The outer lines of the two triangular ends of the medallion have the so-called running-dog motif. The rest of the central area is decorated with geometric and florally inspired motifs. The border is well proportioned and consists of a band followed by two narrow borders. The band has a decoration of cross-shaped, graduated lozenges, alternating in color, separated by triangles. The innermost border has a decoration of small rosettes joined together by short shoots which cross halfway. The outer border has a continuous design of hooks, in two colors, which create a double direction in the decorative pattern.

PERSIA (Kurdistan, Sehna)

Carpet Museum, Teheran

Design Floral
Date Early 20th century
Size 128 x 192 cm (4′ 2″ x 6′ 4″)
Warp Silk
Weft Cotton
Pile Wool
Knot Ghiordes
Density 80 knots per sq cm (500 per sq in)
Principal colors Red, yellow, brown, cream, and mustard
Description Rug with floral decoration. The central area has the same motif repeated over and over—an eight-petaled flower—eight *boteh,* whence the Persian name of *hasht-gol,* meaning eight flowers, to indicate carpets belonging to this group. Between these handsome flowers we have regular lozenges formed by detailed floral motifs. The border consists of a double border with a central band. The borders have a rosette design with the rosettes joined together by tiny leaves; the band has flowers alternating with geometrically designed shoots.

PERSIA (Eastern Persia)

Museo Civico, Turin

Design Carpet fragment with animal and floral design
Date 16th century
Size 60 x 110 cm (2′ x 3′ 7″)
Warp Wool
Weft Silk
Pile Wool
Knot Sehna
Density 41—42 per sq cm (260 per sq in)
Principal colors Various shades of red, blue, green, yellow, and olive; pink, orange, black, violet, cream, and white
Description Fragment of a carpet of very high quality which can be immediately associated with similar fragments scattered around the world in a variety of museums. The design consists of large shoots with leaves and rosettes or budding flowers, across the background, and large flowers and animals, singly or in combat. One guard stripe and a wide central stripe are what remain of the border.

80

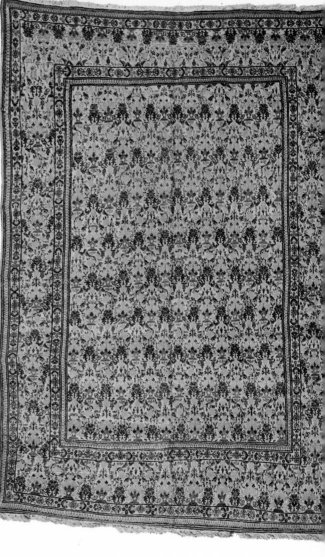

PERSIA (Western Persia)

Private collection

Design Floral
Date Late 19th century
Size 135 x 203 cm (4′ 5″ x 6′ 8″)
Warp Cotton
Weft Cotton
Pile Wool
Knot Sehna
Density 48 knots per sq cm (300 per sq in)
Principal colors Cream, pink, brown, gray, and yellow
Description The central area has the same decorative motif repeated in horizontal bands all over. The design is of a vase, from which issue floral garlands with pairs of nightingales. This motif is known as the *Zill-i Sultan*—the Shadow of the Sultan—and alludes to the son of Shah Nasir-ud Din, who was the governor of Isfahan in the 19th century. The border is wide, unlike the customary border in carpets of this type. It consists of a double border with a wide band in between. The latter is decorated with the same ornamental motif as the central area of the carpet. The borders themselves have very simple and stylized floral designs.

PERSIA (Western Persia)

Private collection

Design Rug with geometric decoration
Date 19th century
Size 120 x 212 cm (4' x 7')
Warp Cotton
Weft Cotton
Pile Wool
Knot Sehna
Density 15–20 knots per sq cm (95–125 per sq in)
Principal colors White, orange, blue, yellow, green, brown, and red
Description The center is dominated by an elongated geometric form, a scallop-edged rectangle with recessed areas in the short sides, containing highly stylized floral motifs in the center. These include rosettes, buds, and lozenges, as well as other plant and floral forms. The remainder of the central area is decorated with angular and triangular forms, respectively, at the sides and in the middle of the short side. The remaining part of the central area has a decoration like that in the central rectangle. The border is well proportioned, consisting of a band within two identical borders. The borders have a continuous design of shoots with small blooms and flowers, alternating in direction. The central band has a motif of handsome flowers with leafy stems and small buds.

PERSIA (Nain)

Private collection

Design Naturalistic
Date 19th–20th centuries
Size 150 x 230 cm (5' x 7' 6", approx.)
Warp Cotton
Weft Cotton
Pile Wool and silk
Knot Sehna
Density 100 knots per sq cm (625 per sq in)
Principal colors Red, blue, green, white, cream, brown, yellow, and pink
Description The field has repeated bands with naturalistic decoration. The motif is reintroduced every three bands. The bands are not arranged with geometric regularity and have a roughly similar decoration. The main design is one of bushes with leaves and flowers, which are both elegant and detailed. In addition to the plant motifs the field has many animals, mainly birds either perched on branches or in flight, gazelles and leverets. The design is an open-ended one and the overall effect is one of great harmony. The border is well proportioned and consists, as usual, of two edged guard stripes and a central stripe.

Other groups, which are important from the typological aspect and which we shall discuss in the illustrations, may be of excellent and even exceptional quality, but do not help in defining the historical development of the art of carpet making. These include carpets with tree motifs, "garden" carpets, *boteh* motifs (a form of floral derivation, consisting of a leaf that is very wide at the base with the tip shaped like a hook), carpets with arabesques of the *mihrab* (prayer) type. But by their very existence they remind us of how vast Persian production has been and still is. They also remind us of how incredibly widespread, in both time and space, this important artistic activity has been.

In recent years Iranian carpet production has suffered markedly, and adversely, from political events. During the reign of the late Shah, looms were abandoned for more lucrative jobs in the petroleum-related industries. Today the shortage of wool is the main obstacle in the way of a revival of this craft. As a result, other countries have recently started producing considerable quantities of high-quality carpets with Persian designs. So nowadays it is not hard to find Persian-designed carpets being manufactured in Pakistan, or Eastern European states (in particular Bulgaria and Romania), or the Maghreb (North Africa). But the huge number of Persian carpets still on the market is far from drying up; furthermore, imports have always been on a massive scale. In a report to the Foreign Office at the end of the 19th century, submitted by the English consul Preece, we find the following figures for the export of carpets made in the Isfahan *sola:* in three years (1896/7, 1897/8 and 1898/9) the volume of merchandise, in bales (each one weighing some 70 kg/160 lbs) was, respectively, 1911, 611 and 2214. A large amount, and even if Isfahan was embracing trade from large surrounding areas, this volume (which does not, unfortunately, make a distinction between ancient and modern carpets) gives a clear idea of the extent of this trade, even if only in purely economic terms.

When the Ottomans took Tabriz in 1514 and again in 1534, this had important consequences in many artistic sectors. As well as procuring a wealth of materially very rich pickings, Constantinople found itself welcoming a host of highly talented architects, artists, and artisans. The Turkish craftsmen soon realized the superiority of the Persian knot when it came to making more refined designs and they started using it for some of their carpets. Thus we find carpets knotted

PERSIA (Western Persia)

Private collection

Design Floral
Date 20th century
Size 150 x 250 cm (5′ x 8′ 4″, approx.)
Warp Wool
Weft Wool
Pile Wool
Knot Ghiordes
Density 12 knots per sq cm (75 per sq in, approx.)
Principal colors Various shades of red, blue, and green; white, yellow, black, and brown
Description The central area is completely dominated by stylized tree designs: cypress trees, broad-leaved trees, willows, and trees in blossom arranged according to a precise decorative pattern, in bright colors, rounded off by rosettes, animals, and human figures, all depicted geometrically. The border is in three sections.

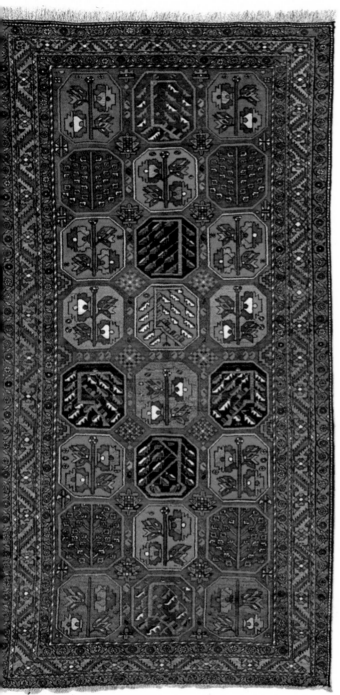

PERSIA (Bakhtiyar)

Private collection

Design Floral and geometric
Date Late 19th century
Size 125 x 210 cm (4′ 1″ x 6′ 11″)
Warp Cotton
Weft Cotton
Pile Wool
Knot Ghiordes
Density 15 knots per sq cm (93–94 per sq in)
Principal colors Various shades of red, green, and blue; orange, brown, yellow, white, and black
Description The checkered decoration of the central field has three horizontal and eight vertical rows of octagons. There are three different groups of motifs. The areas between the various octagons have stylized floral motifs, squared lozenges and small *boteh* motifs. The border is decorated by two identical guard stripes and an edged stripe in between.

Eastern Anatolia. Two elderly women sitting on a doorstep.

by Turks using the Sehna (Persian) knot with a decoration (sometimes smacking of Iranian influences) that is floral with large lanceolate leaves and bouquets of flowers (particularly roses, tulips, and carnations, but also hyacinths and palmettes) which are typical of the 17th century and are found in the decoration of the beautiful tiles made in Iznik (formerly Nicaea, now in Turkey), of the great mosques in Istanbul, Edirne, and Bursa. This group of carpets has been located in various places (among others, Damascus and Cairo), but it seems certain that it is essentially Turkish and produced either in Bursa or Istanbul.

Anatolian Carpets (18th–19th Centuries)

The Anatolian carpets of the 18th and 19th centuries found their way to many parts of the world. Even though they are not of paramount interest to the documentation of the iconographic development of the carpet, they are very much part of its history. We have all heard of the names Ghiordes, Kula, Ladik, Mujur, and Milas, to mention just a handful of the most famous. These carpets are generally known as "prayer rugs," and they are of good quality. The Ghiordes type of niche (Ghiordes is in Asia Minor, a few kilometers/miles from the other major center of Kula) is supported on two columns which then extend into floral festoons. In the first examples the borders with floral motifs that become increasingly abstract borrow from earlier designs. The lamp motif in the center of the

ANATOLIA (Ghiordes)

Private collection

Design Prayer rug
Date 19th century
Size 120 x 170 cm (3′ 11″ x 5′ 7″)
Warp Wool
Weft Wool
Pile Wool
Knot Ghiordes
Density 17—18 knots per sq cm (110 per sq in)
Principal colors Yellow, cream, various shades of red; brown and black
Description The central area has a not very large niche, with the sides of the arch steplike, decorated by a line of floral motifs along the inner edge, and by a representation of the mosque-lamp design, with stylized budding tulips at the top of the niche. Above the niche there is a very indistinct decoration, floral in origin. Beneath the niche are two transverse bands: the first has a design of stylized palmettes linked together by shoots and leaves, and the second is identical to the one mentioned earlier. The border, as is customary in this type of rug, is very wide and consists of a double border with a wide central strip. The inner border has a continuous stylized design of carnations with serrated leaves. The outer border has a similar design. The strip is divided into narrow bands of varying colors decorated with floral motifs.

ANATOLIA (Milas)

The Cleveland Museum of Art

Design Prayer rug
Date 19th—20th centuries
Size 109 x 168 cm (3′ 7″ x 5′ 6″)
Warp Wool
Weft Wool
Pile Wool
Knot Ghiordes
Density 12—13 per sq cm (76—77 per sq in)
Principal colors Various shades of red, yellow, cream, green, violet, blue
Description The central area is extremely small: most of the area of the rug is taken up by the border which is a very important element in this type of rug. The inside edge of the niche has a continuous motif made up of short segments surmounted by small circles. The inside area of the niche is decorated with geometric designs: stars of various colors that are joined together with a central lozenge. The remainder of the central area is decorated with a network of large and stylized flowers joined together by steles. The borders are usually striped with small bands of the barber's pole motif. The inner border, decorated with rosettes of alternating colors, is placed between bands with a wavy motif. The central strip has lozenge-shaped motifs decorated with small geometric figures, rosettes, and stylized flowers. The rug is rounded off by a border with small octagons or rosettes.

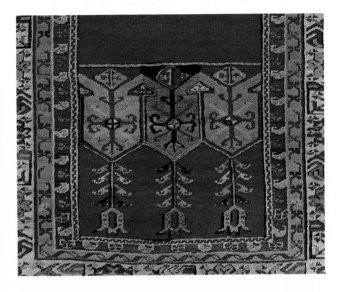

An example of stylized tulips beneath the niche, from a Ladik carpet.

niche is common but not indispensable. A further distinctive feature of the Ghiordes type consists of two transverse bands (one on top, the other below) which enclose the field of the carpet before the border begins. The most commonly used colors are warm shades of red and blue, with some use also of white, yellow, and other colors. The Kula carpets are similar to the ones just described, but differ principally in the border and coloration. The carpets from Ladik, a town near Konya, are quite elegant.

In the earliest examples (known as the "column" type) they have a triple-pointed arch supported by double columns, above or below the niche, and there is a band or strip with a motif of alternating arrowheads, which extend into the highly stylized tulip design. This is a particularly pleasing decoration, possibly because it is not too sober, but of undeniably good taste.

The looms of Mujur, in central Anatolia, produce robust carpets of the prayer rug type with a pointed niche and very stylized motifs both in the outlying spaces and in the borders. The colors used are bright and lively, but not displeasing to the eye. The carpets here are tentatively dated 18th and 19th century. They are made of wool (cotton is also used in some cases) and knotted with the Turkish knot. We have already mentioned that in a very large number of cases, it is the woman who knots the carpets. This is especially true with carpets made on village or nomads' looms, whereas in the urban carpet industry—particularly old industries—both men and women did this work. An

ANATOLIA (Ladik)

The Cleveland Museum of Art

Design Prayer rug
Date Late 19th century
Size 105 x 195 cm (3' 5" x 6' 5")
Warp Wool
Weft Wool
Pile Wool
Knot Ghiordes
Density 8 knots per sq cm (50 per sq in)
Principal colors Turquoise, cream, red, black, and ochre
Description At the center is the niche formed by a broken line and decorated with a tree-inspired design showing marked stylization. There are also stars, rosettes, and other geometric elements. Beneath the niche there is a narrow panel with floral motifs and five stylized tulips, introduced by large arrowlike forms containing three stars formed by hooks. The area above the niche is decorated with two elegant shoots, spiked leaves, and flowers. The border is quite wide and wider on the long sides of the rug.

ANATOLIA (Ladik)

The Cleveland Museum of Art

Design Floral and geometric rug
Date 19th century
Size 113 x 168 cm (3′ 8″ x 5′ 6″)
Warp Wool
Weft Wool
Pile Wool
Knot Ghiordes
Density 6–7 knots per sq cm (40–41 per sq in)
Principal colors Various shades of red; yellow, brown, ochre, orange, cream, and black
Description At the center there is a rectangular form with zigzag outlines. A series of floral motifs are arranged to a simple pattern: four below and four above, along the short sides, and the same number vertically along the long sides. At the center of the rectangle a *boteh* with fringes is contained within an irregular geometric figure. The rest of the central area of the rug is decorated with four plant shoots arranged around the rectangle, represented by a broken geometric line. The shoots, with indented leaves, support stems with rosettes, carnations, and possibly tulips. The border is quite small, consisting of a double border with a central strip. The strip has a very stylized plant decoration of alternating colors.

ANATOLIA (Kirsehir)

The Cleveland Museum of Art

Design Prayer rug
Date 19th century
Size 119 x 152 cm (3′ 8″ x 5′)
Warp Cotton
Weft Cotton
Pile Wool
Knot Ghiordes
Density 7 knots per sq cm (44 per sq in)
Principal colors Red, blue, yellow, green, in various shades; brown, cream, and white
Description At the center of the rug there is a pointed niche, ending with an arrowhead motif. The diagonal sides have a steplike design. The interior of the niche is decorated with a stylized tree of life. The central area of the rug is rounded off by two corner sections with zigzag motifs along the edges and stylized flowers at the center, and a panel frieze decorated with arrowhead motifs in alternating directions. The border consists of a double-striped border with a central strip divided into five narrow bands. The inner border has floral designs with geometrically designed small buds and flowers in the center. There are similar motifs on the outer border. The five bands forming the central strip are of different colors and have the same motif, staggered in adjacent bands.

ANATOLIA (Yuruk)

Private collection

Design Geometric
Date 19th–20th centuries
Size 100 x 150 cm (3′ 3″ x 4′ 11″, approx.)
Warp Wool
Weft Wool
Pile Wool
Knot Ghiordes
Density 9 knots per sq cm (56–57 per sq in)
Principal colors Red, various shades of blue; green, yellow, white, violet, mustard, and black
Description The central section is dominated by a large elongated hexagonal lozenge with a rhombus at each end, decorated with geometric motifs. In the middle of the lozenge there is a star-shaped figure containing geometric designs surrounded by stepped rhombi ending in arrowheads. At the corners of the rug there are floral forms, rosettes, and octagonal stars inside more-or-less regular octagons. The border is quite wide. A first border has a continuous shoot motif with flower buds and is followed by a band with triangles. The central strip has a design of serrated leaves alternating in color and direction. The rug is rounded off by a border decorated on three sides with the same floral motif as the inner border; the design of the upper side shows a different decoration of oblique geometric bands.

important object is the carpet that a girl knots for her own dowry: the refinement and quality of this carpet shows her skill as a carpet maker. And this is certainly appreciated and valued not only in an aesthetic sense, but also for economic reasons, because a skilled carpet maker represents a good investment for the family. For this reason the carpets and other knotted objects in a girl's dowry are of a very high quality, technically speaking, and much sought after by collectors. As a rule people attribute the Kis-Ghiordes group to this category, but there is no serious scientific basis for so doing.

Carpets from the Caucasus

The harsh geographical features of the whole Caucasian and sub-Caucasian region, with huge mountainous areas and dozens of valleys that are hard to get to and from, make it particularly difficult to establish the exact origin of a given typology, and it is hard to make absolute classifications in more than a few cases. In addition, down the centuries numerous migrations took place, and peoples of differing ethnicity tended to overlap, and this has further complicated the task of the expert. In one and the same area—and not a very large one at that—we can find many peoples with different languages, cultures, and religions. In this respect the history of the Armenians is symptomatic: there is no doubt that the Armenian civilization was one of the most advanced, and today it still proudly upholds all the elements of the great force it once was. Unfortunately, art historians seem to be divided into two camps: there are those who maintain that, at least in its origins, "Armenian-ness" embraces much of Anatolian art, and those who restrict Armenian art itself to a very limited period of time, relegating it to very narrow confines or ignoring it altogether. Neither camp, obviously enough, does proper service to the consciousness of this extraordinary and extremely vital culture. Unfortunately, carpets and rugs also suffer from the same schizophrenic situation. Not all Caucasian carpets are Armenian, but they are certainly a very important stage in the art of carpet making.

The Caucasian region (Georgia, Daghestan, Azerbaijan and Armenia) has been a constant melting pot for various civilizations that have become merged with the culture of the area. The nature of this area has always been a composite one, open to outside influences which have in turn become assimilated and

The northern shore of Lake Van in eastern Turkey. This region produces some of the most brightly colored and commercially sought-after kilim.

modified. The various individual contributions to this "cocktail," though recognizable in terms of origin even when stylized or distorted, form a whole that becomes more or less typical of the Caucasian area, this being understood as the sum of the four regions concerned. Each one, therefore, has its own individuality, but retains close relations with the others. This is especially evident precisely where carpets are concerned. There are a great many typologies. The most characteristic and important are those with the dragon motif, as already mentioned. During the 1930s there was a lot of lively argument between those who supported the idea that the origin of this was probably Armenian (Armenaj, Sakisian) and those who disagreed with this theory (Arthur Upham, Pope); the controversy, as such, is now over: it seems very likely that the region where the carpets were knotted and made was the Kuba region, in the eastern Caucasus, home of a great many Armenians, and the dragon motif—not necessarily imported from the East in the form in

which it appears in the carpets—has its cultural base, in all likelihood, in the Armenian tradition.

The accentuated stylization of animals, as we see it in the numerous examples that have come down to us, all relatively late in the day, may be one of the reasons why the design—which is certainly not traditional in Islam—spread and has been accepted by Moslems (the *vishap* dragon is typically Armenian as an ancient literary-cultural tradition rather than an iconographic tradition, at least not in this form). The assertion that these carpets come from Kirman—as already mentioned, at least as a possible source—is plausible on a technical level, but less so in stylistic terms.

It must be accepted that there is a "traditional" Armenian-Caucasian motif in an imported arrangement of the gridlike space: the carpets of Kirman, like the so-called Sanguszko group, which show a depiction of dragons but with phoenixes, cannot in fact be stylistically related to the Caucasian carpets, and conse-

CAUCASUS (Kazakistan or Karabagh)

Private collection

Design Geometric
Date 19th century
Size 140 x 305 cm (4' 7" x 10')
Warp Wool
Weft Wool
Pile Wool
Knot Ghiordes
Density 12 knots per sq cm (75 per sq in)
Principal colors Various shades of red, brown, cream, and gray; black, yellow, and pink
Description Carpet with geometric decoration. The central section has diagonal bands with a background of different colors arranged to a precise pattern; these bands have the same geometric motif—a floral design—with alternating colors. The frame is quite small, consisting of a double striped border and a wider central band. The identically decorated borders have small geometric motifs alternating in both color and direction. The central band has a design of octagonal stars alternating in color and joined together by diagonal leaves. As is customary in examples of this typology of carpet, the color scheme is particularly bright.

CAUCASUS

The Textile Museum, Washington

Design Carpet with stylized dragons
Date 17th century
Size 239 x 544 cm (7' 10" x 17' 10")
Warp Wool
Weft Wool
Pile Wool
Knot Ghiordes
Density 12–15 knots per sq cm (78–91 per sq in)
Principal colors Red and blue in various shades; brown, green, white, cream, and yellow
Description The central area has a close-knit grid of lozenges containing, in alternate rows, stylized dragons, stylized palmettes, and pairs of *chi-lin* and lions. The design is apparently a very dense one, but it is

based on a not particularly original pattern. The dragons have stylized designs and harmoniously combine the Persian tradition—especially from central-southern Persia—in the iconography of the dragons, with the upper Mesopotamian and Armenian tradition. The border is virtually nonexistent and limited to a narrow border decorated by a highly stylized plant and floral design.

View of the central region in the Caucasus. The snow-capped mountain in the background is Elbrus (5629 m/18,468 ft), the highest peak in the Caucasus.

CAUCASUS

Private collection

Design Geometric
Date 19th–20th centuries
Size 95 x 280 cm (3′ 1″ x 9′ 2″)
Warp Wool
Weft Wool
Pile Wool
Knot Ghiordes
Density 25 knots per sq cm (155–160 per sq in)
Principal colors Red, blue, yellow, all in various shades; pink, black, white, and brown

Description The central area has two large geometric figures, roughly square in shape, separated by three elongated geometric scrolls. The design of the two medallions is identical. At the center there are very stylized floral motifs surrounded by pointed elements. The four corners have the motif of a square with radiating hooks on each side. The scrolls are decorated with geometric designs, including rosettes and octagonal stars. The background of the central area has various types of rosettes and stylized birds. The border is quite elegant and large. The central strip has a pseudo-Kufic design with different colors, not arranged in a specific order; little care has been taken to merge the designs at the corners.

CAUCASUS (Kazakistan)

Private collection

Design Geometric
Date 19th century
Size 160 x 210 cm (5′ 2″ x 6′ 11″, approx.)
Warp Wool
Weft Wool
Pile Wool
Knot Ghiordes
Density 12 knots per sq cm (75 per sq in)
Principal colors Red, blue, and green, all in various shades; yellow, white, brown, gray, and black
Description The central area is noticeably small. The border is divided into six main bands and represents the major decorative element. The central area has a very elongated octagonal form with serrated edges, decorated with a central row of four florally inspired designs, alternating with two additional rows of similar designs, in a different color, one on either side of the central row. The border is very wide and the individual bands are often striped with small bands of alternating color. There is a border with stylized circular floral motifs with alternating colors and a band with plant shoots with leaves and flowers or berries. The main band is set between two borders of rosettes with alternating colors and has a decoration consisting of stars with eight points, likewise with alternating colors.

quently the Persian dragons, which are naturalistic, are not related to the more geometric dragons of Kuba.

In a sense there is something disconcerting about the gap that exists between the first appearance of a carpet depicting a dragon—the Berlin carpet—and the second phase which arrived in the 17th and 18th centuries. R. Hubel has raised many perplexing points about the age of carpets depicting dragons and phoenixes. They do not really concern us here, given that they have to do only with the iconography. If it is possible, but not probable, that the Berlin carpet can be dated in the 17th century, we still have the Siena fresco to prove the existence of this type of carpet in the mid-15th century.

The oddest feature in these carpets with dragons and phoenixes—whether one looks at painted or woven examples is of no importance—is the subject, which is Chinese, as has been repeatedly asserted, and the marked stylization of the rendering of the design. Chinese dragons crop up quite often in Islamic art from the late 13th century onward, and more widely in the 14th century. But the motif of the dragon set against the phoenix, typical of the balance between *yin* and *yang* and a symbol of imperial harmony, is certainly not an export-prone motif, and in fact we do not find it so often depicted on blue and white porcelain, one of the most highly prized products of the Orient—although it appears more frequently from the 16th century onward. In Istanbul, among the treasures of the famous Topkapi museum, there are four albums with miniatures and ornamental designs of Chinese inspiration, containing various examples of dragons versus phoenixes, sometimes actually engaged in combat with each other (the way we see them in Persian carpets which represent this cosmic clash in a concrete way), which can be dated—although there are considerable discrepancies among experts over this—certainly not before the beginning of the 15th century.

All these designs are made—by hand and at different times—in a naturalistic style which has nothing whatsoever to do with the strict schematic pattern of the Berlin carpet. It is hard to explain this stylization of design, unless one brings in aspects such as lack of technical skill in rendering the subject more in line with the model used. Or perhaps it is a design made from memory, without any precise model, of something that greatly impressed the craftsman to such an extent that he was driven to try and reproduce the

CAUCASUS (Kazakistan)

Private collection

Design Geometric
Date 20th century
Size 150 x 200 cm (4' 11" x 6' 7")
Warp Wool
Weft Wool
Pile Wool
Knot Ghiordes
Density 8—15 knots per sq cm (50—95 per sq in)
Principal colors Red, blue, black, white, and cream
Description ·In the center of the rug, there is an octagonal medallion with a narrow light-colored band on the inside edge, decorated with geometric motifs; salient among them is a sort of dark four-leaf clover with a hooked lozenge at the center with an eight-pointed star. Around this medallion, there is a complicated geometric design which is specular in relation to the lengthwise axis. At the four corners there are trapezoid forms which contain octagonal stars. The border is in three parts of equal dimension, with two identically decorated bands, although with different colors and set in opposite directions, with mainly triangular geometric motifs. Between these two bands there is a third with a "T" design, using alternate directions and colors.

motif. But here we can refer back to the age-old question of the difference between Anatolian carpets—which are highly geometric—and the more naturalistic carpets made in Persia (but definitely not in the 15th century). In conclusion, it is certain that the subject is of Chinese inspiration. It has also been quickly stylized (with a lack of stylistic precision—one can see the third feather of the upper phoenix) corresponding to a precise technical or stylistic requirement—or both. But it is certainly strange that the motif fades into nothingness, with nothing before it and nothing after it, thus belying that maxim which holds that "for centuries carpets have been knotted to the same design"; and dragons—though not of this type—do not recur until the 17th century.

These carpets undoubtedly have a lengthy history (they span four centuries, from the 16th to the 19th) which is reflected in the evolution of their iconography, as shown by the approximately fifty examples that have been handed down to us and manifestly belong to different periods. The space of the carpet is divided on the basis of a geometric division into lozenges or diamonds, and a grid; the designs of the individual dragons are angular, stylized, and between them we find floral motifs that are reminiscent of the Persian Vase group. The evolution, or perhaps the "degeneration" of the design comes about because of a progressively accentuated stylization and abstraction of the forms which are given an increasingly large dimension. The material used is wool (but cotton is also used in 18th-century examples), knotted using the Turkish method. The colors are usually very bright with very beautiful shades of yellow and red. Kuba produced carpets with a strong floral decoration very like that of carpets made in the same period in Kurdistan. The design consists of stylized alternating flowers with backgrounds of various colors which give a geometric dimension to the decorated space. Then the motifs become progressively broader in size and tend toward a more marked abstraction. The carpets of the Shirvan district (also known commercially as Baku and Kabistan) are very well known because of their technical and artistic quality. The same applies to them as to the carpets discussed above, there being an analogy with knotted carpets from the Kurdish region. They frequently have decorative motifs, floral and arabesqued (both types being borrowed from old Anatolian carpets). The borders often have a motif inspired from stylized Kufic script. The Shirvan district also produces carpets in the form of prayer rugs.

CAUCASUS (Talish)

Private collection

Design Geometric
Date Late 19th century
Size 106 x 240 cm (3' 6" x 7' 10")
Warp Wool
Weft Wool
Pile Wool
Knot Ghiordes
Density 12—13 knots per sq cm (80 per sq in)
Principal colors Red, blue, green in various shades; cream, yellow, white
Description The very long and narrow central field is decorated with crosswise bands with geometric motifs and stylized birds. The border is very wide, consisting of a double border with a broad central edged band. The borders are identically decorated with interconnecting octagons. The central band has a design of rosettes in alternating colors and separated by small four-part rhombi. The decoration of the rug is very sober, although use has been made of very simple geometric motifs. The decoration is achieved by means of a simple but original pattern, showing clearly the impressive artistic skills of the weavers.

CAUCASUS (Daghestan) →

The Cleveland Museum of Art

Design Prayer rug with geometric design
Date 19th century
Size 98 x 158 cm (3' 2" x 5' 2")
Warp Cotton
Weft Cotton
Pile Wool
Knot Ghiordes
Density 16—17 knots per sq cm (103 per sq in)
Principal colors Cream, red, green, azure, blue, and yellow
Description The upper part of the central area has a band which follows a broken outline and forms the profile of the niche. The inside of the latter has a network of lozenges, with indented inner lines, decorated with geometric or florally inspired motifs. There are also stylized animal forms. The border consists of two bands of equal width edged by narrow borders. The first band has a small inner border decorated with crosses and circles of different colors, and a lozenge design, almost like the *gul* of Central Asia, within a double zigzag line. The second border, edged by two small borders (barber's pole design) is formed by short diagonal bands of varying colors decorated with geometric motifs.

CAUCASUS (Talish)

The Cleveland Museum of Art

Design Geometric carpet
Date Late 19th century
Size 112 x 300 cm (3' 8" x 9' 10")
Warp Wool
Weft Wool
Pile Wool
Knot Ghiordes
Density 10—11 knots per sq cm (65—66 per sq in)
Principal colors Various shades of green, turquoise, red, cream, and yellow
Description Carpet with geometric decoration. The central area of the carpet is very small and of a very specific shape, with the length dominating the width very conspicuously. It has no decoration apart from the edging of double-barbed arrowheads. The decoration of the border is, by contrast, highly decorative, and represents the largest part of the carpet. But it still retains the customary design which consists of a wide band between two narrow borders.

CAUCASUS (Daghestan)

The Cleveland Museum of Art

Design Geometric
Date 19th century
Size 107 x 151 cm (3' 6" x 4' 11")
Warp Cotton
Weft Cotton
Pile Wool
Knot Ghiordes
Density 12 knots per sq cm (75 per sq in)
Principal colors Blue, yellow, cream, green, brick red, brown, and azure
Description The central area is dominated by staggered rows of *boteh* with the tip turned to the right. *Boteh* are taken to be flowers, given that each one has a short stem with two lateral elements—the leaves. The interior of the *boteh* has geometric checkerboard designs, small lozenges or transverse and oblique stripes. At the bottom the central area is decorated with very stylized animal figures and, at the sides of the *boteh* rows, has swastika-inspired geometric designs. The border is in three parts of equal width, consisting of two borders edged with small narrow bands, and a central band.

CAUCASUS (Daghestan)

The Cleveland Museum of Art

Design Naturalistic
Date 1890
Size 126 x 157 cm (4′ 2″ x 5′ 2″)
Warp Cotton
Weft Cotton
Pile Wool
Knot Ghiordes
Density 17–18 knots per sq cm (110 per sq in)
Principal colors Yellow, dark green, pink, azure
Description In the center a tree covers nearly all the decorative area. Birds are perched on the branches, including a somewhat stylized peacock. Beside the trunk there are two deer with their heads stretching upward to feed from the lower branches. The well-proportioned border consists of a double-edged border and a central band. The inner border, which has a motif of daisies alternating with small circles, is edged by two small bands with a barber's pole design. The central band has a continuous motif of diagonal, stylized, serrated leaves, and "wine-glass" motifs in the center, all alternating in direction and color.

CAUCASUS (Kuba)

Bardini Museum, Florence

Design Floral carpet
Date Early 18th century
Size 163 x 229 cm (5′ 4″ x 7′ 8″)
Warp Wool
Weft Wool
Pile Wool
Knot Ghiordes
Density 15–16 knots per sq cm (95 per sq in)
Principal colors Green, yellow, red, and blue, all in various shades; pink, olive, brown, gray, and cream
Description On the red background of the central area there are alternate rows of rosettes and flower buds with rows of palmate leaves, staggered so as to create a certain movement and a less predictable decorative pattern. The area between the rows is filled with shoots with flowers and leaves. The border consists of a narrow inner border decorated with corollae of small flowers and a wider band that has a motif of stylized lilies, alternating in direction and color.

95

CAUCASUS (Tchi-Tchi)

Carpet Museum, Teheran

Design Geometric
Date 19th century
Size 107 x 142 cm (3′ 7″ x 4′ 7″)
Warp Wool
Weft Wool
Pile Wool
Knot Ghiordes
Density 19 knots per sq cm (120 per sq in)
Principal colors Various shades of red; black, yellow, cream, brown, gray
Description The long, narrow central section has horizontal bands decorated with rows of five rosettes alternating with rows of three octagonal motifs with steplike lines and an eight-pointed star in the center. Between the various bands there are two-colored elements that divide the area; the inner edge has a design of reciprocal stylized lilies. The border is noticeably wide and consists of four bands edged with borders that have a barber's pole decoration. The inner border has a V design with alternating colors and directions. The next band has rhombi with different background colors decorated with octagonal stars. The third band has a V design similar to that of the innermost border, although the shades of color used differ.

CAUCASUS (Baku)

Private collection

Design Floral
Date 19th century
Size 160 x 375 cm (5′ 4″ x 12′ 6″)
Warp Wool
Weft Wool
Pile Wool
Knot Ghiordes
Density 16 knots per sq cm (100 per sq in)
Principal colors Various shades of red, blue, and brown; green, yellow, cream, black, and white
Description The center has three hexagonal medallions with stepped edges, set at the same distance from one another, decorated in the middle with a rosette and flowers along the edge. The remainder of the central area is decorated with horizontal bands of staggered *boteh* set in alternating directions. The central section is rounded off by the four corners decorated with flowers joined together by short stems. The border consists of a central, double-edged band and a small narrow outer border with a barber's pole design and a flowering plant shoot.

CAUCASUS

Private collection

Design Geometric and floral
Date 19th century
Size 244 x 455 cm (8' x 15' 2")
Warp Wool
Weft Wool
Pile Wool
Knot Ghiordes
Density 16 knots per sq cm (100 per sq in)
Principal colors Red, blue, green, all in various shades; yellow, orange, and cream
Description A carpet with geometric and floral decoration. The arrangement of the decoration in the carpet follows a geometric format, but the decorative elements are all floral, though stylized. The design is open-ended and could be extended to a larger area. The motif is of a large lozenge formed by four spiked leaves with flowers, decorated inside by a stylized cypress tree with a pair of flowering shrubs on either side. Where the points of the central lozenges meet, there are octagonal medallions with a central rosette and eight radial flowers. The border is very small, consisting of an edged border, decorated with lily motifs, using two different colors. The decorative format of this carpet with its large lozenges calls to mind the examples of the dragon group, of which it appears to be a variant.

CAUCASUS (Shirvan)   ⟶

Private collection

Design Geometric
Date 19th century
Size 132 x 231 cm (4' 5" x 7' 10")
Warp Wool
Weft Cotton
Pile Wool
Knot Ghiordes

Density 15–16 knots per sq cm (97–100 per sq in)
Principal colors Various shades of red, blue, and yellow; black, pink, white, and gray
Description The central area has three lozenges decorated with geometric motifs—mainly rhombi, octagons, and other closed figures. Above and below these lozenges, which are joined together, there are two rectangular areas decorated inside by hexagons with geometric motifs like Central Asian *gul*. The remainder of the central area is decorated with a host of geometric motifs similar to those in the lozenges. The outside of the central area is edged by a design of stylized lilies. The border is smallish. It consists of a double border and a wider central strip.

CAUCASUS (Shirvan)

The Cleveland Museum of Art

Design Prayer rug
Date 19th century
Size 80 x 135 cm (2′ 8″ x 4′ 6″)
Warp Cotton
Weft Cotton
Pile Wool
Knot Ghiordes
Density 12 knots per sq cm (75 per sq in)
Principal colors Various shades of green; cream and red
Description The central area of the rug is narrow, and the border large, consisting of two double borders surrounding the central band. The outline of the niche is formed by a band decorated with geometric designs, creating a segmented arch. The inner part of the central area, which is filled almost completely by the niche, is decorated with rows of floral elements joined together by stems and shoots. Apart from the band outlining the niche, the central area is rounded off by two corner sections decorated with stylized flowers and geometric motifs. The borders have a similar decoration. It consists of geometric and stylized floral elements. The band has hexagonal designs of different colors decorated with W forms separated by triangles set against the vertex. It is almost a variant of the "crab" motif.

CAUCASUS (Shirvan)

The Cleveland Museum of Art

Design Geometrically designed prayer rug
Date 19th century
Size 108 x 150 cm (3′ 7″ x 5′)
Warp Wool
Weft Wool
Pile Wool
Knot Ghiordes
Density 12 knots per sq cm (75 per sq in)
Principal colors Ochre, cream, brown, all in various shades; yellow and gray
Description In the middle of the field there is a lozenge with geometric elements; the remaining area is dotted with sorts of *gul* with eight-pointed stars. Although not precise, it is possible to single out an arrangement of three rows of motifs. At the top there is a band in the form of an arch decorated with lozenges. Although it does not divide the central area into two or more sectors, it suggests the idea of a niche and hence of a prayer rug. The border is well proportioned, consisting of a double border with the edged band in the middle. The inner border has a design of rosettes separated by vertical elements. The central band is edged by two bands with the barber's pole design, and has a zigzag design of stylized serrated leaves with geometric elements.

Geometric motifs in a Caucasian carpet, made by semi-nomadic shepherds in Kazak, the principal city in the Kazak region.

CAUCASUS or WESTERN PERSIA

Bardini Museum, Florence

Date 17th–18th centuries
Size 140 x 200 cm (4′ 6″ x 6′ 8″)
Warp Wool
Weft Wool
Pile Wool
Knot Ghiordes
Density 20 knots per sq cm (125 per sq in)
Principal colors Pink, blue, yellow, red, white, black, orange, green, and brown
Description A fragment of a carpet with floral decoration. Various parts are evident, but none of them is sufficient to be able to make any definite reconstruction of the original design, which was very probably decorated with medallions. In the area on the left there is a large branch with small spiral forms at the sides, decorated with flower buds and rosettes. Next we see two small trees facing each other, the first smallish with stylized leaves and rosettes, the other larger with delicate spotted fruit as well as leaves.

The bleak and rocky mountainous landscape is interrupted by verdant valleys near rivers or lakes. Band-i Amir in Afghanistan.

Left: Samarkand in the USSR. The Gur-e Mir is the tomb of the great Mongol "general" Tamerlane, who died while preparing to conquer China in 1405. This magnificent city was the seat of power of his huge empire.

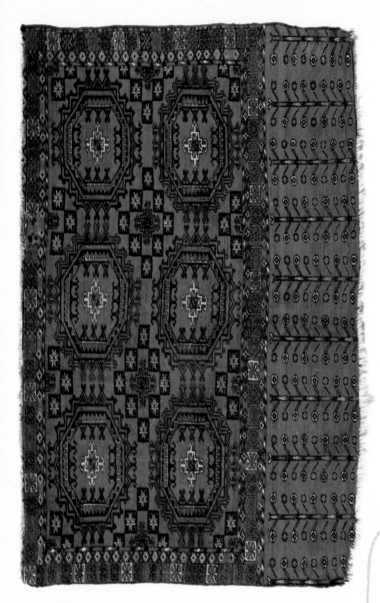

CENTRAL ASIA (Salor)

Museum für Völkerkunde, Hamburg

Design Geometric
Date 19th century
Size 72 x 115 cm (2′ 4″ x 3′ 9″)
Warp Wool
Weft Wool
Pile Wool and silk
Knot Sehna
Density 50 knots per sq cm (310—315 per sq in)
Principal colors Various shades of red and blue; ivory, green, orange
Description Chuval with geometric decoration. The field is dominated by two rows of three *gul* of the Salor tribe; these are octagonal in shape with star-shaped geometric designs at the center. Between the two rows of octagons, and above and below them, there are lozenges and half-lozenges formed by squares with small stars. The design could be extended ad infinitum with this pattern. The guard stripes do not form an actual border, but they round off the composition, and have small square and lozenge-shaped motifs with starlike shapes. The right side of the rug has a row of floral designs supported by extremely stylized stems.

Some have a decoration based on the *boteh* motif which is repeated, on different backgrounds, in each part. Other important and famous centers producing carpets (after which the respective typologies are named as well) include Karabagh and Derbent. Kazak carpets are also very well known.

Western Turkestan

Geographically speaking, western Turkestan is roughly delimited to the west by the Caspian Sea, to the east by the city of Bukhara, to the north by the Aral sea, and to the south by the present-day Iranian border. Traditionally, as far as carpets are concerned, we can also include certain areas bordering on Afghanistan and Baluchistan. These territories were inhabited by tribes originating from Turkey and Central Asia. They were nomadic or semi-nomadic and had been settled in this region from earliest times.

It is an extremely difficult task to reconstruct the history of these peoples, if one is to go beyond the

CENTRAL ASIA (Tekke)

Museum für Völkerkunde, Lübeck

Design Geometric
Date 19th century
Size 26 x 88 cm (10" x 2' 11")
Warp Wool
Weft Wool
Pile Wool
Knot Sehna
Density 32 knots per sq cm (200 per sq in)
Principal colors Various shades of red; green, brown, ivory, blue, and yellow
Description The special interest of this small rug resides in its rarity and in its function, which is probably that of a "door mat" at the entrance of a nomad family tent. In the field the design consists of rows of *gul* of the Tekke tribe. Lower down there is a fairly wide panel with small geometric motifs. The small lower guard stripe with small lozenges and star-shaped motifs has been made with the *kilim* technique. It is fairly common to find such rugs made by the semi-nomadic tribes of central Asia. In fact all the furnishings of these tribes were made by the womenfolk inside their tents.

CENTRAL ASIA (Tekke)

Private collection

Design Geometric
Date 19th century
Warp Wool
Weft Wool
Pile Wool
Knot Sehna
Density 29–30 knots per sq cm (185 per sq in)
Principal colors Various shades of red, blue, and cream; brown
Description This is a very fine example of the group of carpets and rugs produced by the Tekke tribe, and known in the west as "Bukhara carpets"—Bukhara being the main trading center of the region. The field is divided into large rectangles and decorated with two rows of eight large *gul* typical of the nomadic production of this tribe. The border is quite wide, consisting of various guard stripes and a wider central stripe. The width of the border on the long sides is greater than on the short sides, where there are two horizontal panels. The decoration of the guard stripes and central stripe follows the customary geometric pattern.

In the boundless arid landscape of Central Asia, villages consist of rudimentary tents made of mud, brushwood, and matting. At dawn the only living soul here is a woman going to her tent.

most salient features of their material life which has changed so little down the centuries. We have no written documentation. What is more, the complete absence of written sources is a general problem where Persia and Turkey are concerned, as well. Written documentation from the Orient tells us nothing about the great Safawid and Ottoman workshops. Nor do we have any information about later periods, closer to our own modern era. Western historians who have dealt with things Asian have paid no attention to these problems (they have busied themselves with more urgent historiographic investigations), and in the Orient little or nothing has been done, even with regard to the study of carpets at the artistic level. In Turkey things appear to be changing, though at a slow pace, and we can only hope that our colleagues who have access to the material and sources in the various archives will produce historical studies on this subject just as quickly as they are able. Such studies will undoubtedly clear up some of the many problems to do

with attribution and style, which are still open questions at the moment.

The principal tribes were in turn divided into a host of subtribes that kept in contact with each other, although they were partly autonomous in terms of organization and social life. The main Turkmen (or Turkoman) tribes were the Salor, Tekke, Yomud, Ersari, and Saruk (the last four having a common origin); the Ersari tribes were divided into the following subgroups: Bashyr, Daly, Kisil Ayak, Ulma Bedast, Unish, Otli Telpe, and Kanich. The Kanich were divided into fourteen subgroups. The history of the relations between neighboring tribes was never a peaceful one. In fact, there was a long series of skirmishes and civil wars provoked by economic reasons and for reasons of political supremacy. The Persian historian Rashid ad-Din (1247–1318) writes in his monumental *History of the World* that the six branches of the Ogusa tribe each had an animal totem. He refers to the camel, the wolf, the ewe, the

104

dog, the deer, and the fox. The division into six—and the founder of the family, Ogus Khan, had six children —followed a cosmological criterion. The six groups were in fact the sun, the moon, the sky, the star, the sea, and the mountain.

Finding a dog among these animals is a matter of particular interest. For Moslems the dog is regarded as an impure creature. But for nomadic herdsmen of any religious persuasion, the dog represents a firm ally for the safety of the flock. But these practical reasons are compounded by other religious and spiritual reasons which indicate some degree of superficial penetration by the message of Islam among the Turkmen tribes—and it is worth noting how the Turkmen nomads had developed predominantly oral epic forms and literature. It is the dog, or even more often the horse, that accompanies the shaman on his celestial journeys which are of such importance in the life of these peoples and in their animistic spiritual life. Hence the frequent depiction of this creature as it appears—extremely stylized it is true—in the Tauk Nuska *gul.* With regard to the symbology, another very important source as a repertory of images is provided by the *tamgha,* or cattle brands. These motifs, which appeared in very remote times and are now regarded as ornamental designs, refer to extremely interesting archetypes, because they are associated with animal sacrifices and the fertility cult. These highly stylized *tamgha* motifs are also found in the decorations of horses' harnesses and trimmings (the horse was the most valuable property of the Turkmen tribes of Central Asia), and in the jewelry and amulets which are among the most elegant and refined products of the very ancient art of goldsmithery in Central Asia. From these numerous features, and from the recurrent motifs, we can get some idea of the great complexity and of the unsuspected social organization which form the cultural background of these now almost extinct civilizations.

The best-known Turkmen tribe is the Tekke who make magnificent carpets—possibly the best known of all the many types produced in Central Asia. The Tekke live in two main regions: Achad and Merv. The Salor tribe is the oldest group (and wars constantly with the Tekke), although from the latter half of the 19th century, its importance has been dramatically clipped by a series of bloody battles. The Salor live near Pendeh. The same region, more or less, is inhabited by the Saruk, who are also found in northern Afghanistan. Between Merv and Pendeh we find the

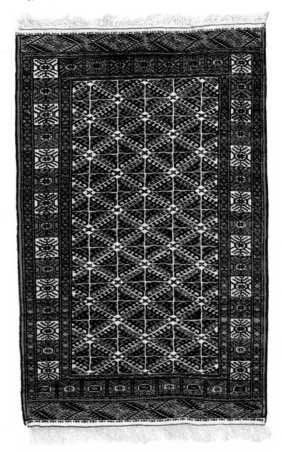
A typical product of the Yomud Turkmen tribe.

Kizil Ayak who are a subgroup of the Ersari. Between the Caspian Sea and the Aral Sea are the Chodor, who are ethnically associated with the Yomud, although their knotted and woven products are conspicuously different. The Yomud tribes, which like the others cannot be considered as a homogeneous entity but rather an entity made up of several groups, live in two main regions: south of the Aral Sea in the khanate of Khiva, and on the southeastern shores of the Caspian Sea. The Ersari tribe, which has remained at a fairly consistent level of population, was found in the Kerki area (more or less halfway along the Amu Darya river), while the ethnically related Beshir colonized the khanate of Bukhara, again on the Amu Darya.

The Turkmen tribes had always been nomadic or semi-nomadic sheep farmers. Among these people the art of carpet making and knotting (which was always only done by women) was not so much an additional activity but rather a central factor in their social and economic life. In fact, all the different ob-

Diagram showing examples of gul, *central Asian emblems typical of the Turkmen tribes: 1. Saruk. 2. Salor. 3. Tekke. 4. Yomud. 5. Kepse, Yomud. 6. Dyrnak of Yomud. 7. Ersar. 8. Tauk Nuska of Arabatch. 9. Bokhara. 10. Afghan.*

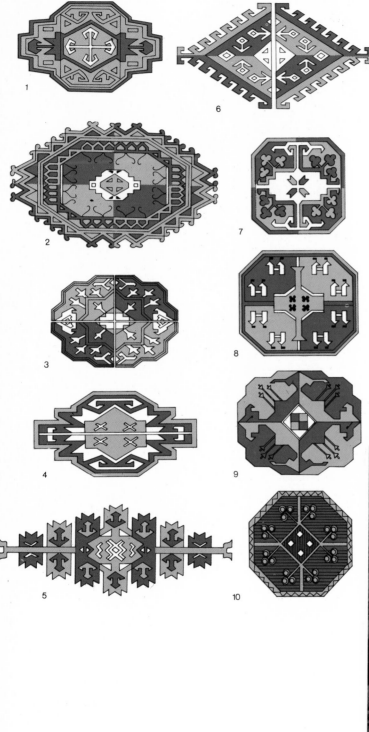

jects used for day-to-day living were knotted, from cots and cradles, to tent fasteners, to long decorative bands, to sacks and bags in which grain and all the various other everyday items were kept. These bags varied in form and design, depending on their use. The saddle was given particular emphasis as a major symbol of power, as were the harnesses and trappings of horses and camels. Designed to embellish the interior of the tent, the carpet thus came to be one element, and possibly not the main one, among several products that were woven and knotted. If carpet weaving and making bags and other similar things is a characteristic that hallmarks almost all the nomadic peoples in the Middle Eastern region, the Turkmen tribes certainly lead the field in terms of the importance of this activity in the life of both the individual and the community. And these activities are still carried on today mainly for personal requirements, and only to a lesser extent for trading purposes. Western interest in these products has come to the fore only recently.

Nowadays, however, carpets made by the Turkmen tribes are among the most keenly sought after by collectors, and their commercial value has risen enormously. This interest has been bolstered, and to some extent heralded and encouraged as well, by numerous publications dealing with these carpets (not least

CENTRAL ASIA (Tekke)

Museum für Völkerkunde, Hamburg

Design Geometric
Date 18th century
Size 37 x 110 cm (1′ 3″ x 3′ 7″)
Warp Wool
Weft Wool
Pile Wool
Knot Sehna
Density 55 knots per sq cm (340–345 per sq in)
Principal colors Various shades of red and blue; green, ivory, brown, and yellow
Description Rug with geometric decoration. The design, which is the customary one in rugs of this type, consists of lines of *gul* of the Tekke tribe, separated by other geometric motifs (each one identifiable by a precise Turkish term), which are also typical of rugs made by central Asian nomads. The border stripes are very narrow, with designs from the geometric repertoire which consist mainly of concentric lozenges and linear motifs. This rug shows very high quality, both in the technique of the very exact knotting and in the choice of materials. The finest rugs woven in central Asia are the handiwork of young women preparing their dowries.

CENTRAL ASIA (Yomud)

Private collection

Design Geometric
Date 19th century
Size 144 x 279 cm (4′ 9″ x 9′ 2″)
Warp Cotton
Weft Wool
Pile Wool
Knot Sehna
Density 14.5 knots per sq cm (90–95 per sq in)
Principal colors Red, blue, black, white, and cream
Description The field has diagonal rows decorated with *gul* belonging to the Yomud tribe. The *gul* have alternating background colors from row to row. In the field we also find plenty of *abrash* effects, undoubtedly due to the use of naturally dyed wools. The border is quite small, which is a typical feature of this type of carpet. The central stripe is decorated with a continuous motif of rhombi. At the ends of the short sides there are two horizontal panels decorated with small *gul* in diagonal rows, with the colors alternating from row to row.

the English edition of the classic work by Bogoljubov), which have greatly swollen our knowledge about them. One of the most intriguing aspects of carpets and rugs made by nomads is the use of color, or rather the subtle variations of tones and shades shown in their products. At one time the constant and unvaried use of the same decorative repertory was regarded as a defect in these carpets—a lack of originality; but today justice has at last been done to these extremely refined objects, by recognizing the wide range of decorative possibilities obtained with very simple but amazingly effective means—all of which testify to an ancient tradition which has been carefully honed down the centuries. The first connoisseur, collector, and authoritative scholar in this field was the Russian General A. Bogoljubov (who was the regional governor at the turn of the century). He collected a considerable number of carpets and other products and shared them with the world at large by his books. The Turkmen carpets and rugs made in the western region are easy to identify by their decorative style. They are hallmarked by the repetition inside the field of the carpet of *gul*. These are star-shaped or floral-geometric stylized motifs which date back to Central Asian traditions. They are arranged in rows, running vertically or diagonally.

The changing social and geographical situation of these tribes complicates the student's task; sometimes different *gul* (belonging to two clearly distinct tribes) are to be found in a single carpet. In some instances the design provides the key for determining the origin of a carpet. When there is some doubt, one

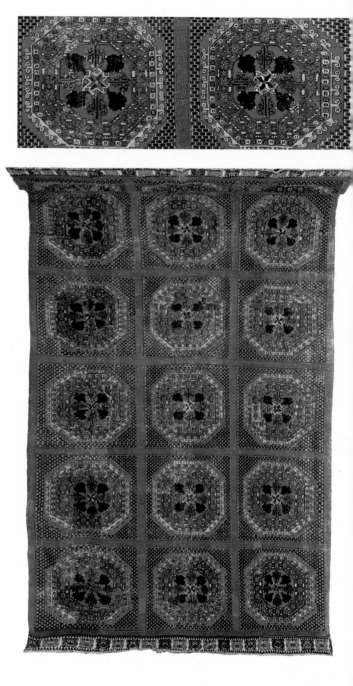

SPAIN (Alcaraz)

The Cleveland Museum of Art

Design Geometric
Date 15th century
Size 233 x 413 cm (7′ 9″ x 13′ 9″)
Warp Wool
Weft Wool
Pile Wool
Knot Arab-Spanish
Density 15–16 knots per sq cm (95–96 per sq in)
Principal colors Various shades of red; azure, yellow, violet
Description The field is divided into six vertical and three horizontal lines of squares, all decorated with the same motif. In each square, against a background formed by a close-knit grid, there is an octagonal medallion. In the middle of this there is a radial "Catherine-wheellike" star-shaped motif and, in relation to the axes, small arabesque designs. The remainder of the decoration consists of concentric rings of arabesque motifs, much smaller in size. There is no border. The short sides have a narrow panel decorated with a detailed motif of small lozenges alternating with lanceolate designs.

The mosaic dome above the mihrab of the great mosque in Cordoba, Spain. This monument embodies a spectacular blend of Byzantine and Islamic art which testifies to the versatility of the decorative language used in Islamic art. The octagonal pattern also features in the carpet on the previous page.

Eighteenth-century Spanish carpet from Alpujera.

SPAIN (Alpujera)

Private collection

Design Geometric
Date 17th century
Size 87 x 115 cm (2′ 10″ x 3′ 9″)
Warp Wool
Weft Wool and cotton
Pile Wool
Knot Ghiordes
Density 11—12 knots per sq cm (73—75 per sq in)
Principal colors Various shades of red and yellow; gray, green, black, brown, and cream
Description At the center of the field there is a rectangle decorated with a flower-patterned vase showing pretty red coloring against a light-colored ground. At the sides of the rectangle there are two small stylized cypress trees. The rest of the decoration consists of rows of vases of two different shapes, from which issue stylized blooms on stiffly depicted stems. The border consists of two fairly wide stripes. The inner stripe consists of squares decorated with stylized designs of rosettes, lilies, and vases. The outer stripe has a zigzag design decorated with small and variously colored circles, alternating in the parabolas.

can then look closely at all the various technical characteristics (warp, weft, and pile, with their respective structures; initial and final bands; edges and borders) that enable one to gain a more precise idea about the carpet. But it is not always possible to establish with any certainty the origin of a carpet, and this probably accentuates the veil of mysterious uncertainty which provides so much excitement for anyone who takes an interest in Oriental carpets for the pure fun of it.

The *gul* (meaning "flower" in Persian, which is apparently how it should be understood) was originally the motif, ornament, and even emblem of each particular tribe. As time passed this practice became gradually more and more diluted as is demonstrated by the *gul* of the Salor which lost its originality when the tribe was defeated in the 19th century by the Tekke and Saruk. The *gul* of the vanquished was taken on by the vanquisher. The most correct names for defining the carpets made by the Turkmen are those of the original tribe with a specific *gul*. This applies in the case of the Tekke, Yomud, Ersari, Saruk, and Chodor (or Chaudor). In a commercial sense, however, these carpets are often known by the names of the towns and cities acting as trading and sales centers. Thus we find, among the most familiar, Bukhara, Merv, Khiva, Pandeh, and Beshir, and in some cases these terms have stolen the limelight from the real, correct terms. The carpets were woven and knotted on movable horizontal looms using the Persian knot (Sehna or Senna knot). At the ends there may sometimes have been a couple of rows of Turkish or Ghiordes knots. The Persian knot is normally quite dense. The material used was mainly wool (white sections were woven with cotton). The commonest colors included many shades of usually quite dark red, brown, and blue.

Chemical analyses have shown that aniline and other artificial dyes, even when they had become widespread in other Oriental countries, were used sparingly by the tribes of Central Asia. In many cases only a few colors and a few small parts of the carpet show the use of artificial dyes.

Peripheral Areas of Carpet Production

From the historical and cultural viewpoint of carpet production (ancient and modern), Anatolia, the Caucasus, Persia, and Turkmenistan are the classic regions where the art of carpet weaving and knotting has best developed and enjoyed a certain continuity which can be documented in certain cases. This is because of several environmental, social, and economic factors, which have persisted through the ages and gradually turned the carpet into an industrial product, regardless of the fact that today it is still being made with a stress on craftsmanship. Only now and then has this set of circumstances found similar conditions in other geographical areas. And although these regions have produced carpets, some of them of top quality, they can be considered only peripheral in relation to the central position occupied by the regions listed above. Despite this, the contribution made to the art of knotting by Spain, Egypt, Maghreb (northwest Africa), eastern Turkestan (Central Asia), and China is important and sometimes original as well, and undoubtedly worthy of mention. The European countries present a different case altogether which will be tackled further on.

Carpets of the Iberian Peninsula

The importance of the inroads made into Spain by Islam is enormous. The Arab conquest took place around the years 710–712 and Arab dominion, which was at first total and then only partial, lasted until 1492, when the "Catholic Kings" reconquered the land. The knotting of carpets is an art that goes back a very long way in the Iberian peninsula, and has close ties with an ancient tradition of high-quality textiles. The existence of Spanish carpets can be traced back, on the basis of literary sources, to the 12th century,

but other sources inform us about an "industry" that already had a firm footing in the 13th century (Eleonora of Castile, married to Prince Edward, came to London in 1255 with a great many Spanish carpets, which are recorded by the inventories of the furnishings in her residence). Spanish carpets were exported, mainly to Egypt, and this is proven by 13th-century fragments found at the Fustat excavations. They can be identified by various details: the type of knotting, first and foremost, which is quite specific (see the chapter dealing with techniques) and commonly called the Arab-Spanish type. It was used by the Copts in Egypt. And it is of significance that Coptic peoples were active in Spain as far back as the 10th century. The introduction of the knot into Spain is attributed to artisans who followed this particular faith. Other distinctive features are the materials used, the colors, and the type of Kufic script at the borders, which appear to be different from other carpets and which, when compared with later examples, suggest an Iberian origin. The style of these carpets, from the late 13th century onward, is called *Mudéjar* (the name given to Moslems living under a Christian monarch), and combines Moorish and other Western elements. The most famous carpets are those of Chinchilla, Letur, Alcaraz, and Cuenca. Among the numerous typologies of Spanish carpets there are some that boast a certain originality. A certain type of carpet with a noble coat of arms in the center of the field (often repeated) on a background with motifs consisting of small octagons, hexagons, or adjacent squares, dates back to the 15th century. The borders have geometric or animal designs, or Kufic inscriptions. Oriental motifs (the Anatolian origins of some of the stylized animals is obvious) are mixed together with other evidently Spanish motifs. In fact one very interesting aspect (which is peculiar to all the Islamic art of Spain) of the art of carpet making in the Iberian peninsula is a clear syncretism between motifs of different origins and provenance that have been reworked and blended together with remarkable decorative skill to create a high level of ornamental style, which is thoroughly original and typical of this culture.

In the second half of the 15th century, possibly coming from Alcaraz, we find carpets that are mentioned in a letter penned by Queen Isabella of Castile. They have a geometric design like that of the Holbein group. In fact they are known as Spanish Holbeins. The motif consists of octagons in square compartments with stars and other geometric forms inside. Broadly speaking there are three main tendencies in this type of carpet. They differ in the variety of the design of the octagons and of the decorative elements inside them. The borders have a stylized floral design, often known as the "scorpion" motif, because it resembles the shape of this small animal's body. From the end of the 15th century craftsmen adopted specifically Western motifs, in particular floral motifs in the Gothic taste. One of the most fashionable designs was a free interpretation (allover and repeated) of the flowering pomegranate tree. Here were the first telltale signs of what was to take place on a more massive scale in the 16th century when motifs peculiar to fabrics, brocades, and arrases or tapestries used in the Italian and Spanish Renaissance were adopted for carpets and rugs. We find a greater stylization of the unrecognizable pomegranate motif and the use of arabesqued designs. The latter were quite different from what the same term means in Islamic art.

Carpets from Egypt and the Maghreb

Carpets have certainly been produced in Egypt from ancient times onward, even though we unfortunately have no archaeological documentation. At Fustat, or Old Cairo, which has been mentioned several times already, finds have been made, including Anatolian, Persian, and Spanish fragments, as well as fragments made by Coptic Christians, but there is no typology to tell us where the place of production was. At the present time only one group of carpets can be attributed to Egyptian looms: a group of so-called Mameluk carpets manufactured in Cairo in the early 16th century, although for a long time they were thought to have been made in Asia Minor, Damascus, or even Morocco. According to some scholars (notably Dimand) these carpets do not predate the Ottoman conquest of Egypt, the year 1517. This hypothesis is backed up by Kühnel and Erdmann who date them as late 15th century. They have geometric designs. The center has an octagon or octagonal star with the remainder of the carpet divided into geometric compartments of various sizes, arranged symmetrically. The border has motifs with long scrolls alternating with other polygons. The entire space of the carpet is filled with small decorative elements, the most common of which is the so-called papyrus motif (a sort of small umbrella, usually arranged in groups of three) which

EGYPT (Cairo)

Museum für Islamisches Kunst, West Berlin

Design Geometric (Mameluk)
Date 16th century
Size 132 x 210 cm (4′ 4″ x 6′ 11″)
Warp Wool
Weft Wool
Pile Wool
Knot Sehna
Density 17–18 knots per sq cm (108–110 per sq in)
Principal colors Various shades of red; yellow, azure, gray
Description The central field is dominated by a square which contains a regular octagon. The decoration consists of successive bands, still octagonal in form, to the middle of the field where there is an octagonal star inscribed within a circle. The outermost octagonal band has octagonal stars halfway along each side. The four triangular corners have squares decorated with small "papyrus" designs. Above two sides of the square there are rectangular panels with stylized rosettes, pairs of trees, and a fine sixteen-pointed star. The border of the rug is well proportioned. The borders themselves are in two sections and have a continuous floral and wavy motif. The wider strip has a series of elongated scrolls alternating with lobed octagonal medallions.

probably derives from a very old Egyptian design. The most widely used material was wool. The knot is the Persian sort. The colors are bright but of limited range (there is a conspicuous tendency toward monochromy) from red to blue to green.

One of the most discussed topics where carpets are concerned is their possible symbolic meaning and the formal analogies that can be singled out. C. G. Ellis has recently, and somewhat provocatively, proposed the *mandala* as a formal model: this is a typical form found in Tibetan and Nepalese art. Others see in the central octagon the typical design of a fountain, which existed aplenty in Cairo, thus tracing interesting parallels with classical art which, with its mosaic forms, was responsible for the tiniest decorative elements, and is an example of the survival of earlier traditions in a younger but more receptive culture. In a sunny country such as Egypt the fountain was a very popular motif, and one that was used like the motif used in the garden carpets of Persia, designed in other works to evoke Paradise, and consequently a place of solace in the broad sense. The stress on the central section, the octagon (formed by rotating one square over another at an angle of 45 degrees), which sometimes contains a square right in the middle, and the radial and circular appearance of the whole composition suggest a different interpretation. At the center of the symbolic carpet we find Mecca (Makkah) and at the center of Mecca we have the Ka'ba. Mecca, the birthplace of the Prophet Muhammad, is the very

heart of the world for the Islamic believer, the place toward which he addresses his prayers five times a day, and the place toward which he will be faced when he is buried. What is more, the pilgrim who travels to the holy city for the *Hajj* (this is one of the five "commandments" for being a Moslem, these being: 1. a profession of faith; 2. praying five times a day; 3. ritual alms-giving; 4. the pilgrimage or *Hajj* to Mecca [if you have the wherewithal to do so]; and 5. the month-long fast called *Ramadan*) walks around the Ka'ba seven times in a rite known as the *tawaf*. This is how the building (covered with a black cloth with Koranic inscriptions embroidered in gold) is both the place to walk around—a very ancient practice found in other religious cultures—and at the same time the place from which the faith is spread. Incidentally, one of the most frequently found "souvenirs" in the house of a *Hajj* (and also found in many mosques in most of the Islamic world) is a modern carpet or fabric with the Ka'ba in the middle radiating the faith in all directions throughout the world. Why the number eight? Because the octogram can be drawn with a single line, like the pentagram, and is regarded as one of the symbols of the Prophet (Jajczay). In addition it should not be forgotten that the two rotated squares form the plan of the Dome of the Rock in Jerusalem. As has been shown by Oleg Grabar, this building, built about a rock and by tradition the spot where Abraham made his sacrifice and the place where Muhammad set off on his *miraj* or journey to heaven, had an important socio-political function: it was the monument to the victory (above all seen as an ideological conquest of faith) of the two great rival cultures, the Sassanid and the Byzantine; and all this in the greatest center of religious tradition that man has ever known. But the contingent historical reason—which was put in some doubt by Grabar—that led to the construction of this building in the year 684–685 (65 H) and its completion in 691 (72 H) by the Caliph Abd al-Malik, was the revolt of the son of a friend of the Prophet who controlled the city of Mecca and stopped Syrians making their pilgrimage there. So the *tawaf* rite was "diverted" to Jerusalem. At an early stage the Prophet also directed his prayers toward the city, and only subsequently actually went to Mecca himself. The octagon is thus the symbol of the Dome of the Rock (which is not a mosque, but a kind of sanctuary) and was in turn compared to the Ka'ba in the minds of the faithful. If this hypothesis, which is not provable and also provocative, is correct, the three or five octagonal medallions often depicted could be explained in terms of the three leading cities (Mecca, Jerusalem, and Medina) or the five basic rules of the Islamic faith. The suggestion that one can see in the motif of Mameluk carpets a geometric design deriving from architecture is also implicit in the interpretation of carpets as designs deriving from fountains. The hypothesis has recently been put forward that the cruciform or cross-shaped plan of many Armenian churches may be the basis of, and responsible for, certain cross-type designs of carpets made in the Caucasus. But two major motifs remain outside this all-embracing reconstruction of events: the "papyrus" and "umbrella," and the medallions that occur at the edge of carpets. The papyrus can be explained, from

this viewpoint, as the representation of the palm tree. In later representations this tree is associated—particularly in Ottoman depictions on ceramic panels—with the mosque at Medina, where it is one of the symbols most used by the decorators. The border, with elongated scrolls alternating with round scrolls, may symbolize the Koranic inscriptions on the palm tree that covers the Ka'ba (in all probability an ancient practice), but without being too explicit as would be the case if the scrolls contained Koranic extracts. Mameluk carpets are thus a souvenir of the pilgrimage or a representation of it. Obviously, we do not claim to have proved anything, other than that there are many plausible explanations for a carpet, especially when the approach made is not technical or stylistic, but symbolical.

In the other parts of North Africa—in the Maghreb—carpet making must have started in ancient times as well. But the conditional tense has to be used because this is only a hypothesis, albeit a logical one, given that there is nothing surviving to enable us to document the possibility of an autonomous evolution in this sector. Today carpets are made that imitate the vast Persian repertoire, especially the more popular modern one. As already mentioned, the old Moroccan carpets are more akin to the so-called Mameluk carpets, which had also been attributed to this region of Egypt. More recently the carpets made by the Berbers have been fairly successful commercially. They have a simple decorative plan (dark-colored lozenges on a light background) and a long, thick pile, both features well-suited to the modern taste for the somewhat flat. They are certainly of little significance in terms of typology, but they do indicate the poor productivity of the area.

Southern Egypt. In a small village the inhabitants break from their jobs and gather around to watch a young dancer accompanied by gypsy players.

The Dome of the Rock in Jerusalem is one of the buildings most cherished by Moslems. The external plan is octagonal and all the geometric ratios on which the construction is based have to do with the number 8. The eight pillars in the ambulatory are situated at the vertices of an eight-pointed star. Inside, the holy rock is surrounded by a structure obtained by rotating two squares at 45 degrees.

A silk-and-gold standard captured from the Moslems at the battle of Las Navas at Toulouse in 1212. Note the central area dominated by the octagon which calls to mind both the octagonal form of Mameluk carpets and, even more sharply, Spanish Holbein carpets. The central part of the standard is surrounded by circular forms painted with varied Moorish-style decorative motifs. The script is typical of Spanish-Moorish art.

An 18th-century Tibetan mandala, now in the Guimet Museum in Paris. Experts have recently detected the formal similarities between the design of the Tibetan mandala and that of Mameluk carpets—but there is no claim that either one acted as the model for the other.

EGYPT (Cairo)

Osterreichisches Museum, Vienna

Design Geometric (Mameluk)
Date 16th century
Size 290 x 540 cm (9' 6" x 17' 8")
Warp Silk
Weft Wool
Pile Silk
Knot Sehna
Density 31 per sq cm (195 knots per sq in)
Principal colors Red, green, yellow, in various shades; white and black
Description At the center there is an octagonal star containing a second one in which the starlike figure is markedly softened. The heart of the design is, again, an octagon, with points at each corner, where there is a design of concentric stars. Between the two octagons, the central one and the almost star-shaped one, there is a band with geometric motifs with the end segment in the shape of a curl; then there are octagonal lozenge-shaped areas which contain the papyrus motif. This same motif also decorates the octagonal star. The remaining part of the area is decorated with octagons (the basic pattern), stars, and arrowlike triangular shapes. The decoration echoes contemporary works in wood and the decoration of the *mimbar* (pulpits) found in mosques.

← EGYPT (Cairo)

Bardini Museum, Florence

Design Geometric
Date 16th century
Size 190 x 270 cm (6′ 3″ x 8′ 10″)
Warp Wool
Weft Wool
Pile Wool
Knot Sehna
Density 18 knots per sq cm (112–115 per sq in)
Principal colors Black, red, white, light green, yellow
Description The whole central area is highly decorated. At the center there is a conspicuous octagonal star which dominates the whole decorative area. The geometric figure of the octagon is taken as a basic pattern for the decoration of the carpet which revolves around this design. The principal star is made up of various octagons. The rest of the field has eight geometric forms, four rectangles, and four squares. The four rectangular forms are intersected by the four points of the star, with four triangles decorated with the papyrus motif arranged opposite them in the other direction.

EGYPT (Cairo)

Bardini Museum, Florence

Design Geometric carpet (Checkerboard type)
Date Late 17th century
Size 230 x 315 cm (7′ 7″ x 10′ 4″)
Warp Wool
Weft Wool
Pile Wool
Knot Ghiordes
Density 13–14 per sq cm (85 per sq in)
Principal colors Red, dark red, light and dark blue, yellow, olive, white, black, gray, and brown
Description A carpet with geometric decoration of the so-called Ottoman design. In this carpet, although the decorative motif could be extended further, it can be considered to be finite. The decorative design consists of thirty-two squares that contain the same number of hexagons. The hexagons are not interrupted by the horizontal lines that form the squares; we thus have four continuous rows of eight hexagons each, which create the visual impression of elongated lozenges. Between the rows of hexagons there is an hour glass (Clepsydra) motif or, if we see it as staggered, a lozenge divided into four parts by the right-angled lines of the squares. The design of this carpet is clearly similar to the one of the Mameluk group.

EGYPT (Cairo)

Kunstgewerbe Museum, Frankfurt

Design Floral
Date 16th century
Size 147 x 190 cm (4′ 10″ x 6′ 3″)
Warp Wool
Weft Wool
Pile Wool
Knot Sehna
Density 18 knots per sq cm (112–115 per sq in)
Principal colors Red, yellow, brown, blue, black, and gray
Description The center has an extremely elegant floral design, with four buds arranged in the shape of a cross surrounded by spiked flowers. A similar decoration occurs at the corners of the central area. The borders have the same decoration of rosettes in alternating colors. The strip is very wide with palmettes and flowering buds, set in alternating directions and joined together by winding spiked leaves and shoots with small flowers.

EGYPT (Cairo or Istanbul)

Musée des Arts Décoratifs, Paris

Design Floral
Date 16th century
Size 188 x 273 cm (6′ 2″ x 8′ 11″)
Warp Wool
Weft Wool
Pile Wool
Knot Sehna
Density 30 knots per sq cm (185–190 per sq in)
Principal colors Red, blue, cream, all in various shades, green, yellow, mustard, and brown
Description In the middle of the central area there is a circular, not very large, medallion, decorated with a central rosette and radiating flowers and buds. Quarter-medallion sections appear at the corners of the field. This is decorated with a close-knit series of "fleshy" floral and plant motifs linked together by slender shoots. There are large feather-shaped leaves, rosettes, palmettes, and flowers designed like contemporary ceramic art. The border is small, consisting of a strip edged with narrow borders decorated with floral motifs. The central strip has palmettes set in alternating directions, joined together by flowering shoots.

MAGHREB (Algeria)

Türk ve Islam Müzesi, Istanbul

Design Geometric
Date 19th century
Size 125 x 220 cm (4' 2" x 7')
Warp Cotton
Weft Cotton
Pile Wool
Knot Ghiordes
Density 10 knots per sq cm (63 per sq in, approx.)
Principal colors Red, yellow, black, white, and brown
Description At the center there is a rectangle, with four more smaller rectangles above and below. The five rectangles are divided from one another by a small stripe which has the same repeated motif of octagonal stars. The central rectangle has a lozenge decorated, both inside and out, by a checkerboard design. The border consists of a guard stripe with a zigzag decoration and a point inside the triangles. The carpet is rounded off by stripes on the short sides decorated with geometric motifs.

MAGHREB (Morocco)

Türk ve Islam Müzesi, Istanbul

Design Geometric
Date 19th century
Size 50 x 116 cm (1' 8" x 3' 10")
Warp Wool
Weft Wool
Pile Wool
Knot Ghiordes
Density 6 knots per sq cm (37–38 per sq in)
Principal colors Red, yellow, blue, pink, brown
Description A rug with geometric decoration. This rug was made in the royal palace in Rabat in the 1850s or 1860s. The field is dominated by two medallions linked together along the vertical axis, in the form of elongated scrolls. The border is very small, consisting of a stripe edged by a simple wavy design. The design of the rug does not seem to come from the North African region, and was probably imported from Anatolia.

This miniature, painted c. 1615 (now in the British Museum) shows Jahangir weighing the equivalent in precious stones and artistic objects of Prince Khurram, following a tradition that is still carried on today. Note the floral carpet with medallion beneath the scale pan with the prince. Jahangir and the attendant are barefoot on the border of the carpet. In the foreground we can see some of the gifts given by the prince's subjects.

The Mogul was a very keen tiger hunter. In this detail from a painting, mounted and armed huntsmen surround a tiger while Akbar and Jahangir, on a finely bedecked elephant, get ready for the kill.

Indian Carpets

The history of the Indian carpet is closely linked with that of the Moghul dynasty in India (1526–1858), founded by Babur (or Babar), a Turk belonging to the Central Asian Chaghatay tribe, who reigned from 1526 to 1530. He was directly descended, on the paternal side, from Tamerlane. The heyday of the carpet in India has been fairly lively and intense, although for mainly climatic reasons the use of carpets has never been that widespread, with the exception of well-to-do households and princely courts.

The Moghul art of carpet making, but not only this style—in fact we could talk in terms of the entire Indian art of the period—is heavily indebted to Persia. The Indian emperor Humayun, father of the famous Akbar, for some time in exile at the court of the often-mentioned Shah Tahmasp, returned to India with a large company of Persian artists (who were happy to leave Tabriz, not least because Tahmasp had undergone a change of heart as far as the arts in general were concerned) and many of these artists were extremely accomplished miniaturists or illuminators.

The Moghul sovereigns were great patrons of all the arts. During their reign there was a progressive and interesting merger between the decorative motifs of Persia and India. The period during which this development took place was the reign of the emperor Akbar I (1556–1605), a man concerned with having knowledge of different cultures, and who was also responsible for various important architectural achievements. Akbar, who is a full-fledged painter

himself, played an essential part not only as an all-round champion of the art, but also as a front-runner inspirer and ideologist of a new taste—which turned out to be long-lived and earned the status of a "school." This new taste merged two different realities, Indian tradition and Persian doctrine. The result, as seen in many artistic works, is undoubtedly most impressive.

Illuminations and miniatures were commissioned in great numbers by the emperor and depict a great many carpets with a predominance of Iranian carpets of the medallion type from the Safawid period. Among the types of carpets woven on Indian looms we find carpets clearly inspired by the Persian models made in Herat but in colors which do not abide by the original design. This typology has become known as the Indo-Persian carpet. The Moghul craftsmen developed a style that adhered more closely to the Indian taste by introducing new floral motifs (using a more naturalistic inflection than the sometimes highly stylized and thus stiff Persian motif) and animal motifs. The golden age of the carpet was the reign of Akbar's son, Jahangir (1605–28), who was responsible for rich, lush floral style, again markedly naturalistic in flavor. These carpets borrowed the plan of the Persian carpet and then enriched it with a greater profusion of beautiful flowering buds (roses, lilac, bellflowers, violets, peonies, and lilies, as well as the ordinary repertoire) and wild animals (crocodiles, tigers, rhinoceroses, elephants, as well as dragons

Jaipur in India. Flower vendors in the square. The flower has always been a basic feature of Indian culture and art.

INDIA

The Textile Museum, Washington

Design Naturalistic
Date 17th century
Size 82 x 88 cm (2′ 8″ x 2′ 11″)
Warp Wool
Weft Wool
Pile Wool
Knot Sehna
Density 32–33 knots per sq cm (200–205 per sq in)
Principal colors Red, yellow, blue, black, cream, violet
Description The field has the extremely naturalistic depiction of two large elephants having a fight, set against a very bright red background. The inclusion of the elephants in carpet design is a typical feature of Indian artistic expression, and represents an easily identifiable symbol in the production of knotted carpets. This fragment of a larger carpet is extremely interesting because of the quality of the craftsmanship, the very clearly defined design, the excellent wool used, and the bright colors. None of the border has been preserved.

INDIA

Metropolitan Museum of Art, New York

Design Prayer rug with floral design
Date 17th century
Size 103 x 155 cm (3′ 5″ x 5′ 1″)
Warp Wool
Weft Wool
Pile Wool
Knot Sehna
Density 45 knots per sq cm (280–285 per sq in, approx.)
Principal colors Various shades of green; red, pink, cream, and mustard
Description In the middle of the niche there is a beautiful plant in bloom —either a sunflower or, more probably, a chrysanthemum. The flowering plant is flanked by two tulips at the base, where it meets the ground. The corner sections have a similar decoration to the central flowers, but the colors are different. The border is well proportioned and elegant, consisting of two edged guard stripes enclosing the central stripe. The guard stripes are identical and have a decoration of rosettes of alternating colors. The stripe also has a floral decoration: a pretty shoot with fleshy leaves joins together four-petaled flowers with rosettes.

INDIA

Private collection

Design Naturalistic
Date Late 19th century
Size 123 x 181 cm (4' x 5' 11")
Warp Cotton
Weft Cotton
Pile Wool
Knot Sehna
Density 34–35 per sq cm (215–220 per sq in)
Principal colors Various shades of red, blue, green, and yellow; white, black, cream, brown, and orange
Description In the middle of the central field there is an oval medallion framed by a spiked garland, decorated with a scene depicted in a pictorial style. The scene shows a handsome style, even if there is a certain geometric rigidity and stiffness about the design itself. The rest of the field is very densely decorated with elegant vases with handles holding large bouquets of flowers among which there are numerous small birds. The border is of normal proportions, consisting of a double guard stripe with a larger central stripe between them.

INDIA

The National Gallery, Washington

Design Carpet with naturalistic and floral decoration
Date 17th century
Size 180 x 300 cm (5' 11" x 9' 10", approx.)
Warp Cotton (?)
Weft Cotton (?)
Pile Wool
Knot Sehna
Principal colors Various shades of red, brown, and blue; yellow, green, cream, orange, pink, and gray
Description The field has a series of designs of animals arranged without any precise pattern. Set against the red background we also have elegant plant and flowering shoots in a very spacious and generous design. Numerous animals are depicted: elephants, gazelles, ibex, lions, leopards, rhinoceroses, and crocodiles; there is also no shortage of legendary creatures, such as dragons, *chi-lin* and winged hounds. The detail shows the large elephant with a man mounted upon it, in a section of the carpet that is a good example of the blending of floral and animal motifs and the precise attention to detail.

The Taj Mahal at Agra in India, built between 1632 and 1648, is the mausoleum of Mumtaz Mahal, the wife of Shah Jahan. The architecture of this most impressive of buildings, made of marble with fine engravings, is an extraordinary example of the perfect balance achieved by the Indo-Islamic art of India. Light, form, and decoration blend together perfectly and create a unique image that expresses this particular style to perfection.

and Chinese legendary four-footed beasts called *chilin*) taken from the rich repertoire of illuminations executed by artists who at least inspired and probably also painted the cartoons for the carpets. This style reached its peak of maturity under the next monarch, Shah Jahan (1628–58), who, among other things, had the Taj Mahal built. In his reign we find magnificent carpets that give one a glimpse of the opulent decadence of the subsequent periods. Technically speaking Indian carpets are excellent. The knot used is the Persian one with a very high density, ranging from about 12,000 to 19,000 knots per square decimeter (750–1200 per square inch). The wool that was used for the vast majority of these carpets is often so thin that it can be taken for silk. Silk carpets are rarer and reach extremely high knot densities, in some

cases 39,000 per square decimeter (2450 per square inch)!

Carpets of Eastern Turkestan and China

The Chinese Turkestan region extends east of Samarkand, north of Tibet and west of the great loop of the Yellow River (Hwang-Ho). It is almost totally made up of deserts and mountain ranges. It was crossed by the great caravans which plied the so-called Silk Route from east to west and back again. The oases along this route became major trading centers and, to a lesser extent, the site of factories and workshops.

The carpets of eastern Turkestan are known in the trade as Samarkand carpets, after the name of the last great caravan center, lying to the west of the Tarim basin. It was here that the carpets were brought to be sold. The civilization of this vast area is known to us mainly because of the accounts given by archaeological expeditions made by Western missions at the beginning of this century (Sir Aurel Stein, Albert von Le Coq, Paul Pelliot), which led to major discoveries that have testified to the existence of an ancient and original culture with decorative motifs widely influenced by Indo-Hellenistic, Persian, and Chinese art. Archaeologists have unearthed countless fragments of carpets, but unfortunately these fragments have not always been in the best state of preservation. Furthermore, it is worth mentioning that it is not impossible to attribute the first knotted carpets, and hence the invention and diffusion of this technique, to this remote but undeniably dynamic part of the world.

We should mention the cities of Turfan, Khotan, Yarkand, and Kashgar, all of which were extremely important caravan centers and in constant contact with the great civilizations of East and West. In the carpet production found in eastern Turkestan, which was actually quite limited, we find a blend of Persian, Chinese, and Central Asian motifs, with the distant echo of Timurid designs. For during that period (Tamerlane's reign) Khotan and Kashgar were on the outskirts of the empire. All of which goes to show the natural tendency of this region to act as a bridge between the culture of China and the culture of Iran. The oldest carpets that have come down to us (18th century) have rather stiff and stylized floral motifs. This is the case with the pomegranate tree growing from a vase, which was a typical product of the region. The knot is Persian. Warp and weft are often cotton, but the pile is woolen and only rarely silk.

The situation of China in relation to the art of carpet making is somewhat specific. It was in China that silk was "invented"; there was a strong textile tradition and matting had been widely used since ancient if not earlier times. Furthermore, various particular types of furniture were used in the Chinese continent, including tables and chairs, in contrast with the Oriental philosophy of the carpet which is, certainly, a work of art but also a utilitarian object, like ceramics, fabrics, and metals that could also be very finely decorated and still be ultimately designed for practical purposes. The discovery of fragments in Central Asian areas to the northwest of the territories colonized by the Chinese shows that the art of knotting was already known in ancient times to peoples whose exchanges with

Chinese people are archaeologically proven. Many literary sources refer to the presence of carpets in China (although they do not mention actual factories). We should also bear in mind the paintings already mentioned in an earlier chapter, the frescoes (the Buddhist ones of the T'ang period, 618–906, at Tunhuang in Central Asia are particularly significant), and numerous other indirect evidence which is not always that helpful in showing the effective presence of knotted carpets in China. Mats made of fabric (silk or of the *kilim* type) were made not only in pressed wool but often tally just as well with the descriptions given and do not contradict the images painted.

One sure fact, which is fairly obvious given the premise from which we have started, is the increase of references and representations in the periods dominated by peoples and tribes coming from Central Asia, who brought with them their beliefs and their social customs, at least in the early stages of this dominion and before the assimilation of the "barbarian" semi-nomadic conquerors by the highly civilized sedentary peoples. It is therefore very likely that the Mongol peoples of Central Asia had—as we have already mentioned—an ancient tradition of carpet weaving, even though no examples of their art have come down to us, not even in the form of fragments, and we must make do with contemporary paintings or literary sources on which to base our meager observations and knowledge. Judging by these sources, their carpets had a geometric design, in the last anal-

129

A Chinese silk carpet from the Ch'ien Lung period (1736–95), decorated with nine (yang number) rampant dragons. The carpet with stylized figures shows dragons with five claws, typical attributes associated with the holiness of the emperor. At the sides of the carpet we see the sea (four times represented in accordance with a precise Chinese cosmography) with the repeated stylized motif of the three sacred mountains. Note also the interesting cloud design with the two "flaming pearls" completing the background.

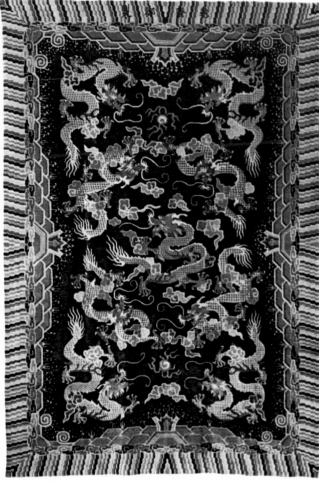

TURKESTAN (Khotan)

Private collection

Design Geometric
Date 19th century
Size 89 x 315 cm (2' 11" x 10' 4")
Warp Cotton
Weft Cotton
Pile Wool
Knot Sehna
Density 4–5 knots per sq cm (28 per sq in)
Principal colors Various shades of turquoise, orange, and yellow; brown, white, and red
Description The field has a series of large circular lobed medallions, and other smaller geometric figures decorated with pomegranates, a symbol of fertility and hence prosperity. The other medallions are decorated with swastikas, rhombi, and rectangles, all intersecting, and small geometric figures, among which we can see chrysanthemums and double pairs of bats, a symbol of perpetual happiness. The corners are decorated with linear geometric designs of the ideogram—indicating "long life." The border is wide and has three stripes, with the central one being the widest. The broad central stripe has a rather elegant geometric decoration, typical of the Chinese decorative arts, deriving from the motif of the three sacred mountains.

ysis not very unlike that of old Anatolian fragments, though on a larger scale. Nor have Chinese carpets from later periods survived. We have no direct knowledge of carpets before the second half of the 18th century. The reason for this is technical, though possibly not primarily technical. The wool used in Chinese carpets is of poor quality—poorer than that used in Turkish or Persian products. This Chinese wool is perfectly all right for other uses—materials for example —but is too soft and weak for carpets. Furthermore, the knots are spaced further apart, which has a considerable effect on wear and tear, and less tight, and the pile is usually longer—and all these features do little, in their various ways, to promote the preservation of the carpet.

The Chinese carpets that have come down to us, which are more recent than they actually look, have decorative schemes from the late Ming period (1368–1644) and from the Ch'ing period (1644–1912), as can easily be observed from other forms of artistic expression (porcelain, fabrics, etc.) which have been handed down to us in large numbers. Chinese carpets almost certainly never predate the K'ang hsi period (1662–1722), and the bulk of the production can be attributed to factories and workshops that were active during the reign of Ch'ien lung (1736–95). The Chinese had developed an artistic civilization in which the symbolic plays a fundamental part, and a vastly more important one than in the contemporary cultures in the rest of the world. This rule also embraces those carpets in which the symbols, with their complex language, constitute the main if not the only part of the decoration. The vast majority of carpets have a series of images, like a sort of puzzle, which when deciphered inevitably sort themselves out into augural or celebratory propositions. In addition to these puzzle-like or symbolic carpets we find carpets with mythological scenes or naturalistic landscapes, both being inspired from the contemporary pictorial arts. Technically speaking the Chinese carpets are of reasonable quality. They are woven on vertical looms using the Persian method. At the borders and ends there may sometimes be a row or two of Turkish knots to bolster the structure of the carpet. The knots are not that dense. Wool is used (often goat's or camel's) and the warp and weft are often of cotton. There are also carpets made only of silk.

TURKESTAN (Yarkand)

Carpet Museum, Teheran

Design Geometric
Date 18th–19th centuries
Size 181 x 372 cm (5′ 11″ x 12′ 3″)
Warp Cotton
Weft Cotton
Pile Wool
Knot Ghiordes
Density 10–11 knots per sq cm (63–64 per sq in)

Principal colors Various shades of red, blue, and yellow; black, pink, violet, and brown
Description In the middle of the field there are three medallions standing out against the red background of an oval stepped shape. The central, four-pointed medallion has a central cross; the other two, which are almost round, have a square surrounded by eight stylized rosettes. The remainder of the field, with a different background color, is decorated with rather stiff shoots. The border consists of an inner guard stripe with the continuous motif of very stylized shoots and two stripes of equal width. The first is decorated with a lily motif, the second by a double set of Greek crosses.

Right: Ceramics from the T'ang period (618–907) known as san o ts'ai or "three colors." The ceramics were first engraved and then colored with lead-based paints. When this technique was used—and it was hard to use in a controlled way because the colors tend to run—often to great artistic effect, it enabled Chinese potters to achieve results of an exceptional quality. The same technique was used with less success by potters in the Near and Middle East.

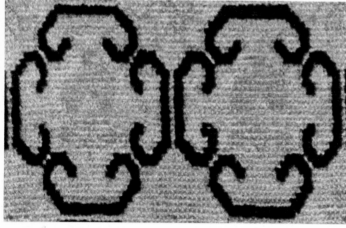

CHINA (China)

Metropolitan Museum of Art, New York

Design Geometric
Date 18th century
Size 342 x 360 cm (11′ 5″ x 12′)
Warp Cotton
Weft Cotton
Pile Wool
Knot Sehna
Density 6–7 knots per sq cm (40 per sq in)
Principal colors Various shades of blue and yellow; green and mustard
Description The field is dominated by a simple decorative design that, repeated, fashions the actual decorative motif. Small medallions are formed by pairs of hooks or brackets and enclose a bat-shaped motif. There are lozenge-shaped areas, which are staggered in relation to the rows of small medallions and contain peach blooms in a darker color than the yellow background. The central stripe is wide and has a motif that is commonly used in Chinese carpets: a design of swastikas joined together. The significance of this carpet, with the repeated bat and peach bloom motifs, is obviously auspicious and is emphasized by the stripe with the swastikas, which infinitely increases the importance of the message.

132

CHINA

Private collection

Design Naturalistic
Date 19th century
Size 142 x 206 cm (4′ 8″ x 6′ 9″)
Warp Cotton
Weft Cotton
Pile Wool
Knot Sehna
Density 5–6 knots per sq cm (33 per sq in)
Principal colors Various shades of red, brown, and cream; pink, yellow, gray, and black
Description At the center of the field there is a roundish oval medallion decorated with a deer and a heron, Taoist symbols of longevity, against a naturalistic background. Around the medallion there are four butterflies, and two beautiful peach blooms are placed above and below the medallion, again with a precise symbolic meaning. The decoration of the corners consists of very elegant blooms supported by geometrically designed stems. The border is well proportioned, consisting of a guard stripe and wider main stripe. The softened shades of color and the pleasing sobriety of the design are typical features of this type of carpet.

Europe and the Art of the Carpet

As soon as Oriental carpets made their first appearance in Europe they were a huge success. They were imported by the thousands, especially by merchants doing business in the coastal cities of Italy. From the Middle Ages onward there was not a single well-to-do family that did not have one or more fine carpets to its name. It was the very idea of the carpet that was intriguing. That soft, warm object with its detailed and colorful decoration could instantly replace the ancient art of mosaics which had fallen by the wayside over the centuries, and this was one of the reasons for its enthusiastic reception. As a result carpets came to be made in Europe (mainly in France and England, but also in Germany and Holland), displaying a taste and a spirit far removed from the original. Production in France, using Oriental techniques and usually the Turkish knot, started between the 16th and 17th centuries. The first person to embark on this venture was P. Dupont, who set up a workshop in 1606, in the Louvre, in Paris, with the help of Henry IV. His disciple, S. Lourdet, was given premises at Chaillot in the Hospice de la Savonnerie, and it was this name—Savonnerie—that was to hallmark French knotted carpets (from Aubusson where they were woven). In 1825 the workshop was merged with the Manufacture Nationale des Gobelins, and moved there. The most fertile period of production occurred from the mid- to the late 17th century. The taste that inspired the European carpets echoed that of the contemporary decorative arts inside the great palaces of the sovereigns and nobles at court. When they were not outright copies, these carpets often borrowed the decorative motifs—be it floral, landscapes, or mythology—which were usually neo-classical, from the walls and especially the ceilings. There was also a considerable amount of decoration in the rococo style. Even though these carpets did not have a very high knot density, production showed a high level of technical quality, and the French carpets in particular stood out because of their rich repertoire and the subtlety of the motifs. In their own genre they were masterpieces that were to have a wide influence on the factories in the rest of Europe.

In England there are dated carpets (one of the oldest dates is 1585) that are clearly a Western copy of contemporary Oriental models. Because there is no documentary evidence of English looms which produced carpets in that period, it has been suggested

FRANCE (Savonnerie)
Private collection

Design Floral
Date 17th–18th centuries
Size 171 x 215 cm (5' 8" x 7' 2")
Warp Wool
Weft Wool
Pile Wool
Knot Ghiordes
Density 15 knots per sq cm (95 per sq in)
Principal colors Various shades of blue, yellow, and cream; red, brown, green, and pink
Description The rectangular central field has a complex floral bouquet as the decorative motif. Thanks to the attention to detail, we can identify roses, lilies, chrysanthemums, cornflowers, and other species. The pale colors against the dark background stand out starkly, creating a very agreeable decorative effect, very much in line with the taste of the day. In some cases, with these carpets, the decorative scheme is juggled quite radically, and it is not even relevant to talk of a field, which becomes delimited by a narrow guard stripe with leaf designs. The border is very wide indeed and is a decorative replica of the central field.

FRANCE (Savonnerie)

Musée de Versailles

Design Naturalistic and floral
Date Started in 1681
Size 520 x 900 cm (17' 4" x 30')
Warp Wool
Weft Wool
Pile Wool
Knot Ghiordes
Density 15 knots per sq cm (95 per sq in, approx.)
Principal colors Blue, yellow, red, green, black, white, brown, gray, pink, and orange
Description This is one of the most famous carpets ever woven in France. It was the seventh in a series of ninety-three ordered by Louis XIV for the Grande Galerie in the Louvre. These carpets are now at Versailles and have been since the palace was turned into a museum. The whole decorative arrangement, both in terms of the spatial distribution and the iconography used, smacks of the monumental pictorial art of the time. The warmth of the colors and, above all, the typical design of this carpet are its paramount features, and represent the best artistic production of the time in Europe.

that they were made in Flanders. But the present level of our knowledge is not such that we can pinpoint the precise place of origin of these carpets, and all our theories need substantiating. The design belongs to the so-called Ushak-star group (with noble coats of arms), with slight distortions in the design vertically (because of the less compact structure of the carpet, in other words to a fairly marked difference between knots along the horizontal axis and knots along the vertical axis) and a density of about 1400 knots per 100 square centimeters (16 square inches).

Before long, however, the French models spread abroad (craftsmen from the other side of the Channel immigrated and brought with them technical know-how and designs on a large scale) and carpets were decorated with essentially European motifs. The most famous workshops were set up in Fulham, Exeter, and Axminster, and the carpets made in these places bear their names. We should also mention the work-shops of T. Moore at Moorfields. Here carpets were produced from plans or in the style of the architect-cum-decorator Robert Adam (1728–92). William Morris (1834–96), who has been mentioned earlier as one of the main champions behind the acquisition of the Ardabil carpet, included the carpet in his wide range of interests in the crafts, and the workshop with which he was associated produced certain carpets in the unmistakable floral and plant-rich style peculiar to that artist. It must also be added that Norris was a very well versed connoisseur of carpets. In fact, a Moghul carpet, now in the Museum of Fine Arts in Boston, and one of the most elegant products of that period, was bought by an American collector at his suggestion.

Carpets Without Knots

Kilim (Ghilim)

When compared with the knotted carpets, those made using other techniques (*kilim, sumak,* fabrics) differ in one basic feature: the absence of a pile. From this we have another way of labeling them, which is "flat carpets." Because they have no pile, these car-pets offer less protection against the cold, even when they are woolen. Furthermore, the knotted carpet has a more compact structure which makes it much more solid and long-lasting. The advantages of non-knotted carpets are the speed with which they can be made,

A typical Caucasian sumak *carpet from the 19th century. The colors and decoration are typical of the area.*

The loom used for the famous Valtellina (Lombardy) pezzotti *(patchwork carpets), a fine illustration of local craftsmanship.*

their more convenient size for transport purposes (particularly useful in the case of large carpets), the possibility of using them on both sides (double face) with the exception of *sumak,* and the much lower cost. The area covered by them is virtually the same as for knotted carpets in the relevant historical period, and even wider from the 19th century onward because the relative techniques found an ideal area of growth among those peoples who were weavers by tradition. The presence of *kilim* side by side with the major products made using knots is demonstrated in two ways: by the end borders of the carpets which are often made using this technique, and by the examples that have been preserved which are not actually that numerous because of their perishability.

Artistically speaking the *kilim* are characterized by an evident prevalence of geometric motifs, although there is no shortage of often good quality examples of figurative scenes using the same repertoire as knotted carpets. The designs are fairly detailed and have bright juxtaposed colors. In the decorated border strips we often find those popular motifs (combs, animals, and small trees) which date back to ancient superstitions and beliefs held by the craftsmen. One of the commonest practices was to insert woolen threads or objects into the fabric as a protection against the evil eye. In Turkey *kilim* are fairly widespread, as they are in the Caucasus (there are a few fragmentary examples with the dragon motif and some are also dated) and throughout Persia. The highest production was achieved by the semi-no-

madic peoples of central-southern Iran. There was an ancient tradition in this area, but today it has been affected by the use of brash industrial colors which, luckily, fade after prolonged exposure to light. The other highly productive group was the Turkmen, and it is this group who nowadays makes the most beautiful and original carpets, and still adheres closely to the traditional decorative motifs and colors. The *sumak* are produced in large quantities in the Caucasian region and throughout Kurdistan. These have geometric designs with strips or bands and large rhombi, in addition to the geometric repertoire shared in common with the *kilim.* The color shades are usually darker and warmer.

We find woven, and therefore flat, carpets and rugs in virtually every corner of the world, made either by hand or with fairly rudimentary machines. The most original and interesting, which in fact retain certain traditional motifs resulting from the long period of Ottoman domination, are those produced in the Balkan region. Of these, the carpets made in Bosnia are extremely pleasing to the eye. Certain nomadic tribes in the Saharan and sub-Saharan region produce mats with successive bands of color. This is a pattern that can rightly be considered as universal. In Europe there are still areas—or more correctly islands of culture and craftsmanship—where carpets (or, more simply, blankets) are still being woven, using techniques and designs handed down by ancient peasant and pastoral traditions. This is the case with the carpets of Muntenia (Romania), Tavastland (Finland),

PERSIA (Kashan)

Residenz Museum, Munich

Design Non-knotted *(kilim)* carpet, floral
Date 1601–2
Size 132 x 238 cm (4′ 5″ x 7′ 11″)
Material Silk
Principal colors Various shades of beige, yellow, green shading
Description At the center of the field, in the position usually occupied by a medallion, we see the coat of arms of the Polish king, Sigismund III (1587–1632), edged with a simple guard stripe. Above and below the rectangle containing the coat of arms, there are elongated scrolls decorated all over with floral designs. The remainder of the central field is decorated with floral shoots with palmettes, rosettes, and small flowers, as well as lanceolate leaves.

PERSIA *(Kilim)*

Private collection

Design Non-knotted rug *(kilim)* with geometric decoration
Date 20th century
Size 100 x 160 cm (3′ 4″ x 5′ 4″)
Material Wool
Principal colors Various shades of red; mustard, blue, white, pink, green, and brown
Description The field has a grid of lozenges with fringed edges. The border has a stripe decorated with indented lozenges, similar in shape, with alternating colors. The carpet is finished off by a series of very simple, interlocking guard stripes and zigzag lines. These rugs are made in large numbers throughout the Orient, and in certain parts of Iran in particular. They are a substitute for the more expensive carpet, except in the main reception room.

KURDISTAN *(Kilim)*

Private collection

Design Non-knotted rug *(kilim)* with geometric decoration
Date 20th century
Size 105 x 165 cm (3′ 6″ x 5′ 6″)
Material Wool
Principal colors Red, green, black, blue, white, and yellow
Description Rug with geometric decoration. The field takes up virtually the whole area of the rug. The decoration consists of six horizontal bands with a similar decorative motif, but with variation in color. The basic design consists of fringed and irregular lozenges and rhombi of various sizes. The design is based on geometric motifs coupled with bright colors, and is just one of many. It is typical of this weaving technique, which produces tasteful rugs and carpets but is not always very hard wearing.

CAUCASUS *(Sumak)*

Private collection

Design Non-knotted rug (sumak) with geometric decoration
Date 20th century
Size 120 x 186 cm (4′ x 6′ 2″)
Material Wool and cotton
Principal colors Red, blue, white, black, yellow, and pink
Description The field has repeated horizontal lines with the same highly stylized floral decoration consisting of large flowers, sometimes completely topsy-turvy. There are also geometric designs such as rosettes and stylized S shapes. These small designs are used to fill the surrounding areas. The bright coloring is typical of these rugs, which retain a certain originality in both design and decoration. The border is small and really consists only of a stripe, edged and decorated with rosettes of various colors alternating with simple geometric motifs.

A display of goods and farm produce at the Sunday market in Pisac, the ancient Inca center near Cuzco, in the Urubamba valley in Peru.

CAUCASUS *(Sumak)*

Türk ve Islam Müzesi, Istanbul

Design Non-knotted rug (sumak) with geometric decoration
Date 16th century
Size 60 x 63 cm (1′ x 2′ 1″)
Material Wool
Principal colors Red, blue, yellow, brown, and white
Description This is a fragment of a carpet of considerable interest because of its age. The decoration is geometric and the pattern is one of horizontal stripes. The field is noticeably small in size, and the term "field" in fact hardly applies. The central area has adjacent and repeated lozenge-shaped motifs with fringed edges. The two outer bands have an identical specular decoration dominated by a central stripe with S-shaped designs edged with narrower stripes with repeated geometric motifs, arranged in a fairly simple pattern.

GREECE (Janina)

Private collection

Design Non-knotted Turkish rug with geometric decoration
Date 19th—20th centuries
Size 86 x 148 cm (2′ 10″ x 4′ 11″)
Material Wool and cotton
Principal colors Red, blue, yellow, white, gray, pink, and orange
Description The center of the field is filled with a rectangular area decorated with a brightly colored series of geometric figures that resemble doll-like figures. Above this area there is a triangular section decorated with stylized floral motifs, and there are more floral forms at the corners. The border is very wide, consisting of an edged guard stripe and a very broad main stripe. The guard stripe has a design of octagons with eight-pointed starlike crosses at the center. This type of stylization, known as the "Janina" style, is also found in the borders of many Ghiordes rugs from Anatolia, from the end of the last century onward.

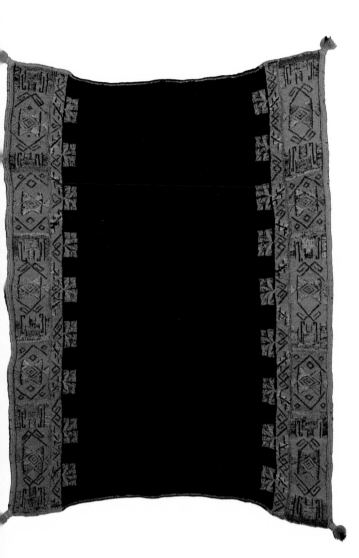

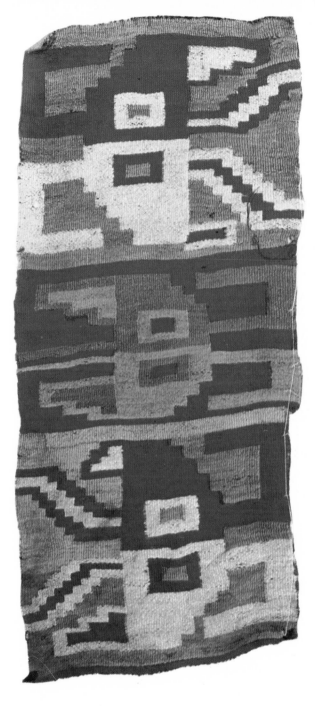

NORTH AMERICA (New Mexico, Acoma)

The Denver Art Museum, Denver, Colorado

Design Rug with geometric decoration
Date 1860–80
Size 101 x 142 cm (3' 4" x 4' 5")
Material Wool
Principal colors Red, black, and green
Description The field is a uniform black color. The two long sides have two brightly decorated stripes which act as borders. The designs are all simple geometric ones. These rugs are typical of the *Pueblos* of Acoma, where this example was made, Zumi, Leguna, and Jemez. The production of mats and other fabrics dates back to bygone times, there being evidence of 12th century fragments, but no single object has been handed down to us intact that can be dated with any certainty before the last century. Conspicuous similarities in structure and decoration have been established between these rugs and Peruvian rugs from Paracas.

PERU (Tiahuanaco)

British Museum, London

Design Rug with geometric decoration
Date 6th–9th century A.D.
Material Wool and cotton
Principal colors Red, brown, cream, mustard
Description The fabric has geometric designs, the precise significance of which cannot be explained with any certainty, but they are undoubtedly charged with a specific, and even social, symbology. This is shown by contemporary ceramics and by the various stone sculptures that have similar motifs, all permeated by a quality of power and forceful expression. The color scheme is also interesting: it is very lively and is found in the best textile production of these peoples who have handed down to us much evidence of their ancient and highly original civilization.

Castile (Spain), the patchwork carpets (*pezzotti*) of Valtellina in Italy, the carpets of Erice and Petralia (Sicily), Pescocostanzo (Abruzzo), Flisi (Sardinia), and various towns in Calabria.

In Latin America the carpets of the Incas are of considerable historical and documentary value. Most of them were made with a technique similar to knotting, and some were flat. Artistically speaking, it has to be said that they are an expression of the complex civilization of the peoples concerned. The same can be said of the mats and rugs woven by the American Indians, which offer interesting evidence of the cultural traditions of those tribes.

Symbology

In our discussion of the historical development of carpets we have already made reference to the symbolic significance of the various motifs depicted in the field and in the borders. This is an extremely complex area in the history of this form of artistic craftsmanship because, down the ages, the original meanings attributed to motifs that today appear to be purely decorative have been muddled and sometimes lost. The absence of any continuity in our documentation and the way it is broken up into various bits and pieces, which cannot always be linked together, make it hard to present an unambiguous and sure-fire reading of the symbolism depicted in carpets. On more than one occasion we have underlined the fact that the origins of the art of knotting date back to nomadic or semi-nomadic tribes with a pastoral (sheep-based) economy. In a society that is not primitive but hallmarked by relatively simple relations among the various social elements, religious beliefs and superstitions, mythologies, the great importance attached to astrology and to astronomical and environmental/climatic knowledge, cabbalistic and magic beliefs, all these end up by playing a fundamental role in day-to-day life and in the relative forms of artistic expression. Proof of this lies not so much in carpets, because few if any have survived since ancient times, as in ceramic objects used for everyday purposes. Large numbers of these have been found and they give us an idea of decoration dominated by stylized representations of animals or the natural elements, in other words the real arbiters of the living conditions of these peoples.

With the development of trade and exchanges and

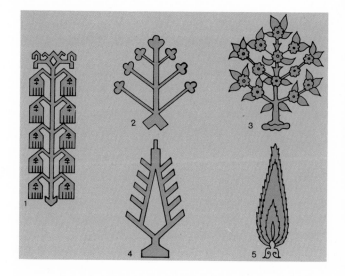

Diagram showing tree motifs common in Persian symbology: 1, 2. The tree of life. 3. Tree in blossom. 4, 5. Cypress tree.

the spread of motifs in the sense of pure decoration, we find a progressive reduction of any precise symbolic significance. In fact by this time the weaver or carpetmaker was "in the dark" as he repeated the designs which he had always seen on carpets, but of whose "true" nature he was ignorant. And in the case of tribes that are still semi-nomadic today—the case of the Qashqa'i of Iran can be applied across the board—conservatism has meant that in some instances the same models were handed down virtually unaltered. For example, it does not make much sense to juxtapose motifs that refer to fire (motifs borrowed from the Zoroastrian cult) with a design of a hand (typical of Islam). Such things occur only when the symbolic language has been forgotten. It should be evident from these remarks that there is little conscious symbolism in the Polonaise carpets from the Safawid period, unless one is to break it down pedantically into each individual element in order to reach the paradoxical conclusion that everything is symbolic (!), given that nothing is haphazard. Much progress has recently been made in the study of the symbological significance of the various typologies of carpets. Much of the merit for this must go to Schuyler Cammann for having brought this basic aspect of the art of carpet making to the attention of academics and connoisseurs alike—for this aspect has been too often neglected in favor of strictly aesthetic or technical analyses, or in favor of commercial evaluations. The only criticism we can level against Cammann is that he occasionally allows himself to be carried away by his deep knowledge of Chinese symbolism, to the

The design of stylized animals is frequently used in the decoration of carpets, kilim and sumak, both old and new. The most commonly used subjects are birds (peacocks, cocks, turtle doves, etc.) and quadrupeds, with a certain preference for camels. The area where these are most common are the Caucasus, eastern Anatolia, and western Iran. Compare the stylized decoration of a Shirvan carpet (below) with that of our design which shows, in order: 1. A camel. 2. A dromedary. 3. A dove. 4. A cock. 5. A peacock. 6. A dog.

point of applying it in quite different contexts that are not always coherent with each other and, above all, cannot always be historically documented. But this is of course a peripheral criticism in the face of the tide of new ideas implicit in his various theses.

A brief list of the possible interpretations of some of the main symbolic motifs (and also of entire carpets) will nevertheless help to illustrate what has just been said.

We have already mentioned the garden carpets, which were produced mainly in northwestern Persia. At the same time these are the representation of an actual Persian garden (an example that has survived is the famous garden of Fin near Kashan) which is in turn rendered in the image of the Islamic Paradise—an illusion inherited incidentally from other older cultures, including the ancient Persian civilization—with rivers, trees in blossom and heavy with fruit, and everything that is most to be desired. The carpet, whose aim is to signify all this even when the form is highly stylized, owes its extraordinary persistence as a motif to the conception of Paradise that is always implied in it. Remaining with the plant kingdom, we should mention the very ancient symbology associated with the representation of trees. A. U. Pope states that the trees of the sun and moon, the latter in particular, with their obvious astral significance, appear in seals dating back to the 4th millenium B.C. and were used (though with nonidentical designs) in the border decorations of 17th-century Persian carpets. The Tree of Life plays a leading role in the Zoroastrian culture and occurs frequently from very earliest times. It comes in various shapes and sizes, including those of the palm tree, but the most popular is the stylization of the cypress, which we find very often in carpets, but only in carpets. The reason for this spread is quite simple: the cypress tree is an evergreen tree, which can thus be immediately identified as a symbol of renewal and eternal life.

One motif that has given rise to varied interpretations is that of the *boteh*. Some see this as a representation of the flame of the temples of the Zoroastrian fire. This is a rather bold and not easily proven hypothesis. It is opposed by those who consider that the motif originated from the degeneration of an arboreal sign (possibly the design of an almond tree or, more probably, of a cypress). There are also those who support the idea that it represents a drop of water.

The simple rosette also has a hidden symbolic

meaning which, depending on the context, may be either solar (in the majority of cases) or lunar.

The various forms of vine leaves, vine shoots, and bunches of grapes date back to ancient symbologies, and are made identifiable by a long itinerary of changes and assimilations, which started in the Sassanid period. They appear in 19th-century carpets as well, with floral motifs. The pomegranate design was an extremely fortunate one. With its countless seeds it well represents the idea of fertility which was close to the hearts not only of the nomadic pastoral societies, but also of the sedentary rural and agricultural

This lively and detailed miniature depicts the Mosque at Medina with the tomb of the Prophet and other trappings. Two palm trees stand at the center of the courtyard, symbolizing the city.

societies. The history of that other plant motif, the papyrus, is somewhat exceptional. It was around in Egypt during the times of the ancient pharaohs, undoubtedly with a precise symbolic role associated with the fertility-giving waters of the Nile, and it was retained in the so-called Mameluk carpets which were made in Egypt. As we have already mentioned, it is also possible that the design is not in fact a papyrus, but represents the palm tree—an important plant in Islamic culture, whose association with Medina and the tomb of the Prophet has been discussed earlier.

We do not know the reason for this unless it was a decorative one entrusted to a motif that had always been a familiar one. We can round off this series of "vegetable" examples with the element that is probably the main one in the decoration of carpets and is also one of the more original inventions in Islamic artistic culture: the arabesque. The form of the arabesque, which is concrete and yet abstract, is typically floral and does not infer any specific botanical species. In our view, the symbolism lies in the schematic essence which can be repeated ad infinitum—in other words, in the representation of the spirit that characterizes a duality (abstract and concrete) of the approach to his subject of the Moslem artist. And this is especially true if the arabesqued carpet is for use in a mosque.

There is also a wealth of animal symbology. The theme of animals fighting is a very frequent one. The most widely depicted scene, the lion (an obviously solar symbol) attacking a prey that is usually horned (a clear allusion to the crescent moon, and a typical lunar representation), is a presentation of a truly universal symbology. Day and night, good and evil, and so on and so forth: in a more imaginative context (generally typical of a more recent period, at least where carpets are concerned) this scene is taken from the theme of the duel between the dragon and the phoenix, in which the myth of the two animals (which is ambivalent in both cases) is simplified and made extreme.

The stylized birds that appear in the Anatolian carpets sometimes seem to be modeled on a cock, an ancient sun symbol, as well as a symbol of resurrection heavy with positive implications. The predatory animals depicted in carpets are often unrecognizable today, and are often difficult to grasp even in ancient models. They often have a propitiatory function. The lion and other fierce creatures depicted on the carpets of the nomadic tribes of southern Iran (in the

Shiraz region) are also said to have the power of keeping ill-luck at bay. In a region scattered with mighty but extinct volcanoes, and a great deal of seismic activity, the dragon motif, which is extremely stylized but always clearly recognizable, must also symbolize something similar. A protection by and also an evocation of the ancient legendary monsters (fish-serpents called *vishap*) that once, according to popular fantasy, lived in the great lakes of Armenia. In a word, a crowded melting-pot of elements that are not always extricable but are always persistently present in the collective memory of the peoples who created and represented these myths.

A silver platter from the Sassanid period, now in the Hermitage in Leningrad. This depiction of ascension clearly draws on the solar symbology of the great bird (the eagle) between two trees. The decoration shows an obvious Hellenistic influence. Pre-Islamic culture was to some extent absorbed by the conquering Arabs and represents a vital basis for understanding subsequent cultural developments.

The symbology that refers to Islamic customs is the most clear-cut—because it deals with a relatively young culture—even if its connotations have become quickly diluted, as is shown by the most characteristic motif, the *mihrab* (prayer niche), which has changed from being a "sign" to a purely decorative motif, sometimes even represented in a baroque taste. The same goes for the mosque lamp which we find almost always associated with the *mihrab*. And we can see it degenerating into a bouquet of flowers. The lamp, which occurs in the niche of a great many carpets (including the Ardabil carpets), represents—according to the correct interpretation made by Cammann—Allah, light of Heaven and Earth, as written in the Koran. But in the Ardabil carpets it represents the sun and the moon. The motif of the mosque lamp—and other motifs as well—occurs not only in the artistic repertory for fabrics, but also for ceramics, architecture, and painting. The jug or pitcher which often appears in so-called prayer rugs or mats is the symbol of purity, physical and otherwise, necessary when presenting oneself before God.

In some carpets—Iranian and also Caucasian—we find the stylized depiction of hands. These hands are not to be interpreted as the spot where the believer should place his own while praying. The form of the stylized hand recalls the way the name of God is written in Arabic. The number five symbolizes a sort of "holy family," consisting of Muhammad, his cousin and son-in-law Alī, his daughter Fatima, and their two sons Hasan and Hosein, all of them particularly revered figures. The comb, which appears in some carpets, is a feminine symbol and virtually represents the signature of the (female) knotter or weaver. With regard to the varied meaning of the different symbols, it is worth noting that there is often an analogy between the imagery of carpets—especially those made for everyday use—and the imagery of tombstones.

The *gul* of the Turkmen tribes are certainly symbolic, even if nowadays all trace of their original meaning has been lost. The motifs on the carpets are mainly geometric and tricky to interpret, unless they slot into easily identifiable categories (*mihrab,* tree of life, etc.).

The practice—common throughout most of the Orient—of having a narrow zigzag, or "reciprocate trefoil" border, or a border with lilies and lozenges set in opposite directions, with different colors, can be traced back to the symbolism of the insuperable mountain, thus of the barrier, or to the idea of protection for anyone sitting inside the border. The corners keep the *jinn* (evil goblins) well away from the carpet, and the practice of making corner designs with this precise purpose in mind is a very ancient one: in architecture, a well-known prototype of this constructional style, with corners jutting outward to repel evil spirits, is the mausoleum tower at Gunbad-e Qabus (dated 1006) in eastern Iran. In a great many cultures the triangle is the symbol of God, and is also associated with the locust or cicada, which has in turn always been associated with the concept of rebirth and celestial life.

Chinese carpets are in a separate group. The art of this people has always had very marked symbolic connotations, from very earliest times. This has remained a constant feature which has, if anything, been enriched down the centuries. In the periods to which we are referring, regarding carpets—the Ming and Ch'ing periods—every single element is in practice symbolic, and clearly and deliberately intended as such. The carpets are decorated with symbols which follow on, one from the next, like a puzzle whose final solution is an augural sentence that suggests the occasion or the reason why the carpet was ever made. A detailed list of the various symbols and their meanings would be too lengthy and disproportionate when

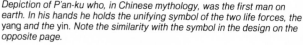

Depiction of P'an-ku who, in Chinese mythology, was the first man on
earth. In his hands he holds the unifying symbol of the two life forces, the
yang and the yin. Note the similarity with the symbol in the design on the
opposite page.

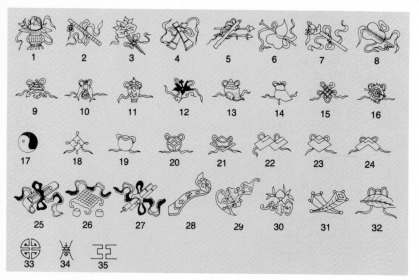

compared with the actual artistic merits of Chinese
carpets, so we shall just give a few which will give the
reader some idea of the complex world of Chinese
symbology.

In many cases the symbological game—which is
what it is—is based on equal sounds but rendered
with different spelling (the Chinese language is very
rich in homophones). For example, the sound *fu* indicates the word happiness, but it also means a bat,
which thus becomes synonymous with happiness.
Thus, five (a propitious number) red (the supreme
color) bats signify the five forms of highest happiness,
which are: long life, wealth, health, a love of virtue,
and a natural and serene death. In the same way, *lu*
means a deer, but it also means wealth; *hu tieh* means
a butterfly, and *tieh* long life. There are very many
cases when this mechanism is triggered off, and numerous sentences that can be composed as a result.
Then there are less conspicuous symbologies. A carp
that jumps to cross a floodgate is in search of immor-
tality (if it manages to make its crossing—with a long
jump through the air—it will change into a dragon, that
is, into a higher being). The fish represents the can-
didate, the channel the examinations, and the dragon
the part of the mandarin. The dragon is an imaginary
animal, made up of parts taken from twelve creatures,
and it is of great importance in Chinese mythology. It
is laden with positive connotations and represents
yang (the male, solar, light—diurnal—principle).
When it has five limbs it represents the emperor. No-

The five-colored parrot, painted on silk, belonging to the emperor Sung
Hui Tsung (1082–1135). This is a fine example of the level of refinement
achieved by the Chinese in the figurative arts. The "flowers-and-birds"
painting genre has always been one of the most popular in China. Pictorial
compositions not infrequently alluded to deeper, hidden meanings.

A detail of a piece of embroidered Chinese fabric from the 19th century. At the center we see a dragon, head on, with five claws (yang number), a garment that only the emperor could wear. Beneath the dragon's snout we see the spiral-shaped sphere which is variously interpreted as a symbol of one of the two heavenly bodies, or a pearl, or even thunder.

body, apart from the sovereign, was allowed to wear garments or have furnishings bearing this insignia. In the event of an imperial gift a limb had to be "amputated" or in any case cancelled. When alone the dragon is represented in the act of following a sphere called the "flaming pearl" which has been variously interpreted as the moon, sun, thunder, and so on. The counterpart of the dragon is the phoenix, the *yin* symbol (*yin* being the female, lunar, dark—nocturnal—principle) as well as a symbol of the empress. When the dragon and the phoenix stand opposite one another they symbolize matrimonial harmony (note the difference with the Iranian world which used the dragon-and-phoenix motif in the Mongol period, but had the two figures doing battle with each other) and, more generally, the sum of two principles which, by alternating and combining, allow the world to move forward.

Among the most frequently used symbols in Chinese art is the swastika—a very ancient and fairly universal solar motif. In Central Asia it is seen as a sign of thunder and thus associated with water (which has a festive sound and a beneficial connotation for peasant populations), and in later periods it signifies "10,000 times," and is, in other words, a reinforcement of the following or preceding symbol, or of the whole puzzle. Finally, the symbolic world of China draws from the well of religion as well. This is why we have the emblems of the eight Taoist mortals, the eight trigrams (from an ancient form of divination), the symbols of the five cardinal points (four plus the central one), the 100 precious objects, and the symbols associated with Buddhism. Each of these figures has its own precise meaning which is immediately understandable to the Chinese. We can in fact say that Chinese people are as familiar with these puzzles as we are with road signs.

Practical Advice about Buying and Caring for Oriental Carpets

The following remarks and suggestions refer to the carpet as an object that is used day to day. They may be helpful for acquiring that minimum of inside knowledge necessary if you are to avoid the pitfalls of the marketplace. At the time of writing there are no foolproof handbooks to assist the would-be purchaser. This is because each carpet is different, even when it comes from the same place and is of the same typology as the one next to it. In fact, never forget that the carpet is a work of craftsmanship involving many different factors, the most important being: the team of craftsmen, or the individual craftsman, and his or their degree of sensibility, the materials used, and the place of production. It is not hard to see that each of these "ingredients" incorporates different possibilities or variables. So the materials may change considerably both in their nature and, in this context, in their quality. And the carpet makers (usually women) may be experienced, or not so experienced. No book can pinpoint all these differences, but there are some good publications (see the bibliography) and excellent guides written for the expert and the layman, which make it possible, for a reasonable outlay, to acquire some basic knowledge about the subject. But this is an extremely complicated area, precisely because of the reasons outlined above, where any form of presumption can have adverse results. Reading a book, even a clear and well-written one, is not enough to master such a vast topic. In fact, our knowledge of it is in a state of continual evolution. Modesty is called for. One does not become a carpet connoisseur by correspondence, even though with a little patience one can store up enough ideas to avoid being "taken for a ride." It is well worth testing out your own ideas (because photographs cannot give the whole picture) by visiting the museums that exist in every major city in the world and now offer a wide range of excellent carpets on display. This will give you an immediate idea of the world's major carpets, and if you discover at this stage a certain passion for them, it is well worth visiting the major auction rooms where carpets can be seen close up and, even more importantly, can be touched. Touching a carpet gives you a precise feeling about it, and this can vary greatly depending on its age and the materials used. In a word, a vital clue for anyone who wants to take a serious interest in

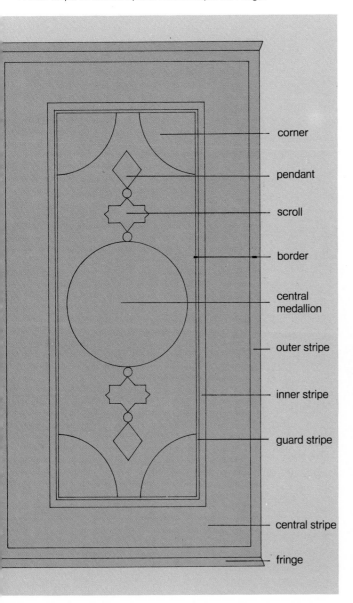

Diagram showing the various parts of the carpet, in order: 1. Corner. 2. Pendant. 3. Scroll. 4. Border. 5. Central medallion. 6. Outer stripe. 7. Inner stripe. 8. Guard stripe. 9. Central stripe. 10. Fringe.

corner

pendant

scroll

border

central medallion

outer stripe

inner stripe

guard stripe

central stripe

fringe

carpets is direct experience, and a constant keeping in touch with the various typologies, ancient and modern.

Buying a Carpet

If such experience is hard or slow to come by and you are keen to buy a carpet, it is best to go to serious firms with a well-established and well-known reputation for honesty, and with an attentive, well-informed, and, above all, experienced staff. Anyone involved lock, stock, and barrel in the carpet business gains absolutely nothing from betraying his client's trust, not least because at the medium-priced level, which accounts for the great majority of carpets now in circulation, profits are based on quantity. The market therefore tries to create a stable relationship with its satisfied customers. It is advisable to tread warily with the numerous firms that vaunt exotic Oriental and high-falutin' names. Such firms have been multiplying in recent years: they rarely have good-quality carpets for sale and continually offer poor-quality products at "closing-out" prices: such carpets are without any artistic merit, and are sometimes knotted mechanically.

If you travel to the East you are advised to select your purchases with the utmost care. Once you have paid the customs duty you will probably save little or nothing. In fact, old carpets—not to mention ancient carpets (and we shall define these terms as they are conventionally used a little further on)—are more expensive in the East than they are in Europe or the United States. But there is one advantage to be had in the Orient: a wider range of choice from a very large repertoire of carpets. And if you have a good eye and are blessed with a little luck, you will be able to purchase carpets which, for one reason and another, are not available in the West. Some of these may turn out to be real bargains, not commercially speaking perhaps, but certainly as collectors' items—and even for the pure amateur.

Carpets have always been relatively expensive (although this was not the case at the dawn of modern carpet collecting when there were still various types of carpets and various geographical areas which were still neglected). In 1767, according to Reitingler, a sum of £13.13 was paid for a silk Persian carpet. We have already mentioned the sum of £2000 rustled up in 1893 to purchase the famous Ardabil carpet; its "Pendant," which is now in Los Angeles, was sold by an antique dealer in 1939 to Paul Getty II for the sum

A carpet that is knotted by hand is inevitably quite costly, hence an important acquisition, for which one is paying for the craftsman's labor and skill. In European houses it is rare for a carpet to fill a completely empty space around which the rest of the furniture and furnishings are arranged. More often than not the carpet must be "matched" with furniture that is already there. In such cases, which are the norm, take your carpet "on approval" to see it in its new surroundings, under the light in your home as it changes through the day, and in artificial light. This acts as some sort of guarantee and no good carpet dealer will be taken aback by such a request.

It is not easy to define carpets by their age. Because there are large gaps in the history of the development of this ancient art, relatively recent carpets have an artistic and historical importance which is in fact much greater than one would expect. In the trade, the convention is to define as *antique* carpets made more than 100 years ago, that is, before about 1860, the date that heralds the arrival of aniline dyes. *Semi-antique* applies to carpets made between 1860 and the first world war; and the term *old* to carpets made between the wars. The rest are obviously *modern*. When it comes to assessing a carpet, be it old or antique, your judgment is best based on fixed criteria which help to establish your evaluation on not merely subjective facts. A basic criterion is the state of conservation of the carpet: this must of course be excellent. In assessing this, examine the carpet several times, on both sides, to make sure that there are no gaps, holes or unsightly repairs or patches. Then it is important to establish the actual age of the carpet by comparing it with those displayed in museums and illustrated in books. When making these comparisons make sure that the colors of the composition tally with the age being suggested or asserted for the carpet, and with its claimed origin, which is the very next criterion to be appraised. The fineness of the knotting (the density of knots per square decimeter/square inch) is the last yardstick to be considered, and not the first as some people mistakenly believe. It is ex-

of £14,050. In absolute terms, the highest price paid was the £23,100, in 1928, for a silk Persian carpet depicting hunting scenes. But there are so many carpets in circulation nowadays that the price scale is huge, and any serious dealer may well turn out to be the best source of advice both in terms of the taste of the purchaser, who may well find the matter of taste tricky as a beginner, and in terms of what to pay for his taste.

tremely variable, and its value is relative rather than absolute, because the density of say 1,000 knots may be good for one type of carpet and absolutely worthless for others. In the illustrated section of this book, the reader will be able to get some idea of the average density, and of the considerable variations of knot density, depending on the place of production and the age of the carpet.

Ancient carpets that are dated, like the Ardabil or Milanese carpets, are quite rare and thus not put up for sale every day. But there are dated carpets (the date, in lunar years and in Arabic figures, refers to the year of Muhammad's Hejira in 622 A.D. and is written, for example, 756 H) that have been made in the last two centuries. In such cases it is advisable to take a close look at the knots that form the figures. In many cases the second figure may have been altered, by being reknotted, to make the carpet a few decades older. This can be detected by examining the knots one by one and comparing them with the surrounding field. Sometimes carpets only look ancient. In the East you will often see carpets laid out on the ground in villages being "aged" by passing animals, by the sun, and by the dust. Similarly, in towns and cities, they will be laid out in streets and aged by passing cars and trucks. This aging operation is then rounded off by a good wash. But such attempts at hoodwinking never manage to achieve the precisely desired effect. As a result, beware of carpets in which some parts are more faded than others, and look at various parts of the carpet. In addition, open it out in both directions to see the base of the knots, which is rarely reached by these aging processes.

It is more complicated and difficult to detect chemical washing which artificially fades and ages a carpet by imitating the natural loss of sheen, resistance and suppleness of the fibers which occurs over the years. This practice has the drawback of leaving the carpet's pile "weakened": when you touch it, it feels too dry and almost "unreal." Furthermore, if you remove one of the knots (which will not do any serious damage!) the fiber should remain good and curved. If it is easily straightened (by twisting it, for example) this is a sign that the carpet is a modern one.

The customs importation seal does not necessarily signify authenticity. Throughout Europe there are carpets that are knotted mechanically and can thus be regularly imported. Not even the guarantee certificate accompanying a customs declaration is sufficient proof of the authenticity of the carpet's place of origin

or of the fact that it is hand-made. A common practice in some parts of southern Italy, for example, and no doubt elsewhere, is to send mechanically knotted carpets to a subsidiary or associate in the East (with nothing more than a warehouse or depot), and then reimport them with a guarantee certificate written in Persian, and of course the relevant customs clearance. Although this may seem a rather roundabout method, the profits are considerable because there is a huge difference in price between authentic hand-knotted carpets and false mechanically knotted carpets. Fairly complex machines for knotting carpets (usually using the Turkish or Ghiordes knot) were in use as far back as the mid-18th century, but it was with Jacquard's mechanical loom, invented in 1805, that this practice spread far and wide, undergoing progressive improvements. It is nevertheless possible to tell a genuine carpet from a mechanically made one —regardless of counterfeit guarantees—by using the following criteria: the characteristics of the design, the never perfectly uniform length of the pile, the differing thicknesses of the warp and weft chains, the side borders, the underside of the carpet with its slight unevennesses which can easily be seen under a magnifying glass, and the small holes that can be seen in a hand-knotted carpet by holding it with the underside to the light. But if there is any doubt it is best to ask the seller for a signed certificate stating not only the place of origin (a problem that can be bypassed in the ways we have already described) but also declaring that the carpet is entirely hand-knotted. The carpet business has always been big business. In addition to the places where carpets are traditionally made, other areas have come to the forefront of the international market in recent years. These areas offer carpets that are not inevitably of poor quality and are good imitations of Turkish, Persian, or Central Asian products. In Pakistan, Bangladesh, central-eastern Europe (Bulgaria and Romania) and the Maghreb, in particular, carpets are made to keep the Western market constantly and amply supplied.

The basis of any knowledge about carpets is the ability to distinguish the materials used, which are, as we have said, basically three in number: wool, cotton, and silk. After a certain amount of practice it will be quite easy to make this distinction simply by touching: wool is warm and fluffy; cotton is cold and dry; and silk is fine, smooth, and fluid. If in doubt, simply burn a piece of the fiber which will react in different ways, depending on what it is. Wool sizzles and melts into a

single lump that smells like burnt hair; cotton leaves a trace of gray ash which disintegrates if touched and smells faintly of burnt wood; silk is like wool, but more so. Given that you know the structure and material of a carpet, and in order to establish that it really does come from a given place and is not an imitation, it is very important to analyze the small details, especially the narrow strips of the borders, which have often been altered if compared with the models seen in books and museums. It is also advisable to compile a sort of table to check whether the structure of the carpet (warp, weft, pile, borders, and fringes) tallies with the design and type of knotting used in a specific region. The width of the borders as compared with the central part of the carpet is not proof of age or originality. It varies considerably with the age and typology of the carpet. In this case it is advisable to adopt the same attitude that we have suggested for the knot density, that is, make relative but never absolute comparisons.

There are plenty of imitation carpets on the European and American markets. The plentiful and good-quality imitations of Turkish carpets called Pandirma are a good buy. It is always better to have a good imitation (which will always be a reasonably good hand-knotted carpet) than a poor original in poor condition. For anyone who wants to start collecting carpets now, our advice would be to choose a limited area of interest or typology, and to bear in mind that it is still possible to come by interesting carpets at prices that are not prohibitive. The *kilim* and *sumak* in particular are generally of a very high quality, with lively designs and colors, and one does not have to pay exorbitant prices for them. The various nomadic or semi-nomadic peoples make excellent carpets (and for less money you can buy bags, saddlebags, and other products that are invariably well decorated and of good quality) which, because of their long-standing cultural traditions, have not undergone any major stylistic changes. The result is that 19th- or 20th-century carpets usually have similar characteristics.

Looking After Your Carpets

In mosques and ordinary homes, shoes are removed before one enters the carpeted interior. This is not so much a habit, but rather a deeply rooted cultural fact for these peoples. It gives the carpet a much longer life than it would have in the West. In so saying we do not mean to encourage the reader to take off his shoes every time he walks on a carpet, but merely to remind him that the wear and tear to carpets caused by footwear is comparable to the effect of sandpaper on a rough surface. A carpet is made with organic substances which have a physiological need for air if they are to be kept in good condition. It is thus a good idea not to keep carpets in places that are too enclosed or dark (although too much light can also be harmful) or damp. Whatever else happens, do not lay carpets under very heavy pieces of furniture. Any carpet laid beneath a dining-room table will come to a premature end because of the rubbing and stamping of feet. The same goes for carpets laid near front doors. If it is not possible to avoid laying your carpets in these places, choose strong types of carpets that are renowned for their robustness. Change their position frequently.

Carpets should be cleaned daily with a soft brush. Depending on their use and position they should be vacuum-cleaned weekly, every other week, or even less often. Do not use carpet-beaters, and avoid elec-

tric ones even more (if you have to beat your carpet, beat only the underside); these treat your carpet with nothing less than physical violence and will eventually ruin it. If you clean your carpet regularly and never too energetically you will get good use from it. But every four or five years it should be washed by a specialist firm. It is very important that this is not done in an amateur way, and in order to avoid irreparable damage being done, you would do well to ask your trusted carpet dealer to recommend an expert. In most cases the major firms have the right equipment for washing and restoring carpets.

If your carpet becomes stained or marked, do not use stain removers unless you are sure of the type of dye used in your particular carpet. Dyes made from natural materials are very sensitive to stains made by organic liquids. Moreover, if they are exposed for a long time to very bright light they will lose their color to some extent, although this will—artificially—create that slight patina which is one of the most pleasing aspects of old and antique carpets.

Worms or grubs associated with wool are quite rare and can be gotten rid of easily by various sound products that will not harm the fibers in any way. A more common pest is the moth which lays its eggs inside the carpet and causes considerable damage. The eggs need peace and quiet in order to hatch, so a carpet that comes in for daily use and wear will not be in much danger. Carpets hung on walls cause more concern: in this case it is a good idea to place a vase with a few feathers in it in the same room because moths prefer this environment for laying their eggs and will leave the carpet alone.

In conclusion, a word about carpet restoration. This is a difficult and demanding job. There are few craftsmen who are really expert and experienced at it. They often charge a lot of money for their work, because it is complicated, and the right choice of materials that will be suitable is not always available in the West. In any event, the cost of restoration should certainly not exceed that of the value of the carpet (as sometimes happens!), and if you are not entirely confident in the restorer, it is best to get him to mend just the worst of the damage (a frequent part that needs attention is the fringe, as the knots gradually loosen). In our view a carpet in a poor state of conservation but with the damage isolated and in control is better than a badly restored carpet.

Oriental Carpet Masterpieces

Explanation of Symbols

MATERIALS

Woolen Warp

Woolen Weft

Woolen Pile (Knots)

Silk Warp

Silk Weft

Silk Pile (Knots)

Cotton Warp

Cotton Weft

Cotton Pile (Knots)

Note:
In the plates the description of each carpet or rug concludes with a map indicating the region or place of its production.

KNOTS

Sehna

Ghiordes

Arab-Spanish

Kilim, Sumak, and non-knotted carpets in general

DECORATION

Floral

Geometric

Naturalistic

Religious

From Anatolia, Egypt, and the Caucasus

ANATOLIA (Central Anatolia)

Türk ve Islam Müzesi, Istanbul

Design Geometric
Date 13th century
Size 240 x 320 cm (7' 10" x 10' 6")
Warp Wool
Weft Wool
Pile Wool
Knot Ghiordes
Density 8–9 knots per sq cm (52–53 per sq in, approx.)
Principal colors Red, blue, yellow, green, brown
Description The center of this geometrically designed carpet is hallmarked by the repetition of the same geometric motif. Staggered octagonal stars in two continuous lines are alternated with small lozenges. Between two rows of stars there is a geometric design, arranged in alternating directions, of an elongated lozenge with lateral double-hook patterns and highly stylized palmettes. The fairly wide border is separated from the central design by an undecorated strip. The design of the border is the classical one with two striped edges that enclose a wider central strip. The edges are decorated identically with rectangles within, which are elaborate hooks formed from transverse segments. The strip has the rectangle motif (but the distribution is invariably rather arbitrary), with a central square containing an eight-pointed star; we also see the diagonals from the rectangle to the square. The latter is decorated around the star with small squares alternating with small lozenges.
History This carpet, with others, was found in the Alaeddin mosque in Konya (central Anatolia) and dates back to the 13th century, the Seljuk period. It is undoubtedly one of the most interesting antique carpets in both size and design, and it enables us to pinpoint an important stage in the history as well as the technical and artistic development of this art.

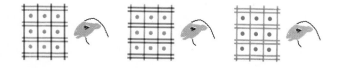

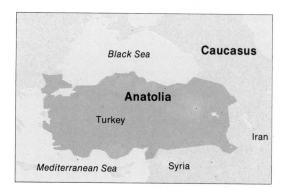

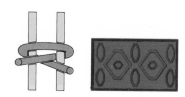

ANATOLIA

Islamisches Museum, East Berlin

Design Geometric, known as the Berlin carpet
Date 15th century
Size 90 x 172 cm (2′ 11″ x 5′ 8″)
Warp Wool
Weft Wool
Pile Wool
Knot Ghiordes
Density 6—7 knots per sq cm (40—41 per sq in)
Principal colors Red, blue, cream, yellow, brown
Description This is one of the oldest and most famous carpets to have remained intact up to the present day. It was acquired by the German scholar W. von Bode in Rome in 1886, and is thought to have come from a church in central Italy. Like the Marby carpet (page 158), it is of very great importance because it represents a significant comparison with contemporary pictorial documentation (one is reminded of the fresco by Domenico di Bartolo in Siena). In fact, it fully confirms the artists' reliabiilty and their fidelity to the model in question. The carpet is somewhat fragmentary. The central section is dominated by two octagons within squares that are decorated with the same pictorial design. The very stylized scene depicts a dragon and a phoenix. We can identify the dragon's clawed feet, tail, wings, and head with a large eye, as well as the horn and three tufts of hair on the neck. The flying phoenix is less detailed: it has three long plumes; the head consists of four small lozenges and two large additional elements. The design is cleverly executed and based on a pattern that was customary at that time: there are slight deformities in the two octagons. The upper dragon and phoenix also have supplementary ornamental motifs: the neck of the dragon is striped, and it has no horn; the body of the phoenix has ovals on it. The corners between the square and the octagon have concentric triangles and hooked strips. The border is quite small and consists of a double-striped edge and a central strip. The edges are decorated with continuous small lozenges. The colors in the inner border alternate, but in no precise order. The existing long edge has no outer border.

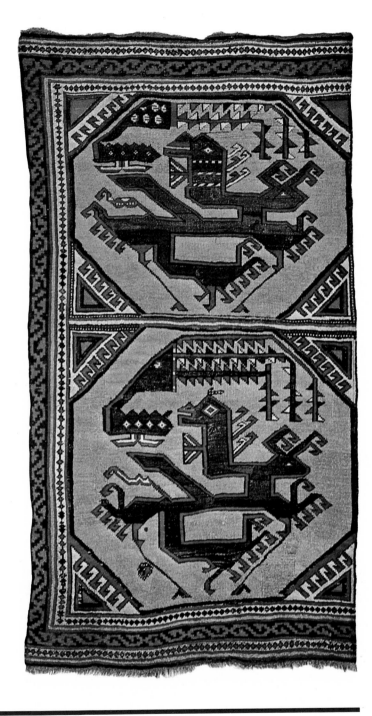

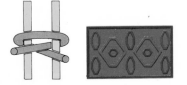

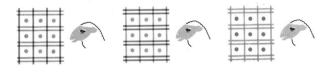

157

ANATOLIA

Historiska Museum, Stockholm

Design Geometric; known as the Marby rug
Date 15th century
Size 109 x 145 cm (3′ 7″ x 4′ 9″)
Warp Wool
Weft Wool
Pile Wool
Knot Ghiordes
Density 8 knots per sq cm (50 per sq in)
Principal colors Red, yellow, green, blue, brown, white.
Description This old geometric rug was found in Marby church in Sweden, and is commonly known as the Marby rug. Numerous hypotheses have been put forward about the place of origin and the date of acquisition, but we have no precise knowledge about either. Analyses have shown that the wool used in the warp comes from Tibet. This is only a fragment of a larger carpet (like the Berlin carpet, page 157), but its great interest lies in the fact that similar carpets appear in contemporary Italian painting. The center is decorated with two octagons within squares, formed by a hooked border; both octagons show the same depiction of birds with a tree standing between them. The motifs are extremely stylized and the tree consists of a symmetrical, specular design. The four corners between the octagon and the square have a geometric design. The border is well proportioned and consists of two borders with identical motifs and a central strip. The design is based throughout on the Greek cross, alternating in direction, and linear in both borders, staggered and separated by diagonal and vertical lines in the central strip.

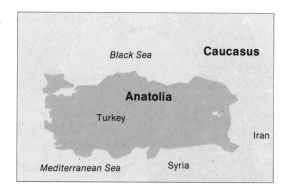

Black Sea — Caucasus
Anatolia
Turkey
Iran
Mediterranean Sea — Syria

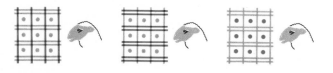

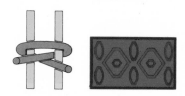

ANATOLIA (Ushak)

Metropolitan Museum of Art, New York

Design Arabesqued, of the Lotto type with coats of arms
Date 16th—17th centuries
Size 145 x 230 cm (4' 9" x 7' 7")
Warp Wool
Weft Wool
Pile Wool
Knot Ghiordes
Density 13—14 knots per sq cm (85 per sq in)
Principal colors Red, blue, yellow, brown
Description An arabesqued rug, of the Lotto type, with coats of arms of the Genoese Doria and Centurione families. The center is dominated by a symmetrical motif with repeated arabesques, which develops at random and has no focal center. At the sides there are four and three lines (one less because the coats of arms are placed at the top left) of elongated lozenges; in the center the area has small rhombi which separate more or less octagonal forms. The design is executed with considerable precision and rigor, and the result is impressively decorative, mainly because of the broken lines which create hard geometric areas. The border is wide and well proportioned in relation to the size of the rug. One border has a naturalistic motif with flowers, steles, and leaves, arranged continuously as in a shoot. The broad strip consists of stylized floral motifs with alternating colors, separated by indented oblique ovals alternating in direction. The outer edge has a wavy geometric motif.

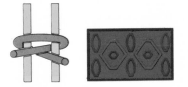

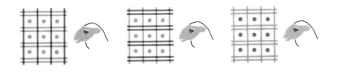

ANATOLIA (Ushak)

Islamisches Museum, East Berlin

Design Prayer rug
Date 17th century
Size 128 x 329 cm (4′ 2″ x 10′ 9″)
Warp Wool
Weft Wool
Pile Wool
Knot Ghiordes
Density 12 knots per sq cm (75 per sq in)
Principal colors Various shades of blue, red, green, yellow, black
Description A prayer rug. This is a fragment of the type of rug known as a "multiple-prayer rug." The rug is dominated by the particularly elegant silhouettes of five niches and half of a sixth niche, within the same number of rectangles. The decoration is very simple, consisting simply of the color contrast which produces the silhouette effect. The border is very small, consisting of a border surrounded by a wider outer strip. The border is decorated with small staggered triangles. The outer strip has a reciprocal design using different colors. Rugs of this type were made at a time when the *mihrab* was tending to lose its original significance and become merely decorative. If such rugs are very large they are used to cover the floors of mosques. This type of decoration occurs in the Kairuan mosque (Tunisia) where a multiple niche design is applied to bamboo matting.

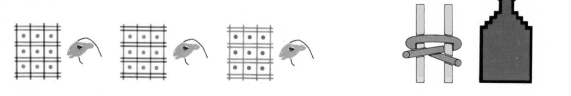

ANATOLIA (Ushak)

Bardini Museum, Florence

Design Prayer rug
Date 17th century
Size 106 x 160 cm (3′ 6″ x 5′ 3″)
Warp Wool
Weft Wool
Pile Wool
Knot Ghiordes
Density 14—15 per sq cm (90 per sq in)
Principal colors Red, yellow, blue, black, white, pink
Description Prayer rug of the symmetrical type with two niches, but without any lamp or other indication of direction. Strictly speaking, the nature of the *mihrab* niche is not respected, and the design of the rug takes on a form that lies halfway between the *mihrab* group and the group with a central medallion. The background is red with a lozenge-shaped medallion at the center, with a vaguely geometric design consisting of four-petaled flowers. Around this is a very stylized shoot with flowers and leaves. The remaining part of the central area of the rug—the four corner sections of equal size—is simply decorated with ovals or small red leaves against a blue background. The border is divided into three strips all roughly the same width, with the central one slightly dominant. The latter has a motif of serrated leaves with long steles arranged obliquely, with alternating colors and directions. In the gap between two leaves we see a somewhat stylized rosette and other plant and floral motifs. The other two strips have an identical design consisting of the repetition of a stele with flowers and leaves which form an alternating trapezoid area. Although this rug is not exceptional in artistic and decorative terms, it is a fine example of a type of rug that was widely readopted and copied in later periods.

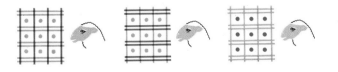

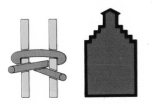

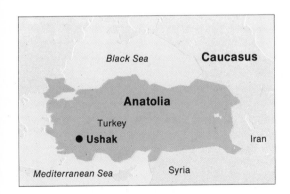

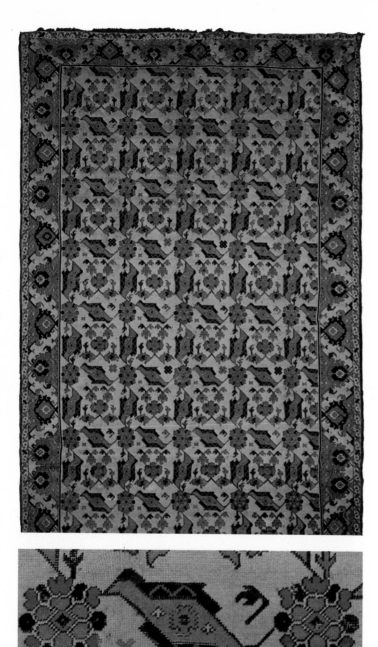

ANATOLIA (Ushak)

Bargello Museum, Florence

Design Floral
Date 16–17th centuries
Size 240 x 490 cm (7' 10" x 16' 1")
Warp Wool
Weft Wool
Pile Wool
Knot Ghiordes
Density 9 knots per sq cm (56 per sq in)
Principal colors White, olive-green, pink, red, blue, black, yellow, orange
Description This type of carpet is also known as the "bird-and-flower" type. The design, which is repeated all over the central part of the carpet, is of a square formed by two pairs of multicolored rosettes, and by the repetition of the same floral shape. This latter consists of a symmetrical zigzag motif occurring twice horizontally and twice vertically, thus forming the square, with the rosettes at its corners. The symmetrical motif, which could be a design of two matching leaves with steles, with a flower at the center, and small plant forms, has been interpreted as a bird. In this case the long lines of the steles become the bird's beak. Inside each square there is a rosette with four large petals. From this rosette two stylized and symmetrical buds with leaves originating from the same stele branch out in the vertical sense of the carpet. In the other direction we see two more flowers, similar to those within the zigzag motif, with separate steles, each one surmounted by two leaves. The border has a broad strip with a narrow outer border. The strip has an alternating triangular motif which depicts a very stylized palmette. The decorative effect is achieved by the alternation of the colors, although the basic motif is repeated. At the center of the longer sides of the carpet, two triangles are joined together in a double-palmette motif. The outer border is quite narrow and consists of the repetition of an S design, or by the stylization of a stele with leaf, intersected at the center by a rectangle and with two small circles at the ends.

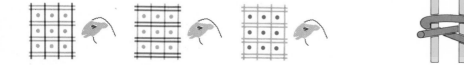

ANATOLIA (Ushak)

Bardini Museum, Florence

Design Geometric
Date 17th century
Size 220 x 390 cm (7′ 3″ x 12′ 9″)
Warp Wool
Weft Wool
Pile Wool
Knot Ghiordes
Density 10–11 knots per sq cm (67–68 per sq in)
Principal colors White, blue, red, cream, green, olive-green
Description A simple decorative motif is repeated against a white background which has now become cream-colored. The motif has been variously interpreted as "Tamburlaine's coat of arms" and as a "thunder-and-lightning" motif, and is generally known by the Sanskrit name of *chintamani.* This terminology would seem to indicate that the design, which is linked to the concept of the fertility of water, comes from Central Asia and the Far East. The decoration, in vertical rows, consists of two short zigzag lines surmounted by three small spheres. This is one of the favorite and most widely used decorative motifs in the Ottoman period. We find it in fabrics, in ceramics, and on the small tiles that decorate some of Istanbul's mosques. The phenomenon of motifs being used on different materials is typical of 17th-century Turkish art which can be traced back to court painters and decorators who worked closely together, and with the various craftsmen from the various workshops—very often at the behest of the Sultan. These rows are staggered to avoid any emphasis on their separateness and to fill the ground more effectively. The wide border has a large central strip enclosed by two narrow borders. These are decorated by steles, leaves, and flowers, all very stylized. The central strip has the motif known as *chi-chi,* also of Oriental origin, repeated several times. This consists of a wide band held at the center by a knot, intersected by shoots with flowers and leaves, and alternating with floral forms halfway between the leaf and the rosette. Little care has been taken to merge the motifs at the corners.

Black Sea

Caucasus

Anatolia

Turkey

● **Ushak**

Iran

Mediterranean Sea

Syria

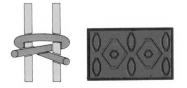

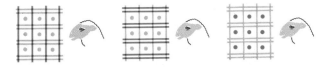

ANATOLIA (Ushak)

Poldi Pezzoli Museum, Milan

Design Geometric
Date 16th century
Size 150 x 220 cm (4′ 11″ x 7′ 3″)
Warp Wool
Weft Wool
Pile Wool
Knot Ghiordes
Density 13–14 knots per sq cm (85–86 per sq in)
Principal colors Dark red, red, black, blue, white, and yellow
Description The central part of the rug is dominated by a large decagonal irregular medallion with two lozenge-shaped pendants at the extremities with the terminal parts lobed and pike-shaped; at the four corners of the central area there are geometric motifs which are like segments of an octagonal star. In the middle of the medallion there is a stylized four-part floral design delimited by a line that forms a square; in the middle of each side of this square there is a small triangle. These lines of the square continue beyond the intersection of the corners and form a complicated motif interwoven with stylized palmette leaves, whorls, and other elements. We also see small flowers and arabesqued shapes in a very geometric style. In the middle of the pendants there is a floral shape enclosed in geometric motifs of leaves with stylized curls and hooks. The corners are decorated with motifs similar to those in the medallion and the pendants, again somewhat stylized. The borders have a repeated S motif—the S being couchant—with curled ends and a serrated lozenge in the center. This design alternates with small circles. The central strip of the border has a hooked design which closely resembles the swastika, alternating with a broad leaf with an indented outline like a carnation. These two motifs are joined around each other by a line which intersects itself at the center of the hooked design and has very curled S motifs. In addition to the border, the shorter sides of the rug have three narrow decorated borders; the outer and inner borders have small leaves or small white dots on a black background; the central border has the same, though scaled-down, motif as the two borders of the main border, but there are no small salient circles. The colors here are red, blue, and white.

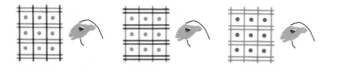

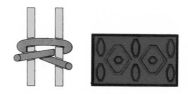

ANATOLIA (Ghiordes)

The Cleveland Museum of Art

Design Prayer rug
Date 19th century
Size 126 x 197 cm (4′ 2″ x 6′ 4″)
Warp Cotton
Weft Cotton
Pile Wool
Knot Ghiordes
Density 13–14 knots per sq cm (84–85 per sq in)
Principal colors: Various shades of red, yellow, brown, white, blue, and green
Description Prayer rug with double niche, and geometric and floral decoration. This typology represents the limit of the definition as *prayer* rug; it would be just as valid to call such rugs floral and, even more so, geometric. The center of the central area has an elongated hexagonal lozenge with the diagonal sides decorated with a hook motif and the straight sides with a continuous design of small stylized flowers. In the middle of the lozenge or, in other words, of the double niche, there is a square formed by stylized floral motifs surrounded on two sides by large leaves. At the two ends there is a palmette with very geometric lines and four stylized rosettes between the palmettes and the central square. The central area is rounded off by two corner areas decorated with floral motifs and serrated leaves. Two rectangular strips with octagonal rosettes and stylized leaves finish off the central area which appears long and narrow. The border is very wide: it consists of numerous small borders, striped and otherwise, plus a central strip divided into five sections. The inner border, which is very narrow and also includes the two rectangular strips mentioned above, has a zigzag motif and introduces a wider, striped border decorated with geometric motifs of floral origin. The strip is divided into five smaller strips, three with a white background and two with a red background, decorated with the same floral motif, staggered on two adjacent strips. The border is finished off by an outer edged border, decorated with a wavy and geometric design which alternates stylized flowers with leaves with the *crab* motif, using alternating colors.

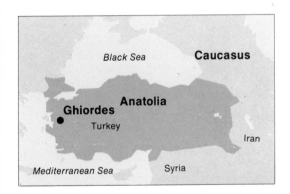

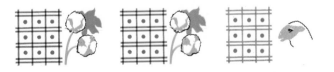

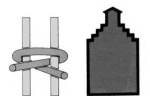

ANATOLIA (Ushak)

Museum für Islamische Kunst, West Berlin

Design Prayer rug of the Kis-Ghiordes type
Date Early 19th century
Size 133 x 197 cm (4' 4" x 6' 6")
Warp Wool
Weft Cotton
Pile Wool
Knot Ghiordes
Density 12–13 knots per sq cm (78 per sq in)
Principal colors Red, blue, yellow, in various shades; white, brown, green, and black
Description Prayer rug with double niche. In the middle of the central area, which is quite narrow, there is a rhombus, indented on the outer edges, containing a four-leaved clover with a rosette in the center. The background of the double niche, which is quite narrow and elongated and hexagonal in form, is decorated with a design of small leaves arranged in horizontal lines. On the vertical axis, above and below the central rhombus, there are two pendants, geometric in design. The straight sides in the inside of the niche have an alternating floral motif, while the oblique sides have large hooks. The corners above and below the niches have imposing designs of leaves and flowers, with *boteh* among them. All the forms are highly stylized. Again, above and below this central section there are two rectangular panel friezes surrounded by a narrow border with leaflike motifs, (almost unrecognizable) ribbonlike shapes and geometric leaf shapes. One border, between two narrow borders with oblique segments, formed by geometric leaflike designs, delimits what forms the central section in the strict sense. Then we have a very wide strip in which sixteen triangular areas are delineated by indented stripes forming a zigzag, formed by three or four rows of small leaves identical to those in the central area, in the two niches. The triangles are filled with designs of rosettes and floral forms. The rug is rounded off by a strip that is much narrower than the previously described one, with a decoration of rosettes surrounded by oblique steles which support stylized tulip corollae and indented motifs used as "filling." The short sides have two narrow green strips, with no decoration, outside the border of the rug.

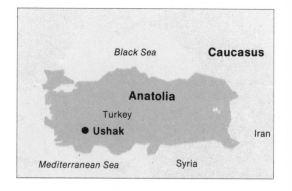

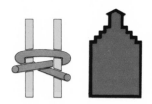

166

ANATOLIA (Ladik)

Bardini Museum, Florence

Design Prayer rug
Date 18th century
Size 120 x 130 cm (3′ 11″ x 4′ 3″)
Warp Wool
Weft Wool
Pile Wool
Knot Ghiordes
Density 20 knots per sq cm (125 per sq in)
Principal colors Red, green, blue, white, black, brown, yellow, pink, olive-green, all in various shades
Description In the middle of the rug there is a triple niche supported by slender columns, a typical feature of this group of rugs. These columns, which are single at the sides and double in the center, are placed on basements and surmounted by capitals which in turn support the large central arch and the two lateral arches, which are tripartite. Above the arches there is an imposing decoration of floral and plant forms taken from the repertoire of motifs that make up the borders of older rugs of this type and of other types. The upper panel has the motif—traditional in this type of rug—of long stems of flowering plants (lilies or tulips) which, in the lower section, form an arrowhead design alternating with a pike-shaped design. The central area of the carpet is surrounded by a narrow border with different colored rosettes, a motif that is also repeated in the outer border of the rug. This is dominated by a wide strip decorated with small lobate medallions, again typical of this type of rug, which have geometric motifs of flowers and stems. Other stylized motifs, on the same axis—two semicircles with small half-stars—are arranged between the small medallions. This carpet is a good example of those motley products known by the term "Transylvanian." Particular features of this typology are the large leaves above the niches, the stylized tulips and the energetic border designs. On the basis of technical characteristics M. Beattie refutes their Ladik provenance and the place where these highly prized carpets were made is still a matter of debate.

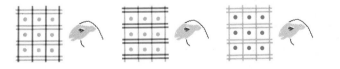

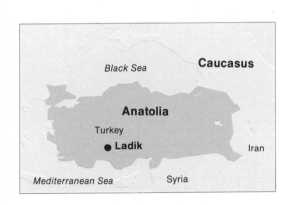

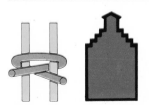

EGYPT (Cairo)

Metropolitan Museum of Art, New York

Design Geometric (Mameluk)
Date Early 16th century
Size 238 x 896 cm (7′ 10″ x 29′ 5″)
Warp Wool
Weft Wool
Pile Wool
Knot Sehna
Density 15–16 knots per sq cm (96 per sq in)
Principal colors Green, red, blue, azure, gray, brown, yellow

Description A so-called Mameluk carpet with a geometric decoration. The design of the carpet develops lengthwise. There is a large medallion in the center. Above and below it there are two more sizable medallions. The decoration is based on geometric figures with an emphasis on the octagon. The central medallion is formed by the intersection of a rectangle with a rhombus, thus forming a star-shaped octagon at the center of which there are various sets of concentric octagons of different colors. The outer sides of the large octagon are surrounded by three geometric forms, two smaller circular ones, between which there is a star-shaped octagon. These crown the design which is again switched back to the form of an octagon. At the four diagonal sides of the large medallion there are the same number of small octagonal medallions. The whole field of the medallions, both large and small, is dominated by geometric designs, Kufic pseudo-inscriptions, arabesques, and a preponderance of the papyrus motif, either single or in groups. The remaining four medallions are symmetrical with a decoration that is similar in each one. The two most central medallions are again octagonal, filled with arabesques, pseudo-inscriptions, and papyri, and as the composition gradually nears the center, it tends to soften and shift from the polygonal form to the circular. This is not the case in the two large remaining medallions where the octagonal format is strictly adhered to, and in the small medallions that surround the principal figure. In the corners of the central section, there are small squares filled with elegant arabesque motifs. As is usually the case with this type of carpet, the field is completely filled with small decorative elements that stand out from the background which tends to be monochrome. The border is quite small, formed by two very narrow borders with shoots and small flowers, surrounding a wider band. This is formed by alternating many-lobed medallions with elongated scrolls: inside them there are floral and arabesque motifs respectively. The background of this band has similar designs. This is known as the "Simonetti" carpet, after the name of its previous owner. It is one of the most elegant and complex carpets of this group. The Mameluk period has been called the "Renaissance of Islam," a term that is certainly unsuitable and misleading in the context of Islamic art. Think, for example, of the great Fatamid era. The typical decoration of the period is extremely elaborate, as shown by this magnificent example which, on a stylistic level, recalls the *horror vacui* of certain metals and may be a fine example of the "monumentality" and at the same time the taste for minute detail

EGYPT (Cairo)

Museo Civico di San Gimignano, Siena

Design Floral carpet
Date 16–17th centuries
Size 230 x 260 cm (7′ 6″ x 8′ 6″)
Warp Wool
Weft Wool
Pile Wool
Knot Sehna
Density 16 knots per sq cm (100 per sq in)
Principal colors Violet-red, red, blue, green, yellow, pink, white, black, and brown

Description This is a cross-shaped carpet, thus rather special. It was made to be used to cover a table, as is evident from the four side sections, which are like flaps. These are made in such a way as to simulate two carpets which cross over beneath a third central carpet. The part used for covering the actual table top has a central circular medallion; at the corners there are small medallion segments. The central area of the carpet has a close-knot floral design with shoots and larger flowers. The four "flaps" have the design of a border with wide bands, and the central area of the pseudo-carpets has a regular floral motif. Halfway along the short side of each of the four flaps, there is a coat of arms, which has not been positively identified. The broad band at the center of the border has an extensive floral motif, while the borders themselves have a pleasing wavy design with detailed floral elements.

History This carpet is said to have belonged to Cesare Borgia who, in turn, is said to have been given it by Paolo Orsini, who, in turn, was given it by his uncle, Cardinal Orsini. In 1502 "il Valentino" went to Senigallia to celebrate the suppression of various rebel leaders, including Orsini. Borgia accepted the gifts and had the bearers killed. This disgusted Nicolo Machiavelli, who was in the company of "il Valentino" and he took his leave. Borgia offered Machiavelli money, but Machiavelli refused it; when offered the carpet, however, he accepted. When Machiavelli was sent from Florence to San Gimignano (Siena), he took the carpet with him and left it there either as a gift to a ladyfriend, or to settle a debt. The carpet is now municipal property. A similar, though less densely decorated, carpet can be seen in the Victoria and Albert Museum in London. Carpets of this type must have been fairly popular in Europe in the 16th and 17th centuries, and even later, as is shown by the numerous examples depicted in contemporary Western painting.

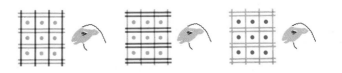

169

CAUCASUS

The Textile Museum, Washington

Design Carpet with stylized dragons
Date 1689+
Size 183 x 445 cm (6' x 14' 7")
Warp Wool
Weft Wool
Pile Wool
Knot Ghiordes
Density 13—14 knots per sq cm (81—82 per sq in)
Principal colors Red, green, blue, all in various shades; white, brown, black, yellow, and cream
Description A carpet with geometric decoration. The long, narrow central area has a gridlike design which divides the space up into a series of lozenges, all roughly of the same size. At the center there is—and this is unusual—an octagonal medallion. The decoration consists of a series of rows of lozenges which alternate, where their decoration is concerned, from highly stylized dragons to naturalistically depicted animals to birds. The vertices of the lozenges are marked out by very bright palmette flowers, and the juxtaposition of the various colors making up the background of the lozenges is very effective. The border is very small, consisting of a narrow border and a slightly wider strip decorated with floral and plant motifs. Some elements, such as the central medallion, the design of the animals, and the color scheme, set this carpet apart from the large group of carpets with dragons. At the top left the carpet has an inscription with a date which might read 1529/1689. The latter date sounds more probable on the basis of stylistic criteria. In fact a later date cannot be ruled out. Charles Grant Ellis gives it a 19th-century dating in his monograph on Caucasian carpets, and even suggests that it was made by Kurds in the Karabagh region. The date was apparently copied unthinkingly by an illiterate craftsman and taken from another carpet.

USSR

Caspian Sea

Caucasus

Black Sea

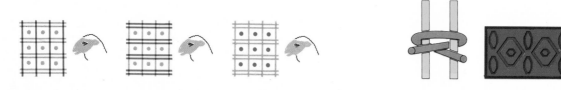

CAUCASUS

Museum für Islamische Kunst, West Berlin

Design Geometric and floral
Date 17th century
Size 224 x 523 cm (7′ 4″ x 17′ 2″)
Warp Wool
Weft Wool
Pile Wool
Knot Ghiordes
Density 13–14 knots per sq cm (85–86 per sq in)
Principal colors Red, blue, green, and yellow, all in various shades; pink, brown, black, white, and violet
Description A carpet with geometric and floral decoration. The central section has a close-knit network of lozenges arranged regularly in this area, with outlines that are not always particularly precise. The network of lozenges is formed by bands of indented segments using two different colors, decorated with flowers on stems and extremely stylized flowers. The lozenges are decorated in alternate rows with floral motifs alternating with pairs of geometric animals, and rows with stylized dragons. The three lozenges that have the stylized palmette buds and the two horned animals facing one another alternate the motifs and colors in the next row. There are two lozenges with the dragon motif, but there are also two half-lozenges at the ends of the central area, decorated with very stylized dragons, the structure of which is not immediately self-evident. The bands that form the lozenges with the dragons are decorated, where they intersect, with medallions containing floral elements. The half-lozenges at the ends of the short sides of the carpet have a bird motif—possibly phoenixes—in a stylized manner. The carpet is rounded off by a narrow border, typical of this type of carpet, consisting of alternating rosettes and palmettes joined together by leaves arranged obliquely on short stems.

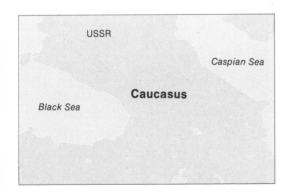

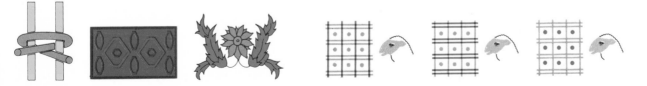

CAUCASUS (Karabagh)
Private collection

Design Geometric and floral
Date 19th century
Size 120 x 495 cm (3'4" x 16'6")
Warp Wool
Weft Wool
Pile Wool
Knot Ghiordes
Density 10—11 knots per sq cm (63—64 per sq in)
Principal colors Red, blue, green, cream, pink, and brown
Description A carpet with geometric and floral decoration. The very long and narrow central section is decorated in the middle with an oval medallion which has a rather stylized floral design. The decoration is specular and symmetrical in relation to the right-angle axes which intersect in the rosette at the center of the above-described medallion. The central area is decorated by a further three medallions on each side, one in the form of an elongated scroll, one with an octagonal star, and one with a lily alternating, with stylized pairs of birds facing one another. The long sides of the carpet are edged on the inside with double-dotted elements. The central area is rounded off by four corner areas, curved in shape, decorated with stylized floral motifs. As often occurs on carpets of this type, the border is noticeably small; it consists of a single border decorated with a continuous design of rosettes and buds alternating with serrated leaves arranged obliquely. The color scheme and the sober decoration achieve a particularly elegant effect in this carpet.

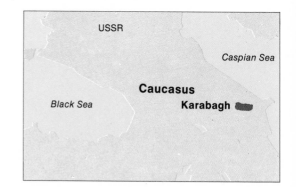

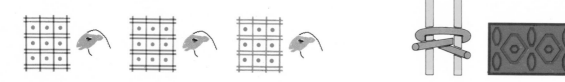

CAUCASUS

Türk ve Islam Müzesi, Istanbul

Design Naturalistic
Date 17th—18th centuries
Warp Wool
Weft Wool
Pile Wool
Knot Ghiordes
Density 14/15 knots per sq cm (90-91 per sq in)
Principal colors Various shades of red and blue; yellow, green, cream, orange
Description A carpet with naturalistic decoration. In the middle of the carpet we see the same scene depicted twice over: a horseman riding among numerous animals, mainly birds. Between the two scenes depicted there are two adjacent rectangular panels decorated with large stylized birds facing each other. The same motif also occurs beneath the first scene and above the second, with the latter remaining incomplete. The depiction of the scene is executed in a slightly coarse style, but not without energy. In accordance with a certain tradition the scene depicted is probably of a hunt and the horseman is probably the Mongol leader Genghis Khan. But this is a popular version which is quite often used for carpets, such as this one, that do not abide by the traditional rules and have not been knotted for commercial purposes. The border section consists of a border, a wider band, and two bands on the long sides. The inner border has a design of simple rosettes of various colors. The wider band has a design of octagons decorated inside with a lozenge motif with stepped edges. The bands on the outside of the carpet on the long sides are decorated with geometric motifs with alternating colors. The carpet is not in the best condition: it shows a great deal of wear in places and has been repaired in many places.

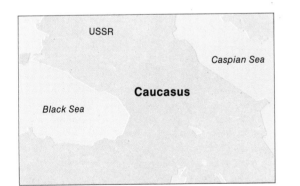

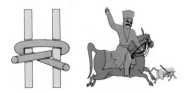

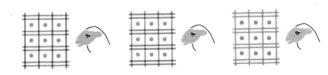

From Persia

PERSIA (Northern Persia?)

Osterreichisches Museum, Vienna

Design Rug with inscribed medallion
Date Late 16th—early 17th centuries
Size 165 x 265 cm (5' 5" x 8' 8")
Warp Wool
Weft Wool
Pile Wool
Knot Ghiordes
Density 16 knots per sq cm (100 per sq in)
Principal colors Red, brown, cream, white, blue, and black

Description A rug with a cross-shaped medallion. The main feature of this rug is the wide use of Arabic script for decorative purposes. The central area is dominated by a pointed, cross-shaped medallion which is asymmetrical. At the bottom there is part of a similar medallion (a single arm of the cross). In each point of the cross the medallion has the words "God is Great." The most conspicuous part of the medallion is decorated with carefully arranged and elegant arabesques which enclose palmettes and other floral forms. The single arm of the lower cross is decorated like the main medallion. In both cases the words "God (Allah) is Great" are upside down. The remainder of the central section is divided into a large number of geometric spaces, rather like a jigsaw puzzle, which are filled with writing. The border consists of two narrow borders with an identical repeated S design, of different colors and set in different directions. The central band is wide. On the short side at the top there is a motif using ribbons and rosettes; the other three sides have a Koranic surah (one of the 114 chapters into which the Koran is divided). On the long sides of the rug there are four medallions set in an impressive arrangement of Kufic script (reminding one of architectural decoration) with the names of God (Allah), the Prophet, and so on. The short sides have a rather worn band with the motif of a hooked stem with leaves. There are two evident patches where the carpet has been repaired. The size of the rug, together with the use of script, the form of the medallions which resemble tombstones, all suggest that this rug was used for funeral purposes.

PERSIA (Tabriz)

Poldi Pezzoli Museum, Milan

Design Carpet with floral decoration and hunting scenes
Date 1542–43 or 1522–23
Size 365 x 570 cm (11′ 11″ x 18′ 9″)
Warp Silk
Weft Cotton
Pile Wool
Knot Sehna
Density 41 knots per sq cm (250–260 per sq in)
Principal colors Red, blue, yellow, green, all in various shades; gray, pink, cream, white, violet, olive, black
Description This carpet is dated either 1542–43 or 1522–23, depending on the interpretation of the last letter in the inscription. At the center there is a handsome polygonal medallion; it is star-shaped with eight large lilylike forms alternating with eight smaller ones. At the upper and lower ends there is a scroll that supports a drop-shaped pendant. A scroll that bears the name of the master craftsman in the workshop and the date decorates the center of the medallion. The background of the medallion consists of a close-knit network of stems with flowers, rosettes, and buds arranged to a geometric layout. In the four large lobes set at right angles in relation to the center there is a pair of goslings, while the others are decorated with a large bird in flight. Eight other large birds appear inside the medallion, the decoration of which is, as usual, symmetrical and specular. The scrolls at the ends of the medallion have two goslings facing each other on an elegant and detailed design of floral shoots. Inside the pendants we see a palmette surrounded by flowers and buds of varying sizes. The corners of the central section of the carpet are decorated with a motif which is a one-quarter section of the central medallion, together with geometric figures corresponding to half the scroll and drop-shaped pendant. The decoration inside the quarter-medallions is identical to that of the central one. The border consists of a narrow border with wavy motifs and a meandering shoot with the leaves of a half-palmette intersecting with another that has small flowers. The wide band contains small oval medallions with floral forms linked by a ribbon motif, sometimes wide and sometimes narrow, with shoots and flowers inside it.

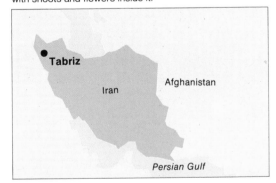

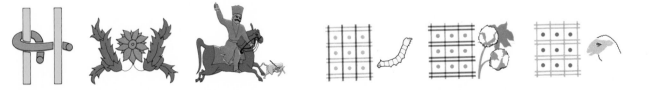

PERSIA (Tabriz)

Victoria and Albert Museum, London

Design Floral carpet, known as the Ardabil carpet
Date 1539—40
Size 534 x 1152 cm (17′ 10″ x 38′ 5″)
Warp Silk
Weft Silk
Pile Wool
Knot Sehna
Density 51—52 knots per sq cm (325 per sq in)
Principal colors Various shades of red, blue, yellow, and green; brown, salmon-pink, ochre, black, and white
Description The middle of the central area is decorated with a radial, lobed medallion with lilylike forms surrounded by sixteen smaller elongated oval medallions joined by buds to the tips of the forms of the central medallion. Above and below the large medallion there are pendants which support a mosque lamp. In the middle of the main medallion there is a closed, eight-lobed figure decorated with floral motifs. The remaining part of the central medallion is decorated with arabesque designs, ribbons, and shoots with small flowers that intersect and create an extremely harmonious sense of movement. The oval, drop-shaped medallions have different-colored backgrounds (four are green, four are red, and the remaining eight are yellow) and are decorated with arabesque motifs, *chi-chi* and small flower buds. The decoration of the corners echoes the decorative pattern and color scheme of the central area. The two lamps are joined to the medallion by a bud and are supported by four strings. The form is that of an upturned cone in the case of the lower one, and a fairly large vase in the case of the upper one. At the bottom, halfway along the short upper side, we find a scroll containing an inscription with the date. The border is well proportioned in relation to the size of the carpet. An inner border is decorated with buds and oblique palmettes joined together by winding leaved shoots. Then we have a border formed by rather curving *chi-chi* and leaf and floral designs, used sparingly. The central band has alternating lobed oval scrolls and octagonal scrolls, similarly lobed, decorated respectively with ribbon designs with flowers and shoots, and arabesques interwoven with flowers.

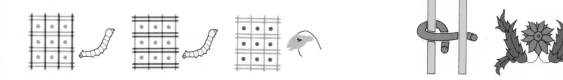

PERSIA (Tabriz)

Metropolitan Museum of Art, New York

Design Scrolled carpet with animal and floral decoration
Date Early 16th century
Size 498 x 340 cm (16′ 8″ x 11′ 4″)
Warp Silk
Weft Silk
Pile Wool
Knot Sehna
Density 96-97 knots per sq cm (600 per sq in, approx.)
Principal colors Various shades of blue, red, and green; pink, white, brown, and yellow
Description A scrolled carpet with animal and floral decoration. The decorative scheme of the carpet is based on small scrolls that have designs of animals, arabesques, and shoots with flowers and leaves. The areas between one scroll and the next are decorated with small ribbons or shoots with small flowers, rosettes, and buds. The basic scheme of the carpet is fairly simple, but the result achieved is one of considerable decorative effect. The center of the design consists of an eight-lobed medallion which contains the design of a dragon and phoenix, surrounded by eight smaller medallions arranged obliquely and radially, with alternating colors and designs, and containing, respectively, birds in flight against a background of floral shoots and arabesqued shoots. Staggered in relation to two adjacent medallions with the dragon and phoenix, or in other words at the center of four of these medallions, there is an eight-lobed medallion which has the design of four lions against an intricate floral background. Four smaller, oblique medallions, with alternating colors and designs, are placed radially around the principal medallion. The small medallions placed between the scrolls with the dragon and phoenix have the same design, but on backgrounds of alternating colors. With this scheme, which is simply arranged and can be repeated ad infinitum, and the intricate arrangement of the background colors, a decorative pattern is created which has a marked ornamental effect. The design is detailed and precise, and great skill has been applied to describe the many details, such as the dragon's tongue or the feathers of the phoenix—a skill that reveals the thoroughness of the most deft of miniaturists.

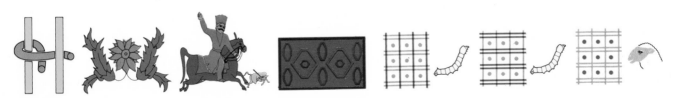

PERSIA (Tabriz)

Metropolitan Museum of Art, New York

Design Prayer rug with inscriptions
Date Early 16th century
Size 161 x 107 cm (5′ 3″ x 3′ 6″)
Warp Cotton
Weft Silk
Pile Wool, with silver brocade
Knot Sehna
Density 85–86 knots per sq cm (530–535 per sq in)
Principal colors Various shades of blue and green; red, ivory, yellow, pink, orange, black, silver
Description A prayer rug with inscriptions. The central area is dominated by a niche (the form of which resembles that of the cupola or dome of a mosque) surrounded by an inscribed band. Inside the niche, at the top, there is an oval scroll, also with an inscription; the remaining part of the area is decorated with very curving ribbons, leaves, palmette flowers, buds, and plant shoots with small leaves and flowers. The area outside the niche has inscriptions which stand out against backgrounds of different colors and irregular shapes. The border is quite wide, consisting of two borders that enclose a wide central band. A special feature of the borders and the central band is that the lower half is decorated with floral motifs and the upper half is inscribed with Koranic verses. The inner border has a decoration of floral buds and leaves of half-palmettes arranged in an elegant wavy motif; the upper part of the short side, also inscribed, is wider than the corresponding lower part. In the lower half, the central band has a close-knit network of slender plant shoots with half-palmettes and flower buds; the lower corners have a decoration consisting of an oblique peony, which is particularly cleverly inserted and most elegant. The upper part of the central band is decorated with three oval inscribed scrolls, one on each side, on a background formed by a subtle design of plant shoots. The ends of the scrolls are marked by four squares inscribed in Kufic with the names of Allah and Muhammad. The outer border has a floral decoration with buds and palmettes with alternating colors joined together by shoots with small leaves and flowers.

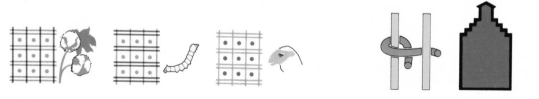

178

PERSIA (Tabriz)

Poldi Pezzoli Museum, Milan

Design Carpet with central medallion with floral and naturalistic decoration
Date Mid-16th century
Size 505 x 240 cm (16′ 10″ x 7′ 10″)
Warp Silk
Weft Silk
Pile Wool and silver
Knot Sehna
Density 60 knots per sq cm (375 per sq in)
Principal colors Various shades of red, blue, green, and olive; pink, violet, brown, cream, white, orange, black, silver, and silver gilt
Description At the center of the carpet there is a lobed, oval-shaped medallion. In other words it is slightly elongated along the vertical axis. At the center of the medallion there is another smaller circular medallion with a rosette; this is surrounded by two pairs of identical flowers set facing each other. Still inside the oval medallion, we then find four pairs of birds perched opposite one another on stems, in a design that is hallmarked by floral volutes, buds, and flowers. The decoration of the carpet is symmetrical and specular in relation to the central axis which runs through the middle of the small central medallion. The whole central section of the carpet is decorated with floral shoots and small flowers. The border consists of an inner border, inscribed all around with verses praising the carpets, and small flowers in the free spaces, a central band and an outer border that is decorated with a repeated motif of plant shoots with palmettes, buds, leaves, and flowers. The central band is dominated by twenty-six large flowers, in two main types, alternating in direction and enclosed in forms which are foliate but also resemble oval medallions. Inside these floral elements there are lions and animal heads (wolves, rams, etc.). The large flowers are joined together by a network of shoots and floral racemes and patterns.
History This is one of the most beautiful carpets ever made. The fact that the "Darius of the Universe" or the Shah is mentioned in the last verses of the inscription, indicating the recipient of the carpet and the presumed date of manufacture, lead us to believe that this carpet was woven for Shah Tahmasp I.

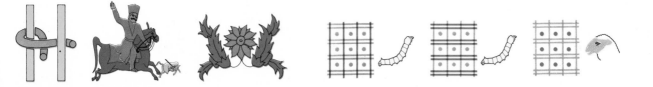

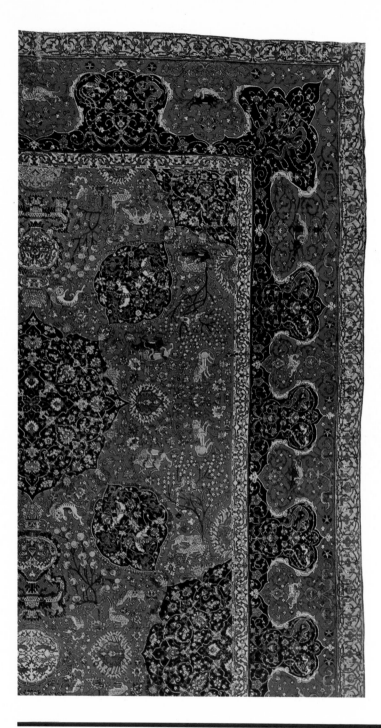

PERSIA (Tabriz)

Victoria and Albert Museum, London

Design Carpet with naturalistic and floral decoration
Date 16th century
Size 549 x 300 cm (18′ 4″ x 10′)
Warp Silk
Weft Silk
Pile Wool
Knot Sehna
Density 71–72 knots per sq cm (445–450 per sq in)
Principal colors Various shades of red, blue, and green; yellow, violet, brown, black, pink, and white
Description This is also known as the "Chelsea" carpet, because it was purchased from an antique shop in that district of London. The central area is dominated by the design of two large circular lobed medallions, each one surrounded by four more oval drop-shaped and lobed medallions. At the center of the carpet there is a small circular medallion with a depiction of four fishes on a background of plant shoots. The whole composition is specular and symmetrical in relation to this central point. Above and below the two large medallions there are vases decorated all over with a pair of peacocks. The large medallions are decorated with a design of arabesques and flowers which leave room in the middle for a four-part lozenge with palmettes. The oval drop-shaped medallions have the motif of two birds in flight against a background that has a circular movement of shoots with flowers and leaves. The rest of the center is decorated, with much attention to detail, by trees in blossom and pomegranate trees, scenes of animals fighting, birds in flight, and birds fighting with each other, lions, and a large number of buds, peonies, and palmettes supported by twisting shoots. The border is no less impressive. The inner and outer borders have different decoration, with certain similarities, consisting of the overlay of various shoots with flowers and leaves. The central band is particularly striking. It is divided into two equal parts which stand out in turn, an effect caused by the change of color of the background and the reciprocal border design. In one band we see animals fighting with one another against a background of interwoven shoots meeting at the center of a palmette; at the top there are *chi-chi* motifs. In the other band the decoration is one of dragons and phoenixes facing one another.

PERSIA (Tabriz)

Museum für Islamische Kunst, West Berlin

Design Carpet with naturalistic decoration
Date 16th–17th centuries
Size 225 x 437 cm (7′ 5″ x 14′ 7″)
Warp Cotton
Weft Wool
Pile Wool
Knot Sehna
Density 30 knots per sq cm (185-190 per sq in)
Principal colors Red, cream, yellow, all in various shades; blue, black, brown, orange, and pink
Description Carpet with naturalistic decoration. At the center there is a circular many-lobed medallion which, in turn, contains a smaller circular medallion decorated with flowers. The medallion has an intricate design of shoots with buds, palmettes, and rosettes, against which we see four pairs of magnificent peacocks facing one another. At the ends of the medallion, along the vertical axis, there is a flower, a small drop-shaped medallion with flowers and simple arabesques, and then a very lovely palmette. The rest of the central area is decorated, both specularly and symmetrically in relation to the right-angled axes at the center of the carpet, with animals and flowers, both of which are depicted with painstaking attention to detail. At the corners there are four roughly triangular sections with birds against winding flowering plant shoots. At intervals of one-third and two-thirds along the long sides of the carpet we see half-medallions decorated with the same motifs as in the drop-shaped medallions. The border is very wide, particularly where the central band is concerned. The borders themselves have two differing interpretations of floral designs with shoots and flowers. The band has a very striking decoration with peacocks facing one another alternating with pairs of large fishes and ducks. The floral background, similar to that of the central medallion, is also an impressive feature.

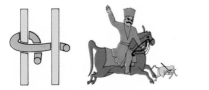

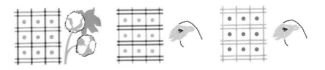

PERSIA (Tabriz or Herat)

Philadelphia Museum of Art

Design Carpet with floral decoration
Date 15th–16th centuries
Size 525 x 359 cm (17′ 6″ x 11′ 11″)
Warp Cotton
Weft Cotton
Pile Wool
Knot Sehna
Density 38 knots per sq cm (235–240 per sq in)
Principal colors Various shades of red, blue, green, and yellow; white, cream, and brown
Description Carpet with floral decoration. The center is completely dominated by the design of trees and flowers, arranged in a specular composition in relation to the central axis. The design makes this one of the possible variants of the type of carpet known as the garden carpet. The large carefully designed trees are arranged in three horizontal rows which also include slender cypress trees and other types of trees in blossom, in some cases with buds coming into bloom. Among the flowers we can identify peonies, rosettes, palmettes, and buds; along the lower short side there are small bushes with leaves and flowers which are also repeated all over the central area, thus rounding off the decoration which, as a result, has a close-knit and de-tailed appearance. The border is well proportioned, con-sisting of a central band between two borders. The inner border is edged by a small band with hook motifs alternat-ing in direction and color; it also has a motif of wavy shoots with leaves that contain, alternately, rosettes and flower buds. The central band has a complicated pattern of three arabesque ribbons of different colors with slender flowering shoots and larger floral forms. The outer border has, on the lower short side, a motif very like that on the inner border. On the other sides it has alternating rosettes and flower buds, joined together by slender shoots bearing small flow-ers.

182

PERSIA (Sehna)

Türk ve Islam Müzesi, Istanbul

Design Naturalistic
Date 19th–20th centuries
Size 41 x 53 cm (1' 4" x 1' 9")
Warp Wool
Weft Wool
Pile Wool
Knot Ghiordes
Density 8–10 knots per sq cm (50–60 per sq in)
Principal colors Red, white, black, brown, and yellow
Description A rug with naturalistic decoration. The whole central area is decorated with a figurative scene, consisting of two figures, one standing, the other sitting cross-legged. Between them there is a tree with graceful branches and two pigeons perched in it. The seated man is a *sufi* master and the standing figure is his disciple. This small rug is not particularly detailed. In fact it has a certain naivete about it. The border is small, consisting of a band decorated by a stylized design with plant and flower motifs. Everything in this very small rug reveals a local product with absolutely no artistic claims. It is an attempt to visualize a theme which is fairly common to popular Iranian tradition. Despite this, we can say that overall the carpet is quite well made and earns our appreciation.

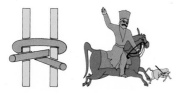

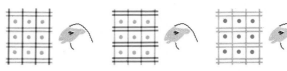

PERSIA (Kashan)

Osterreichisches Museum, Vienna

Design Floral
Date 17th century
Size 135 x 200 cm (4′ 5″ x 6′ 6″)
Warp Cotton
Weft Cotton and silk
Pile Silk, with silver brocade
Knot Sehna
Density 27 knots per sq cm (165–170 per sq in)
Principal colors Various shades of red and blue; yellow, green, black, brown, white, silver, and gold
Description A carpet with floral decoration. This is a good example of the group known as "Polonaise" carpets. The design of the field, which is dominated by lively floral elements that cover the entire surface, is symmetrical and specular in relation to the central axes. The decorative scheme is open-ended, to some degree, and defined by the border. It could well extend beyond these limits because the composition is constructed in such a way that it could continue ad infinitum. In the middle of the field there is a drop-shaped elongated medallion with two floral forms inside it; two multicolored palmettes are set above and below the medallion. The rest of the field, which also has subtle variations of background color, is dominated by a well-balanced movement of fairly large shoots with rosettes, buds, palmettes, and other floral elements. The border is well proportioned, but not particularly wide; it consists of two guard stripes and a central edged stripe. The inner guard is decorated with a continuous motif of oblique rosettes and palmettes, joined together by a slender shoot. The outer guard stripe has a motif of stylized lilies, set one against the other, and of different colors. The central stripe is edged by two small bands resembling the twisted cord motif; it has a lively movement of fleshy S-shaped shoots alternating in direction and joined together by rosettes with alternating colors. The decoration of the central stripe is rounded off by small rosettes. In the corners there are floral forms of highly stylized palmettes.

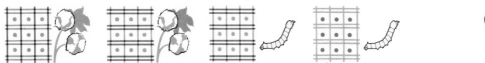

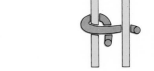

PERSIA (Kashan)

Osterreichisches Museum, Vienna

Design Naturalistic
Date 16th century
Size 320 x 680 cm (10′ 8″ x 22′ 8″)
Warp Silk
Weft Silk
Pile Silk, with silver brocade
Knot Sehna
Density 127 knots per sq cm (790–800 per sq in)
Principal colors Various shades of red, blue, green, and yellow; black, pink, violet, white, brown, and gray, silver and gold
Description The decorative pattern is the traditional one for many carpets woven in the classical period of carpet manufacture. At the center there is a regular eight-sided lobed medallion, and this same motif recurs at the corners. The rest of the central area has a naturalistic decoration. The central medallion has eight lobes and is decorated inside with a design formed by four pairs of phoenixes alternating and set against four pairs of dragons. At the four ends of the axes of the medallion there is, on the long sides, an elongated scroll with two ducks facing each other, set among flowers, surmounted by a lily with abstract half-palmettes. This last motif, in a smaller form, occurs along the horizontal axis as well. The same design as in the central medallion, but reduced to a quarter the size, occurs in the corners of the carpet. The inner guard stripe has the classical design of plant forms and palmettes, with additional human heads, joined together by a subtle motif of plant shoots with spiked flowers. The outer guard has closed floral forms alternating with buds, at the center of which there are human faces; these are joined together by shoots with small leaves. The central stripe is a masterpiece of its type. Against a background of shoots bearing peonies, palmettes, Chinese-type clouds, and multicolored birds, we see winged genies or *urí* separated, in groups of three, by peonies and palmettes.
History Because of the beauty of the images and their particular style, the cartoon for this carpet has been attributed to a famous miniaturist, Sultan Muhammad. The carpet probably found its way to Vienna in 1696 as a gift to Leopold I from Peter the Great.

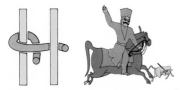

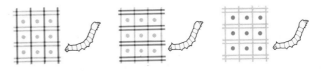

PERSIA (Kashan)

Metropolitan Museum of Art, New York

Design Rug with floral and animal decoration
Date Second half of the 16th century
Size 180 x 238 cm (5′ 11″ x 6′ 11″)
Warp Silk
Weft Silk
Pile Silk
Knot Sehna
Density 88—90 knots per sq cm (555 per sq in)
Principal colors Various shades of green, blue, yellow, and brown; red, gray, olive, black, and cream
Description The field is decorated with isolated animals or animals fighting one another, separated by numerous types of flowers. The animals are mainly quadrupeds, but there are also birds and legendary beasties, such as dragons and *chi-lin*. The animals are depicted naturalistically, with great care being paid to the detail. This also goes for the way in which the flowers, bushes with birds, and the rocks in the lower section are depicted—all real masterpieces of their kind. The design, which has been worked out by an expert and confident hand is well balanced and extremely elegant, and free from all symmetrical strictures. A slender band decorated with small U-shapes divides the central area from the inner guard stripe which consists of palmette flowers and peonies, alternating in both direction and in color. The broad central stripe of the border is decorated with great refinement. Large lotus and peony blooms, depicted naturalistically although in a stylized manner, with alternating colors, are joined together by very elegant shoots with leaves, rosettes, and berries. Between the blooms there are pairs of elegant birds with alternating colors used for their bodies, set facing each other, species by species. They are depicted very realistically in the process of pecking berries from the shoots. Here again there is great attention to detail, as is shown by the representation of the tongue and legs. The outer guard stripe, which rounds off the carpet, consists of double *chi-chi* motifs joined together by small rosettes, alternating with larger rosettes joined together by shoots with small rosettes and leaves. The carpet is an extremely fine one, both because of its naturalistic design and because of the material used—silk—and the faultless execution.

PERSIA (Kashan)

Metropolitan Museum of Art, New York

Design Rug with central medallion and floral decoration
Date Second half of 16th century
Size 168 x 250 cm (5′ 6″ x 8′ 4″)
Warp Silk
Weft Silk
Pile Silk
Knot Sehna
Density 37–38 knots per sq cm (230–235 per sq in)
Principal colors Various shades of brown, blue, and green; pink, red, and yellow
Description Rug with central medallion and floral decoration. This extremely handsome rug displays an undeniably refined taste. At the center of the field there is an octagonal star with a rosette and eight palmette flowers. The star is contained within an elegant octagonal medallion in the shape of a flower with two types of palmettes forming each petal; these are joined together by small floral shoots, in turn joined up by a rosette. At the two vertical ends of the medallion, along the axis, there are two pendants with a scroll containing floral forms, and a lily formed by and decorated with beautiful half-palmettes which form an arabesqued motif. At the corners of the field there is an area decorated with a quarter-section of the central medallion (and half of the pendant on either side) with beautiful palmettes surrounded and decorated by floral shoots with rosettes, buds, and small leaves. The remainder of the central area of the rug is decorated with a busy design of plant shoots with leaves, rosettes, various types of palmettes and buds, the whole effect being one of harmony and symmetry. The border is wide and well proportioned, as befitting a rug in which even the smallest details have been painstakingly worked out. The inner guard stripe has a motif of rosettes alternating with palmettes joined together by a short, slender shoot. The outer stripe, which is wider than the inner one, has palmettes alternating in color, joined together by shoots with smaller flowers. The central stripe has alternating large palmette flowers of differing designs, separated by plant shoots, lanceolate leaves, and smaller flowers.

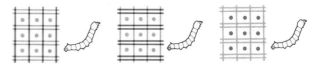

PERSIA (Shiraz)

Metropolitan Museum of Art, New York

Design Floral
Date Late 18th century
Size 135 x 253 cm (4′ 5″ x 8′ 4″)
Warp Cotton
Weft Wool
Pile Wool
Knot Sehna
Density 25—26 knots per sq cm (161—162 per sq in)
Principal colors Various shades of blue; red, pink, and white

Description Rug with floral decoration. The field is geometrically subdivided. Diagonal lines formed by thin shoots with small flowers divide up the whole area into a gridlike network of elongated lozenges. These lozenges are intersected in alternate rows by horizontal and vertical segments which break up the field still further. The basic scheme thus becomes one of a rectangle with two diagonals; at the crossover point, or in other words at the vertices of the lozenge, there is a rosette. The whole field is decorated by the regular repetition of an elegant floral decorative motif containing small carnations, buds, rosettes, and other mostly small floral forms. The border is elegant, well proportioned, and well balanced with the remainder of the rug. It consists of two guard stripes with three bands; these are similarly decorated but with partly different colors; and a central stripe, in between. The narrow lateral bands of the guard stripes have a continuous S-shaped decoration, alternating in direction. At the center there is a motif of rosettes joined up by a slender shoot with leaves. The wide central stripe has a design of hexagonal elongated lozenges, bordered at the top and bottom by a flower, the color of which alternates. At the center of the lozenge there is a small rose from which issue four stems with small flowers and leaves.

PERSIA (Southern Persia)

Metropolitan Museum of Art, New York

Design Prayer rug with floral decoration
Date 18th century
Size 120 x 190 cm (3′ 11″ x 6′ 3″)
Warp Cotton
Weft Cotton
Pile Wool
Knot Sehna
Density 108 knots per sq cm (695 per sq in)
Principal colors Various shades of red and yellow; blue, white, cream, black, green, and gray
Description Prayer rug with floral decoration. The field is dominated by a large niche with a many-lobed contour. At the bottom a curved line, with lily-shaped half-medallions, supports half-sections of cypress trees, the silhouette of which forms the sides of the niche. The decoration in the niche is extremely dense. In the middle, toward the bottom, there is a vase, the form of which recalls Chinese *mei-p'ing* porcelain; from the vase issue flowering shoots arranged to a strict geometric pattern. The very close-knit floral decoration consists of peonies, palmettes, daisies, rosettes, and other floral forms which are hard to identify. At the center of the niche, toward the top, a rosette with several petals, which almost resembles a cockade, indicates the direction for prayer. Like the bottom area, the corner sections also have an extremely complex and intricate decorative design, based on the traditional movement of spiral, wavy shoots. The border is well proportioned, consisting of two edged guard stripes, with the wider central stripe in between. The guard stripes have an identical decoration of rosettes alternating with palmettes and carnations, joined up by a short shoot with foliage. The central stripe has a design of hexagons made up of stems and interposed by beautiful flowers, and decorated with stems supporting pairs of small flowers.

189

PERSIA (Northern Persia)

Osterreichisches Museum, Vienna

Design A so-called Portuguese carpet with floral and naturalistic decoration
Date 18th century
Size 677 x 372 cm (22'6" x 12'5")
Warp Cotton
Weft Cotton
Pile Wool
Knot Ghiordes
Density 50 knots per sq cm (320 per sq in)
Principal colors Red, blue, green, yellow, in various shades; brown, pink, orange, white, black, violet, olive, and gray
Description A carpet of the so-called Portuguese type. At the center, there is a rosette surrounded by four buds and two pairs of birds facing one another. At the same level as the buds, but further to the side, there are four oval medallions with small flowers. Between the medallions there are another four flowers which are similar but smaller. Above these latter there are four pairs of birds facing one another and an indented rhombus with a red background that resembles a design of flames, with an elegant and detailed movement of plant shoots running through it. Different colored bands—yellow, blue, pink, green, and so on—with a very energetic design also echo the form of the rhombus. All this decoration is extremely lively, and the motifs in the corners of the central area are particularly so. We see two ships at sea with figures in European or Western dress: we can make out a woman, an Indian, and a musician. The sea includes various fishes, a sea monster, and a man swimming. The theme here might even be the story of Jonah. The sides have two borders which enclose a wide band. The inner border has large flowers joined together by a winding plant-shoot which has a palmette at the center, set diagonally. The central band has a motif delineated by a blue stripe with small flowers and small white, pink, and green leaves, forming scrolls at the center of which there are oval medallions with large flowers. The outer border is identical in design to the inner one. But the colors are quite different.

History The qualification "Portuguese" derives from the circumstances that some experts attribute to the origin of these carpets, that is, the Portuguese colony of Goa in India, on the basis of stylistic considerations which link them with Indian miniatures of the Moghul period. But these carpets are now, by common accord, attributed to Persia, and most scholars place them in the southern region. K. Erdmann, however, places them in the north, possibly basing his reasons on the proximity with the Caucasian region where these carpets were imitated in later periods.

190

PERSIA (Herat)

Bardini Museum, Florence

Design Floral
Date Early 17th century
Size 280 x 750 cm (9′ 4″ x 25′)
Warp Wool
Weft Wool
Pile Wool
Knot Sehna
Density 19–20 knots per sq cm (120 per sq in)
Principal colors Red, green, blue, yellow, olive, white, black, violet, brown, and pink
Description The decoration is strictly specular in relation to both the vertical axis and to the horizontal axis. The central area of the carpet, which is part of a more extensive design that is in no way finished or delimited, is formed by two small flower buds, opposed at the base, which delineate the vertical axis. At the same level two handsome and many-colored palmettes are set facing each other on the central axis of the carpet. The design also focuses on two more pairs of palmettes placed horizontally and axially in relation to the two central ones. There are also another two brightly colored palmettes which are staggered in relation to the above-described pairs and in alignment with the two buds which we have defined as the central point of the carpet. This, in a few words, is the pattern of the arrangement of the larger flowers. The entire field is then filled by a

series of close-knit floral whorls and spirals with leaves and flower buds depicted in very bright colors. An important position in the economy of the design is taken up by the decorative motif of the cloud or ribbon (chi) which frequently appears as a link-up between the various different elements, and as a "filler." The border consists of an inner guard stripe formed by the alternation of small floral elements. The central stripe is quite wide and formed by quite large palmettes alternating with other smaller ones which are surrounded by four flowers or buds and one or two smaller flowers.

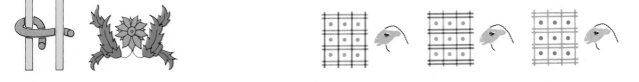

PERSIA (Herat)

Bardini Museum, Florence

Design Floral
Date Late 16th—17th centuries
Size 210 x 490 cm (6′ 11″ x 16′ 4″)
Warp Wool
Weft Wool
Pile Wool
Knot Sehna
Density 25 knots per sq cm (156—160 per sq in)
Principal colors Various shades of red, green, blue, pink, and yellow; olive, white, black, and brown
Description The background of the central field is garnet red and decorated with a dense and detailed design of stems with small inflorescences and palmettes with buds of various sizes arranged symmetrically. The whole carpet is decorated with lotus flowers, palmettes, peonies, floral shoots, naturalistic arabesques, and ribbon motifs (chi), all brightly and variously colored. The pattern of the decoration follows a strict symmetrical logic which becomes evident when one sees the various decorative elements not singly but as a whole, in order to grasp the aesthetic sense of the design and its general refinement. At the center of the carpet we have a small red star that forms the focal point of the carpet, and one of the central points of the design which is open-ended. Beside it there are large fleshy palmettes and two more smaller ones, situated above and below the central axis which one imagines running through the star and the large palmettes. Higher up and, symmetrically opposed, lower down—almost a third of the way up/down the field—we find two more large palmettes that are symmetrical in relation to the vertical axis, enclosed within a large group of peonies, which are circularly arranged independently of the palmettes. Two more of these, again symmetrically situated, appear in the middle of the short sides, corresponding to and axial with the central star. There are large numbers of ribbons and floral spirals in many colors which serve as linking elements for the buds and larger floral shapes. The border has a wide central stripe with quite large palmettes alternating with smaller ones, and interposed by shoots with flower buds and plant designs.

PERSIA (Herat, Eastern Persia)

Osterreichisches Museum, Vienna

Design Carpet with floral and naturalistic decoration
Date 16th century
Size 350 x 742 cm (11′ 8″ x 24′ 9″)
Warp Silk
Weft Silk
Pile Silk
Knot Sehna
Density 50 knots per sq cm (310 per sq in)
Principal colors Various shades of red, blue, and cream; green, gray, brown, black, white, and yellow
Description A carpet with floral and naturalistic decoration. The field has a continuous and dense design of plants and flowers that is symmetrical and specular in relation to the central point, where we also see depictions of animals, either isolated or fighting with one another. The decoration of the large palmettes and buds is particularly striking; these are linked together by lively winding shoots with small flowers and leaves. *Chi-chi* or ribbon motifs act as effective link-up features. There are many animals depicted: some are legendary or imaginary, like *chi-lin* and dragons, but others are real, such as lions, gazelles, deer, leopards, and various species of multicolored birds. The overall effect is most pleasing and successful, in terms of both the design and the decoration. The border is very wide, consisting of two guard stripes and a wide central stripe in between. The inner guard stripe has a delicate design of floral racemes which act as a background to the inscription. There are single flowers set in at intervals. The wider stripe has a very elegant and complex movement of plant shoots which interweave with large, elaborate *chi-chi* motifs. This rare and beautiful carpet is rounded off by an outer stripe formed by *chi-chi* arranged partly in diagonals and alternating with buds and palmettes, also arranged in different directions, and supported by shoots with small flowers.

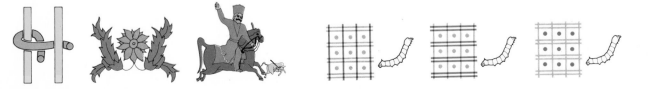

PERSIA (Eastern Persia)

Poldi Pezzoli Museum, Milan

Design Floral
Date Late 17th century
Size 130 x 410 cm (4′ 3″ x 13′ 6″)
Warp Wool
Weft Wool
Pile Wool
Knot Sehna
Density 17–18 knots per sq cm (110 per sq in)
Principal colors Various shades of red and green; yellow, pink, olive, brown, white, and black

Description The center is decorated by four flowers with two large flowers placed at their sides in a medallionlike arrangement formed by leaves. Along the axis running vertical with the four flowers there is a symmetrical decoration with a leaflike medallion, followed further up by a *chi* (ribbon or cloud motif) with a marked curve, almost the shape of the Greek letter Omega. Toward the end there is a floral motif which is elongated and oval in shape. Set axially with the two large lateral flowers there are alternating plant and floral shoots, spiral in form, with large numbers of flowers and large leaf shapes which contain multicolored buds in the middle. The design is open-ended, as is shown by the half-floral forms arranged along all the sides. The field of the carpet is not crowded with decorative motifs, even though the designs are linked together by elegantly designed floral shoots and ribbon or cloud motifs. The border has an inner guard stripe, the customary central stripe, and a narrow outer guard stripe. The inner guard stripe is decorated with green and yellow flowers. The wide central stripe has a very regular design, which is also quite dense, formed by alternating small buds and larger palmettes linked up by slender stems with the suggestion of fine foliage. The decoration at the four corners is merged without any problems, with a palmette set there diagonally. The outer guard stripe has a red background with small white flowers and green leaves.

The carpets of this typology are elegant and decorative. The region of provenance is still a matter of discussion and the term "Indo-Persian" by which these carpets are sometimes known is, in our view, far from satisfactory. Certainly, one can see in these carpets elements both technical and stylistic which indicate an area of northern India and/or eastern Persia. Once again the lack of specific studies which embrace and describe all the known carpets of this typology poses a considerable obstacle when it comes to filling out our knowledge of them.

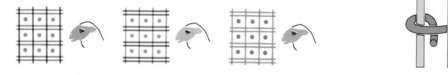

From Central Asia and Afghanistan

CENTRAL ASIA (Baluchistan)

Private collection

Design Prayer rug with floral decoration
Date 19th century
Size 80 x 150 cm (2′ 7″ x 5′)
Warp Wool
Weft Wool
Pile Wool and camel's hair
Knot Sehna
Density 15 knots per sq cm (95 per sq in)
Principal colors Red, blue, black, brown, and white
Description A prayer rug with floral decoration. The field has a simple rectangular niche that is decorated with a very stylized tree of life deriving from a floral and geometric design, with pairs of leaves attached to the trunk, alternating with other leaves on the branches. The upper part of the niche, which is also rectangular, is narrower and the pairs of leaves are attached just to the trunk. The leaves have alternating colors and a geometric style. The niche is surrounded by a double guard stripe with zigzag motifs. At the top, at the sides of the smaller rectangle there are two rectangular panels with leaves like those of the tree. These panels restore the field to its rectangular form. The border is quite small, but it must be remembered that in three-quarters of the carpet it has the niche border running along-side it. It consists of a stripe and outer guard stripe. The decoration, which is geometric in both cases, in the stripe has lozenges with four-part rhombi inside them, alternating in color. The outer guard stripe has a zigzag decoration identical to the one around the edge of the niche.

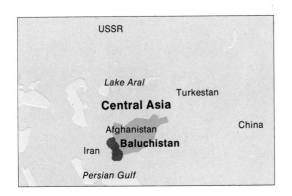

CENTRAL ASIA (Tekke)

Museum für Völkerkunde, Hamburg

Design Geometric
Date 18th century
Size 182 x 233 cm (6′ x 7′ 8″)
Warp Wool
Weft Wool
Pile Wool
Knot Sehna
Density 21–22 knots per sq cm (135–140 per sq in)
Principal colors Various shades of red and blue; green, ivory, brown
Description Rug with geometric decoration. The field is dominated by four rows of ten *gul* (see the detail opposite bottom photograph), all belonging to the Tekke tribe. The design is repeated with great precision and separated by secondary *gul,* typical of the same tribe. The motifs are all geometric and skillfully executed. This rug has a very narrow border formed by a single repeated design, alternating in color and with certain differences in the detail. The design consists of octagons with small stars at the center alternating with lozenges decorated with linear geometric motifs. This is a fine example of this type of carpet, and it is possibly one of the oldest.

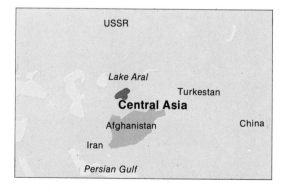

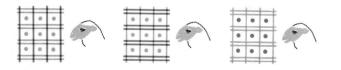

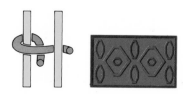

CENTRAL ASIA (Yomud)

Private collection

Design Geometric
Date 19th century
Warp Wool
Weft Wool
Pile Wool
Knot Ghiordes
Density 21 knots per sq cm (135 per sq in)
Principal colors Various shades of red; black, cream, brown, yellow
Description Rug with geometric decoration. The field has the repeated motif—in diagonal lines—of the central Asian *gul* of the Yomud tribe. The typically geometric decoration has remained unchanged over the years, except for a few minor exceptions, giving these carpets a continuity of expression that is hard to find in other types of carpet. The border consists of a single narrow guard stripe edged with small toothed bands, decorated with geometric motifs. The short sides have two horizontal panels with a zigzag, toothed decoration in different colors, the motif known by the term Yomud-pine.

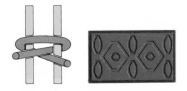

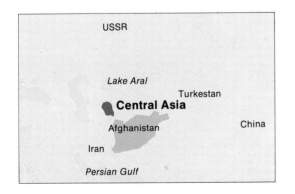

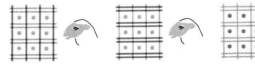

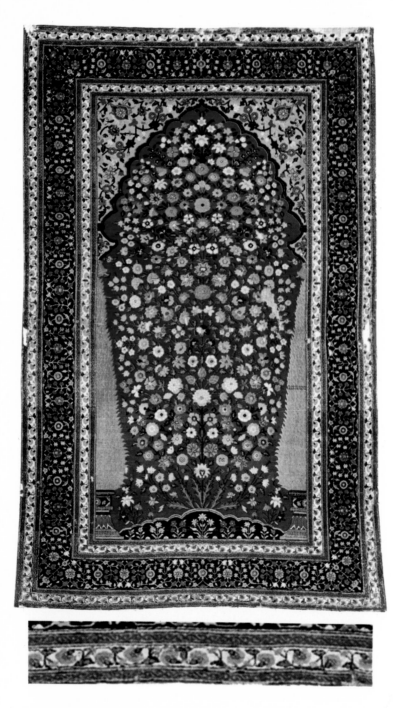

From India and China

INDIA

Osterreichisches Museum, Vienna

Design Prayer rug with floral decoration
Date 17th century
Size 107 x 155 cm (3' 6" x 5' 1")
Warp Silk
Weft Silk
Pile Wool
Knot Sehna
Density 67 knots per sq cm (415—420 per sq in)
Principal colors Various shades of red, yellow, blue, and green; gray, white, brown, mustard, pink, violet, and black
Description Prayer rug with floral decoration. The field is dominated by a large niche, with a red background, containing the principal floral design. From the bottom, we find a curved line, made up of semi-circles, which contains stems with simple flowers. At either side of this line there are basements that are quite elaborate and divided up into various sections, which support ornamental cypress trees —half-trees are depicted—that extend three-fifths of the way up the field. The outlines of the two half-trees form the elegant edges of the niche. The niche is decorated all over with floral motifs; a central stem with different flowers and buds, running along the vertical axis, divides the field into two strictly symmetrical parts which, in turn, have stems with buds, rosettes, palmettes, small leaves, and other flowers. The curved upper part of the niche has a graceful sweep to it. The corner sections, conceived as the hangings of a tent, have two rosettes set in diagonal oval medallions and a graceful and measured movement of shoots with flowers. The wide border consists of two identical guard stripes enclosing a broad central stripe. The guard stripes are in three sections: a narrow central area that has a simple motif of wavy shoots with leaves and a stylized flower and is edged by a continuous motif of alternating S shapes placed between two monochromatic lines. The stripe in the center of the border has alternating rosettes and buds, linked together by a close-knit but not exaggerated design of shoots with small flowers, small buds, and flower corollae. This is a rug which displays a modest taste but a great deal of refinement.

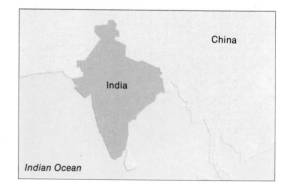

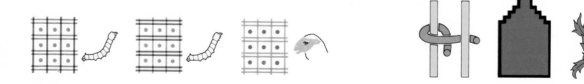

198

INDIA (Amber)

Metropolitan Museum of Art, New York

Design Floral
Date First half of the 17th century
Size 400 x 427 cm (13′ 2 ″ x 14′ 3″)
Warp Cotton
Weft Cotton
Pile Wool
Knot Sehna
Density 24 knots per sq in (150 per sq in)
Principal colors Various shades of blue, red, and green; brown, pink, white, and yellow
Description Carpet with floral decoration. The decorative design of the field is extremely simple, but has a striking ornamental effect. Against a beautiful red background we find seven rows of small bushes with pretty flowers, including carnations, roses, bellflowers, chrysanthemums, irises, and tulips, all depicted naturalistically with great precision and attention to detail. The border is quite small in size, consisting of a central stripe flanked by two narrow guard stripes decorated with a continuous S motif. The central stripe is decorated with palmettes, buds, and rosettes, all alternating with one another, joined together by shoots and surrounded, alternately again, by slender lanceolate leaves that are attached to the previously mentioned shoots. From a decorative viewpoint this carpet is a fine example of Indian taste of the day. But we should also point out the evident affinities on the one hand with Persian art of the Safawid period and on the other with the paintings of herbaria in Europe which, when they were not being copied and reproduced in toto, inspired a great deal of Indian art, and especially the art from that immense natural garden, Kashmir.

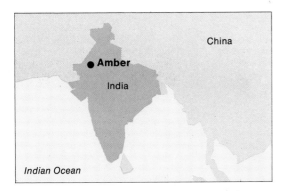

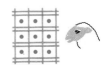

INDIA

Osterreichisches Museum, Vienna

Design Naturalistic
Date 16th—17th centuries
Size 156 x 235 cm (5′ 1″ x 7′ 9″)
Warp Cotton
Weft Cotton
Pile Wool
Knot Sehna
Density 75 knots per sq cm (465-470 per sq in)
Principal colors Various shades of red, blue, brown, and green; cream, white, pink, yellow
Description The whole field is decorated with trees in which we see leaves, flowers, and birds. There are also numerous shrubs with birds perched in the branches and others about to alight or take flight. In the center there is a large tree with a gnarled trunk where, at the bottom of the trunk, to the right, there are two handsome peacocks, one of which is fanning out its tail feathers. On the left of the tree trunk there is an impressive cockerel and a hen. Above the tree there are two large long-billed birds. Although the field is decorated all over, it does not give the impression of being crowded. Working from the inside out, we have a cream-colored line, a red line, a narrow band with a motif of continuous S shapes alternating in direction, another red line, another narrow band with wavy motifs, and lastly a monochromatic line. In addition to these there is a guard stripe with the usual motif of centrally placed flowers joined up by winding shoots, which support a horizontally placed bud, and separated by spiked leaves. The central stripe is enclosed by another narrow stripe with wavy motifs and a monochromatic line, on either side. This central stripe, which is especially elegant, is made up of large flowering plants with alternating designs, colors, and directions, surrounded by floral and plant shoots. Between these flowers we find a pair of spotted animals, facing each other, separated by a small scroll. The style of the decoration, which is clearly related to the art of the miniature, the wealth of the composition, and its particular taste, have suggested that the cartoon for this carpet may have been painted by Mansur, miniaturist at the Jahangir court.

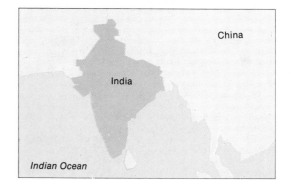

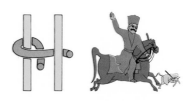

CHINA (Eastern Turkestan, Khotan)

Metropolitan Museum of Art, New York

Design Floral
Date 19th century
Size 282 x 386 cm (9′ 3″ x 12′ 10″)
Warp Cotton
Weft Cotton
Pile Silk
Knot Sehna, with part of the carpet woven with the *sumak* technique
Density 9–10 knots per sq cm (57–58 per sq in)
Principal colors Various shades of blue and pink; white, beige, gold, brown, gray, and silver
Description A carpet with floral decoration and a central medallion. At the center of the field there is a circular medallion containing a sinuous dragon figure, with five-clawed feet, in the manner of the spherical "flaming pearl." The motif, which is similar in substance, is taken up in the four quarter medallions in the corners of the central field. The dragon, which is similar in type to the central figure, is arranged in a different way and depicted in profile rather than head-on. The remainder of the field is decorated with a close-knit design of plant shoots with large "vine leaves," flowers, and other leaves. The border is wide and well balanced. The inner guard stripe has a simple decoration of small light-colored circles against a darker background. Then there is a stripe with a repeated swastika motif, and next the broad central stripe with a design of plant shoots identical to the design that decorates the field of the carpet.

   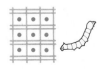

From Other Parts of the World and Non-Knotted Carpets

SPAIN

Islamisches Museum, East Berlin

Design Naturalistic
Date 14th—15th centuries
Size 94 x 303 cm (3' 1" x 9' 11")
Warp Wool
Weft Wool
Pile Wool
Knot Arab-Spanish
Density 17—18 knots per sq cm (110 per sq in)
Principal colors Brown, black, and cream
Description A carpet with naturalistic decoration. This carpet is known as a "synagogue" carpet after the place where it was discovered, and after the type of decoration. It is not in a good state of preservation or repair. The field is divided into two rows of large rectangles, all decorated with the same motif. This is a building with a pointed roof and a large doorway with small-scale geometric designs depicted on it. The border is well proportioned, consisting of a wide central stripe and an outer guard stripe. The central stripe has an elegant and fairly straightforward design of pseudo-Kufic writing alternating with small circular rosettes. The decoration differs marginally on the short and long sides. The outer stripe has the simple design of a double line of small circles. Because of its date and the decorative design used, this carpet is one of the finest produced in Moslem Spain. These carpets (known also as "Mudejar," after the name given to Moslems who lived as subjects of Christian sovereigns) often have motifs influenced by Western taste, especially from the late-14th century onward.

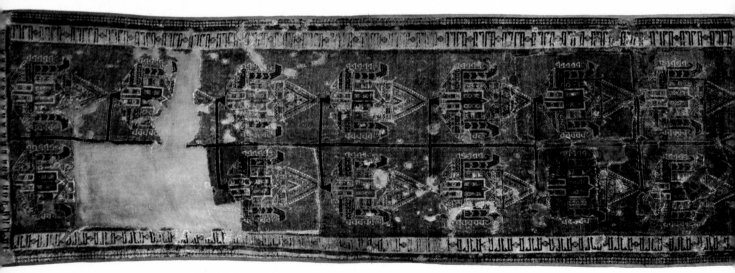

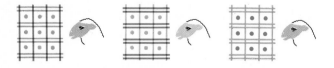

SPAIN (Alcaraz)

Philadelphia Museum of Art

Design Geometric
Date 15th century
Size 268 x 593 cm (8′ 11″ x 19′ 9″)
Warp Wool
Weft Wool
Pile Wool
Knot Arab-Spanish
Density 18–19 knots per sq cm (115 per sq in)
Principal colors Various shades of blue and red; white, yellow-brown
Description A carpet with geometric decoration. The field is dominated by a detailed and close-knit grid of small octagons decorated with stars, likewise octagonal in shape, alternating with mainly animal ornamental motifs arranged in no particular pattern. We can see ducks with their beaks joined, large birds, stylized peacocks facing one another, other stylized birds, quadrupeds, human figures, and lozenge-shaped geometric designs which are very reminiscent of the various Central Asian *gul.* At the center of the narrow field there is a coat of arms repeated three times. The border is quite large, consisting of two stripes of almost identical width. The inner stripe is edged by two small bands with X motifs and dots, alternating X forms set very close together; it also has lines of small lozenges with very stylized S forms halfway along each side. The design is very simple and forms a grid which acts as a well-balanced complement to the principal motifs in the central field. The second stripe has a motif of repeated pseudo-Kufic script with rampant lions on the short sides—and figurative scenes separated by geometric designs on the long sides. Among the figurative and ornamental scenes we see women, trees, lions, and birds. The carpet has a narrow guard stripe with zigzag designs and two stripes, along the short sides, with figurative scenes like those already described—that is, displaying a pictorial taste and inspiration that smacks of Europe—which are typical additions to Spanish carpets of this period. The coat of arms is that of Fadrique Enriquez (26th) Admiral of Castile, who died in 1473.

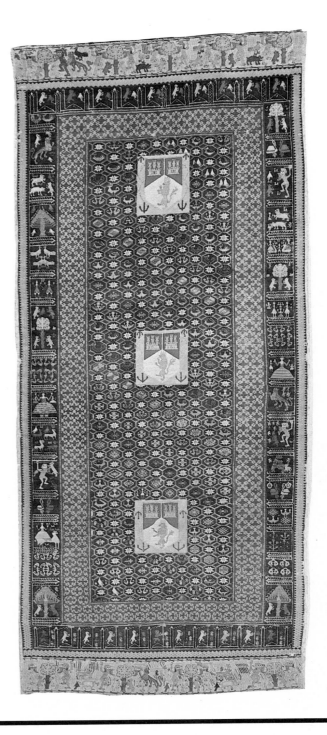

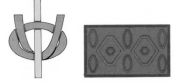

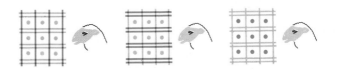

Commercial Terminology

Included below are some of the most commonly used commercial terminology for rugs and carpets.

Generic definitions relating to areas of origin:
Turkish or Anatolian, Persian or Iranian, Caucasian, Afghan, Turkoman or Turkmen, Indian, Chinese, Pakistani, Spanish, Maghreb (North Africa), Baluchi.

The oldest carpet-weaving areas and centers:
Anatolia: Bergama, Yuruk, Milas, Konya, Ushak, Kula, Mujur, Kirsehir, Ladik, Ghiordes.
Caucasus: Daghestan, Kuba, Shirvan, Karabagh, Kazakistan.
Persia (Iran): Tabriz, Sanandaj (Sehna), Kashan, Isfahan, Shiraz, Herat, Kirman, Hamadan, Joshagan, Ardabil (or Ardebil), Varamin, Kirmanshah, Qum, Nain.
Central Asia: Beshir, Pendeh.
China: Kahsgar, Yarkand.
Spain: Cuenca, Alcaraz.

Carpets named after the names of trading centers:
Bukhara, Merv, Khiva, Mossul, Kerki, Samarkand.

Carpets painted by artists:
Holbein, Lotto.

Carpets named after their format:
Kenare (long and narrow, runner), Namas (prayer: 80 x 100 cm/2′ 8″ x 3′ 4″), Sar or Nim (100 x 150 cm/3′ 4″ x 5′), Do sar (narrow and long).

Carpets named after structural features:
Gabe (long-haired, deep-piled, from the Shiraz region).
Keindirli (with quite thick wefts, usually from the Kula region).
Nim baff (carpets made by merging various knotted patches).

Carpets named after their function:
Nemazlik (prayer, in Turkish), *Ja-namas* (prayer in Persian), *Sajjade* (prayer in Arabic), *Selahak* (prayer in Turkoman), *Saf* (collective prayer), *Germetch* (Turkoman rug at tent entrance), *Aiatli* (funeral carpet), *Khalik* (Turkoman, small carpet used for decorating camels on wedding days), *Oyalik* (Turkish carpet in a group that is halfway between the *mihrab* and the medallion design), *Osmolduk* (for camel decoration).

Glossary

Note. This glossary includes the technical, historical, and geographical terms most commonly used in the specific vocabulary relating to carpets that appear either in the introductory section or in the text describing the plates.

abi the color of water, blue-green.

abrash varying shades of a color caused or produced by a lack of uniformity in the dyeing of the fibers.

Achaemenids a dynasty in pre-Islamic Persia, 560—330 B.C.

Ali cousin and son-in-law of the prophet Muhammed.

alum (aluminum sulphate and potassium) material used as a fixative and mordant agent in the dyeing of fibers.

arabesque decorative motif consisting of abstract and open stylized floral designs which can be repeated ad infinitum.

Arab-Spanish knot used in Spanish and some Coptic carpets.

arras fabric woven on a loom by hand.

beam (of a loom) the wooden bar around which the warp and the finished part of the carpet are wound.

Berbers a people inhabiting Barbary, the ancient term for northwest Africa.

border (of a carpet) the part delimiting the field of the carpet, generally formed by two guard stripes enclosing a central stripe.

boteh a decorative motif, probably derived from plants, which is ovoidal and conical in shape, with the tip folded over on itself like a hook.

brocade a specific type of fabric; in carpets this term refers to gold and silver threads, forming rings, which are woven into the warp and weft.

Buddhism the religion and philosophy preached by Buddha (6th century B.C.) and practiced principally in eastern Asia and India.

Cairo (carpet) term used in Venice in the 15th and 16th centuries, indicating that a carpet came from Cairo, or describing a specific detail in the decorative technique.

caravanserai places where, originally, camel caravans stopped to rest and buy supplies; later they became trading centers and in many cases thriving towns.

carding process of combing wool either manually or mechanically.

Chatagay Turkish tribe coming from Central Asia.

chevron decorative motif formed by a series of concentric "V"s.

chi-chi Chinese decorative motif of floating ribbons.

chi-lin imaginary or legendary unicornlike quadruped, typical of the Chinese decorative repertoire.

Ch'ing the last Chinese dynasty, 1644—1912.

column (carpet) a term used to describe Anatolian carpets with a series of columns supporting the *mihrab* (cf.) or niche.

Copt a term describing Christians in Egypt and Ethiopia.

Damascene, Damascus (carpet) term used in Venice in the 15th and 16th centuries to describe specific technical and decorative features of rugs and carpets.

double knot *see* **jufti.**

dragon a legendary creature depicted in Oriental carpets on the basis of the Chinese decorative scheme, consisting of twelve parts from twelve animals depicted in differing styles.

fabric (or textile) something that is woven, either manually or mechanically.

false knot *see* **jufti.**

farsh carpet in modern Persian (Iranian).

farsi baff *see* **Sehna.**

Fatima daughter of Muhammad and wife to Ali.

field (of a carpet) the central area, usually rectangular or square in shape.

fu "bat" in Chinese, and homophonous with *fu* meaning "happiness."

flaming pearl Chinese symbol associated with dragons and with the fertility cult.

garden (carpet) a carpet decorated with the design of a typical Persian garden.

ghilim *see* **kilim.**

Ghiordes the site in Anatolia where Alexander (the Great) had to undo the famous and legendary (Gordian) knot; the term now refers to the principal system of knotting *(Turk baff)* used by tribes and weavers in Turkey.

Gobelins *see* **Manufacture Nationale des Gobelins.**

gul meaning "flower" in Persian; this is the emblem and decorative motif peculiar to each Turkmen tribe.

Hasan son of Ali and Fatima and for Islamic believers, especially of the Shiite faith, a martyr.

heald (or heddle) the part of the loom that raises or lowers the warp chains.

Hegira, hejira the flight of Muhammad from Mecca to Medina in the year 622 A.D., the year that marks the birth of the Islamic era.

herati from the town of Herat: a floral motif used mainly in carpets woven in this region.

Holbein (carpet) named after the painter Hans Holbein the Younger, who often depicted this particular type of carpet.

horror vacui the custom of filling every part of a rug or carpet with dense decoration.

Hosein son of Ali and Fatima and for Islamic believers, especially of the Shiite faith, a martyr.

Hospice de le Savonnerie a soap factory near Paris where looms were set up for the production of carpets.

hu tieh "butterfly" in Chinese, a symbol of longevity.

Ibn Battuta 14th century Arab traveler.

Ibn Sa'id 13th century Arab traveler.

iconophobia the prohibition of images inferred from Koranic passages.

Ilkhanids an Islamic Mongol dynasty from 1256—1353.

Islam from the Arabic meaning "abandonment, submission" and referred by Muhammad to the will of God; the term embraces all the rules contained in the Koran which form the basis of Moslem civilization and culture.

jufti (also double knot or false knot) a knot made on four or more warp chains rather than on the customary two chains.

Karkhana state factory or workshop set up for the manufacture of carpets and other artistic products.

kerm in Persian, "(silk) worm" and also "red," whence the English words "carmine" and "crimson."

kilim a Turkish term used throughout the Orient to describe a flat rug or carpet without knots, made by hand, and double-sided.

kis the so-called *Kis-Ghiordes* rugs and carpets were those woven by young Turkish women for their own use.

Koran the Moslem holy book, dictated by God (Allah) to the prophet Muhammad via the Archangel Gabriel.

Kufic a type of geometric script originating from the Mesopotamian city of Kufa.

lamp (or mosque lamp) a decorative motif used in prayer rugs to indicate the direction of the rug, or for purely ornamental purposes.

loom a structure with various interconnecting parts on which carpets and rugs are woven.

Lotto (carpet) after the name of the painter Lorenzo Lotto, a definition used as a rule in the same way as "Holbein carpet."

lu "deer" in Chinese, and homophonous with *lu* meaning "wealth."

Maghreb name given to the countries of North Africa, with the exception of Egypt.

Mameluks sovereign dynasty in Egypt and Syria, 1250—1517.

Manufacture Nationale des Gobelins from 1825 onward the factory where French rugs and carpets were produced.

Maqsud Kashani supervisor of the famous Ardabil carpet.

mausoleum a large monumental tomb.

mihrab the niche in the wall of the mosque that is directed toward Mecca and indicates the direction of prayer.

minbar a sort of pulpit for the prayer leader.

Ming Chinese dynasty from 1368–1644.

miniaturist (or illuminator) the artist who provides illustrations of particular episodes contained in manuscripts.

Moghul Islamic Indian dynasty, 1526–1858.

mohair from the Arabic-Persian *mohayyar* meaning "choice," referring to high-quality wool from goats.

Mongols a semi-nomadic tribe in Central Asia.

moon tree a very ancient astral symbol.

Moorish (Moresque) the style in both Arab art and civilization in North Africa, Sicily, and in particular, Spain.

mosque the Moslem equivalent of a church.

mudéjar a term used in Spain for Moslems who were subjects of a Christian sovereign.

Muhammad the prophet of Islam.

Muslim (or Moslem) pertaining to or belonging to Islam, from the Arabic-Persian word *muslim,* meaning "belonging to Islam."

Ottomans Turkish dynasty, 1281–1924.

Pandirma name attributed to the best Anatolian carpets from the Kayseri region and embracing the large numbers of imitations of this type of carpet.

patchwork a type of carpet originating from the Valtellina region, consisting of various "patches" sewn together.

phoenix a mythical bird, sacred in various mythologies; in rugs and carpets it is generally depicted as a composite creature, taken from the Chinese decorative repertoire.

pile the upper surface of a carpet, consisting of the knots.

Polonaise or **Polish (carpet)** Persian carpets from Isfahan or Kashan, many of which were discovered in Poland; in 1878 the collection belonging to Prince Czartoryski was exhibited in Paris.

prayer rug a small rug used for prayer, generally decorated with the *mihrab* motif, lamp, or other appropriate design.

pseudo-inscription an imitation of an inscription with similar or partly accurate symbols and actual letters of the alphabet, but without any meaning and used for purely decorative purposes.

pseudo-Kufic an imitation of the Kufic script used for decorative purposes.

Qashqai a semi-nomadic tribe of Turkish origin settled in southern Persia.

qibla the direction of Mecca or, more precisely, of the *ka'ba,* which is the box in the main mosque in Mecca where the black stone is kept.

rococo (style) a term derived from French *rocaille,* which refers to an 18th-century artistic and stylistic movement with a focus on rich and luxurious decoration.

Safawid Islamic-Persian dynasty, 1501–1732.

Sassanid pre-Islamic Persian dynasty, 224–651.

Savonnerie *see* **Hospice de la Savonnerie.**

scroll a fairly elaborate elongated ovoid form, named after a roll of paper with inscriptions.

Scythians a group of Asiatic tribes living in the steppes of Scythia (southern European Russia).

Sehna a city in Kurdistan (now called Sanandaj) after which the knot (*farsi baff*) mainly used by Persian weavers is named.

Seljuks a dynasty of central Asian origin, 1038–1194 in Persia, 1077–1307 in eastern Anatolia.

selvage or selvedge *see* **guard stripe.**

shaih a term denoting a person who is particularly respected and venerated for his spiritual qualities: sage, master, spiritual guide.

shaman a priest of Central Asian tribes capable of entering a state of ecstasy by means of mystical practices, and of being in contact with the spirits.

shotori camel-colored.

Silk Route overland trade route from China to the Near East, known above all for its most valuable and sought-after commodity: silk.

Spanish Holbein (carpet) a carpet similar in type to the "Holbein" but made in Spain.

stylized hand an Islamic symbol denoting five particularly venerated people: Muhammad, Ali, Fatima, Hasan, and Hosein.

Sultan Muhammad a famous illuminator from the Safawid period.

sumak a flat carpet made with threads which "hook" several warp chains, and are cut on the underside of the carpet.

Sung Chinese dynasty, 960–1279.

sun-tree very ancient astral symbol.

swastika an ancient sun symbol consisting of a cross with four equal arms, bent at right angles either to the left or the right.

tabachi a Persian word denoting the coat of dead animals.

Taj Mahal a famous Islamic mausoleum at Agra in India.

T'ang Chinese dynasty, 618–907.

taoist from the Chinese word *tao,* "way"; the name of an ancient Chinese philosophy.

teasel or **teazle** part of the operation of processing wool, to make it soft and pliant.

Timurids a dynasty of central Asian origin, 1370–1506.

Transval (carpet) Anatolian carpets found in large numbers in churches in Transylvania.

tree of life very old Oriental symbol of fertility and prosperity.

turchesca (carpet a la) term used in Venice in the 15th and 16th centuries for carpets of Turkish origin.

Turkmen or **Turkoman** semi-nomadic people of central Asia divided into various tribes.

turk baff *see* **Ghiordes.**

urí female angels who enliven the Islamic paradise.

Vase, carpet with a term denoting a type of Persian carpet made with a given technique, but not necessarily decorated with vases.

vishap a mythical aquatic monster in Armenian mythology.

warp the series of yarns arranged lengthwise on a loom.

weft a yarn or series of yarns woven across the width of the fabric through the lengthwise warp yarns, which hold the knots of the carpet.

yang Chinese term denoting one of the two forces on which the universe is founded; *yang* is the male, solar principle.

yin Chinese term denoting one of the two forces on which the universe is founded; *yin* is the female, lunar principle.

Bibliography

Achdijian, A., *Un art fondamental, le tapis,* Paris 1949.

Azadi, S., *Turkoman Carpets and the Ethnographic Significance of Their Ornaments,* London 1975.

Beattie, M. H., *Carpets of Central Asia,* Birmingham 1976.

Bogolyubov, A. A., *Carpets of Central Asia,* London 1973 (ed. orig. St. Petersburg 1980/1909).

Campana, M., *Il tapetto orientale,* Milan 1945.

Campana, M., *Tappeti d'Occidente,* Milan 1966.

Cohen, G., *Il fascino del tappeto orientale,* Milan 1968.

Dilley, A. U., *Oriental Rugs and Carpets,* Philadelphia-New York 1959.

Dimand, M. S., and Mailey, J., *Oriental Rugs in the Metropolitan Museum of Art,* New York 1973.

Edwards, A. C., *The Persian Carpet,* London 1960.

Erdmann, K., *Oriental Carpets,* London 1960.

Erdmann, K., *Europa und der Orientteppich,* Berlin and Mainz 1962.

Erdmann, K., *Seven Hundred Years of Oriental Carpets,* London 1970.

Formenton, F., *Il libro del tappeto,* Milan 1970.

Gans-Ruedin, E., *Handbuch de orientalischen und afrikanischen Teppiche,* Munich 1971.

Hackmack, A., *Chinese Carpets and Rugs,* New York 1973.

Hangeldian, A. E., *Tappeti d'oriente,* Milan 1967.

Hawley, W. A., *Oriental Rugs Antique and Modern,* New York 1970 (1st ed. 1913).

Hubel, R. G., *The Book of Carpets,* London 1971.

Iten-Maritz, J., *Les tapis turcs,* Fribourg 1975.

Jacobsen, Ch. W., *Oriental Rugs: A Complete Guide,* Tokyo and Vermont 1962.

Landreau, A. N., and Pickering, W. R., *From the Bosporus to Samarkand: Flat Woven Rugs,* Washington 1969.

Martin, F. R., *A History of Oriental Carpet Before 1800,* Vienna 1908.

McMullan, J. V., *Islamic Carpets,* New York 1965.

Mostafa, M., *Turkish Prayer Rugs,* Cairo 1953.

Petsopoulos, Y., *Les Kilims,* Fribourg 1979.

Pope, A. U., *A Survey of Persian Art,* Oxford 1938.

Ricard, P., *Corpus des Tapis Marocains,* Paris 1934.

Ropers, H., *Morgenländische Teppiche,* Braunschweig 1965 (1st ed. Berlin 1922).

Sarre, F., and Trenkwald, H., *Old Oriental Carpets,* Vienna-Leipzig 1926–29.

Schlosser, I., *Der Schöne Teppich in Orient und Okzident,* Munich 1960.

Schurmahn, J., *Caucasian Rugs,* London 1965.

Tattersall, C. E. C., *Notes on Carpet-Knotting and Weaving,* London 1927.

Turkhan, K. H., *Islamic Rugs,* London 1968.

Viale, M. e V., *Arazzi e tappeti antichi,* Turin 1952.

Von Bode, W., and Kühnel, E., *Vorderasiatische Knüpfteppiche aus alterer Zeit,* Leipzig 1922.

Wulff, H. E., *The Traditional Crafts of Persia,* Cambridge, Mass. 1966.

Yetkin, S., *Early Caucasian Carpets in Turkey,* London 1978.

Index

Illustration Credits

ABOUT THE AUTHOR

Giovanni Curatola was born in Florence in 1953. He studied Oriental languages at the University of Venice, and received his Ph.D. in 1976. He has traveled widely in the East, and studied at length in both Turkey and Iran. Concentrating on the decorative arts of the Muslim world, he has published several important studies on the subject. He lives in Venice and conducts his research at the Institute of Iranian Studies of the University of Venice.